O CANADA
CROSSWORDS
BOOK 19

100 ALL NEW Crosswords

GWEN SJOGREN

NIGHTWOOD EDITIONS

Nightwood Editions
P.O. Box 1779
Gibsons, BC
V0N 1V0
www.nightwoodeditions.com

Edited by Margaret Tessman
Proofread by Patricia Wolfe
Printed in Canada
ISBN 978-0-88971-349-9

Contents

1 Water Marks

Go with the flow of these Canadian rivers

ACROSS

1. Conceal a pelt?
5. Formerly, in olden days
9. Puff or huff
13. Blue Mountain runs
19. Spoken, as opposed to written
20. Insect developmental stage
21. Negative responses
22. Zimbabwe's capital city
23. **River that runs around Halifax**
25. Military group
26. Fruit from Florida
27. Old English letter
28. Pie in the sky
30. Entry or entree
31. Take control again, say
33. When doubled, a dance style
34. Calgary's Fairmont Palliser, for example
36. Canuck singers Cochrane and Connors
37. A Blue Jay, in alternate innings
39. Exigencies
43. Enlightenment, in Buddhism
46. Old World animals with antlers
47. Help to understand
49. Geddy who plays bass for Rush
50. Old-style ogler
51. Sports event cry
53. Drive the herd?
54. Emulate Marcel Marceau
55. Narratives
57. Marketers' spiels
58. College chum in L.M. Montgomery's *Anne of the Island*
59. In the thick of the action
60. Lunch box flask
62. Zoroastrian
63. Marbles?
65. **Saskatoon river**
69. She wrote *Little Women*
71. Cornered in BC's Cathedral Grove?
72. Italian food herb
75. Weaving apparatus
76. Hatred
78. It airs *The Graham Norton Show*
80. Sting?
81. It delivers America's mail (abbr.)
82. 1970 Guess Who hit: "Hand Me Down _____"
83. Chess pieces
85. Took the passenger's side
86. Hawaiian garland
87. Buffalo NHLer
88. Meltdown?
89. Like some wedding cakes
91. Cravat
93. Baker's buddy?
95. Large casks
96. Singer's vocal cord bump
98. Glass or Gershwin
99. Lurch, like an airplane
103. 1990 Blue Rodeo album
106. Early leader, at the Queen's Plate?
109. Ontario Curling Association (abbr.)
110. Debilitate
111. Plastics ingredient
112. **Fredericton is situated on this river**
114. Kicked out of the shoe store?
115. Not quite warm
116. Land plan
117. Roswell sightings
118. Fall bloomers
119. Settles a bill
120. Longings for sushi?
121. Former NHL left-winger Roberts

DOWN

1. Dave Thomas played one on *SCTV*
2. Furious
3. Russian country house
4. Alberta destination: _____ Island National Park
5. Widespread disease outbreak
6. Tsars and czars
7. Paintball game sound
8. Late anagram
9. Grinds one's teeth
10. Pertaining to a major artery
11. Common Coquihalla Highway vehicle
12. Like a trip in the '60s?
13. Young hog
14. Grand theft auto?
15. 1976 Margaret Atwood novel: *Lady _____*
16. Piece of window glass
17. Joule units
18. Witnesses
24. Golfer's hat style
29. More slippery
32. Retail repositories
35. Window with a seat
37. Adversaries
38. Abhor exams?
40. 1983 ZZ Top album
41. Relinquish a membership
42. Like a ratty veggie gardener?
43. Badgers' burrow
44. Colonial India home helper
45. Long-range lens description
46. **Winnipeg waterway**
48. **River that encircles Vancouver**
52. Meat-and-potatoes entree
53. 18th-C. violin maker, for short
54. Business woman?
56. Cereal grasses disease
58. "Land _____!"
61. **River in our nation's capital**

8

62. Poser
64. Astonishes
66. Old-style firefighting device
67. Decorative band around a bicep
68. Pawn
69. Gene Vincent hit: "Be-Bop-_____"
70. Doesn't win
73. Unclothed
74. *National Post* piece
77. Chic, in Chelsea
78. Pedantic pig?
79. It bisects Calgary

83. Emus' South American kin
84. University of Victoria attendees
87. More unfeeling, like the geologist?
88. Prepares a sewing machine needle
90. Unreactive
92. Painkiller
94. Actress Tyson's preferred perennial?
95. 16th-C. Venetian painter
97. "The Twelve Days of Christmas" royals

99. Like bread past its prime
100. Bathing sponge (var.)
101. It flowed through Greek gods' veins
102. Flower for a coward's lapel?
103. Canadian Intercollegiate Baseball Association (abbr.)
104. Northwestern Québec town
105. Dalmatian's dot
107. Piece for a diva
108. Notice Intrepid?
113. Milk container sold in some provinces

Canada Cornucopia 1

ACROSS

1. 1997 Shania Twain album: _____ *On Over*
5. Aliens, for short
8. Mafia bigwig
12. Cultivates crops
17. Jet black gemstone
18. Pacific _____ Exhibition
20. Canada's west coast abuts this
21. Canadian rock music trio
22. Amok
23. They're next to ulnae
24. Appraisers' ratings
26. BC-born Buffalo Sabre Reinhart
27. Walk heavily
28. Black, poetically
29. Previous name of BlackBerry Limited (abbr.)
31. Supermodel Campbell or singer Judd
33. Digital document
35. Extend over
37. *Law & Order* network
38. Engine speed, for short
41. Bryan Adams hit: "(Everything I Do) I _____ For You"
42. Of groundbreaking importance
45. Chevrolet model that debuted in 1958
47. Former W Network show: *Say Yes to the _____ Canada*
49. Student docs
51. Impels
52. Positive answer
53. End of a hammer
55. Pores over a layout
57. Skirt for a Scot
58. Actor's prompt
59. Sinewy
60. Navy honcho's butterfly?
64. Like some fast food meals
65. York University degree (abbr.)
68. Almost round
69. Chewy candy
71. Toyota subcompact since 1999
73. Turn attention in a different direction?
75. In every respect
77. Apartment dweller's fee
78. The Family Stone front man
79. May flowers recipient
81. Mad, in Mexico
82. High-end fashion label
84. Japanese stringed instruments
86. HVAC pro's gnarly expression?
87. You tie a tie around this
88. 1990s Edmonton Oiler Miroslav
91. Saturn's spouse
93. Type of pneumonia
97. Shop salesperson
98. Erudite writers, collectively
100. Brownell Jameson who wrote *Winter Studies and Summer Rambles in Canada*
101. See eye to eye
102. McGill University prof, for one
103. Gossip column component
104. Childcare pro
105. Hansen or Fox, to many Canadians
106. Question
107. Paddles

DOWN

1. Essence
2. Duty
3. Canadian TV drama since 2008: *Murdoch _____*
4. Royal Ontario Museum displays
5. Children, in Chicoutimi
6. Traditional Canadian dessert treat: Butter _____
7. Helm controllers, old style
8. Your unc's offspring, to you
9. Some black birds
10. Song of celebration
11. Alberta river
12. Alberta oil patch locale
13. Mites and ticks
14. Change the paint colour
15. Wound
16. Scissors sound
19. Lacking flavour
25. Classic Canadian film: _____ *oncle Antoine*
30. User?
32. Samurai's belt: Uwa-_____
33. C&W star Arnold who sold 85+ million records
34. Epidermis opening
36. Button material
38. Sitar player's music style
39. Entreated
40. Sunday service
43. Syrup of ipecac, for example
44. John or head
46. Bird of _____
48. Central American animal
50. *Chess* duet: "I Know Him _____"
54. Dutch _____ disease
56. Deciduous tree and its fruit
57. Canadian Pace who won six World Cup skiing medals
58. Canadian Christmas classic: "Huron _____"
60. Barbecue spits
61. Black-heartedness
62. Jones of The Monkees
63. Rodent
64. Actor's histrionics?
65. Enter illegally
66. Helsinki citizen
67. _____ Spumante
70. Ghoulish
72. La-Z-Boy piece

74. Tater eater?
76. Bisson who stars in 3-D
80. Money, colloquially
83. PVR button
84. Former Canadian slopes athlete Percy

85. Mace, for example
88. Computer printer action
89. It might cover a pond
90. Beach bird
92. Heavenly body
94. Soul singer Redding

95. Once again
96. Wallops
99. Tokyo, once

Cleanup on Aisle Pun

A laundry list of wordplay

ACROSS

1. Kitten's cries
5. k.d. lang hit: "_____ Chatelaine"
9. Savoury jelly
14. Like an enthusiastic beaver?
19. At the peak of Mount Logan
20. Dairy Queen Blizzard flavour
21. Outburst of artillery
22. Onslaught
23. Hans _____ Andersen
25. Spun around (var.)
26. Quill's kin
27. **Cleanser for an astronomer?**
28. There are 20+ of these on Parliament Hill
30. Film starring Canada's Carrey: _____ *Sunshine of the Spotless Mind*
32. Refugees' retreat?
34. Polaris and Rigel
35. Instrument for Burton Cummings
36. Prepare *Maclean's* articles, say
38. Sounding the alarm
40. "Hey!" quietly
44. College student, for short
47. Kauai garland
49. You might add this with an iron
50. Prickly vine (var.)
51. 100 per cent
52. With regard to
54. Grass or weed
55. Elegant
56. **Polish for a sorority sister?**
58. Fashionable, in *Flare*
61. Sailor's transformation?
63. Rajas' mates
64. Despise
66. Lisa Simpson's brother
67. Egyptian goddess whose name means "throne"
68. **Sponge for an illusionist?**
71. Emerald _____

75. Collector's purchase?
77. Vertical dimension
78. It may be terry or Turkish
79. Lack of compassion
84. 1954 Hitchcock film: _____ *Window*
85. **Product used by a good French friend?**
86. Desired
87. Word sometimes seen on 78-A
89. Change your watch from PDT to NDT
91. Michael Bublé cover: "I've _____ You Under My Skin"
92. Sunflower kin
93. More sly
96. Newfoundland or Canadian Pointer
97. Chromosome bit
98. Chris Hemsworth played this god in an eponymous 2011 film
99. Blimp pilot, for example
101. Goon's cancellation?
103. Everglades avian
105. Prevent, legally
107. Raises one's glass, say
111. Inept sports day race participant?
114. Pantomimes?
116. **Stain remover for a loudmouth?**
117. Fill with optimism
118. Factoid
120. Skewered serving
122. Post on a staircase
123. Gathering place in old Greece
124. In awe
125. "Pardon me" sound
126. Transmits
127. Official Imperial China residence
128. Sobeys counter
129. Bucks' mates

DOWN

1. Nickname for McCartney
2. Group's mindset
3. Infested with annelids
4. Pitched, like 10-D
5. Bit of wit?
6. Québec symbol: Blue flag _____
7. Places in Parliament
8. Beethoven composition
9. Guarantor, for example
10. Car dealership emp.
11. Furthermore
12. 1974 Alice Munro collection: *Something _____ Been Meaning to Tell You*
13. Cough syrup ingredient
14. City near Cologne
15. Civic land grab
16. **Detergent for a successful trader?**
17. Sicilian peak
18. Irish or Scottish dance
24. Formal menswear fastener
29. Locker room substance
31. Sticker
33. Eeyore's creator
35. Run at Whistler
37. Start of a par 4
39. New Mexico locale that means "place of red willows"
41. Sagittarius or Scorpio
42. Snitched
43. Balsam or beech
44. Style of pants or sandals
45. Stewpots
46. Canada's Kate Nelligan starred in this film
48. Disguised, like a PI?
50. 1922 Physics Nobelist Niels
52. Some US gov. cabinet members
53. Pad _____
55. Surgery relic
57. Not concerned, at CIBC?

59. This gives you an urge to scratch
60. **Laundry soap for a sports fan?**
62. "Wanna make _____?"
64. In need of crutches
65. Leamington, Ontario is on this lake
68. Darn
69. Culture medium in a lab
70. Tear into pieces
72. Shape metal
73. _____ loaf
74. Society bluebloods
76. Stratum
78. *Sesame Street* viewer
79. Team that kills flies?
80. Chronicles of Narnia deity

81. Latch _____
82. Buttoned-down garment
83. Grain storage space
85. Fathered, biblically speaking (var.)
88. Cushy job
90. Terry, to Betty Fox
93. *Mardi* or *mercredi*, *en anglais*
94. Manitoba region
95. Grooves
97. Permission
99. Bow shape
100. 1980 hit from Vancouver's Doug and the Slugs
102. "Golly!"
104. Some highlanders
106. Cleanse of clutter

108. Bantu language
109. Student
110. Arises from
111. Some Ottawa players, for short
112. Protected from a gale
113. **Dish soap for an early morning wash?**
114. Genie-winning film director Egoyan
115. Canadian Tire buy
119. British stove
121. Film special effects software (abbr.)

4 Canada Cornucopia 2

ACROSS

1. 1983 "hosers" flick: *Strange* _____
5. Crop grown in Canada's prairie provinces
9. Legume-based Indian dish (var.)
13. Right away abbr.
17. Verdant
18. 1964 Beatles song: "_____ Love Her"
19. Ask a model a question?
20. Ben Mulroney's mom
21. Fungal spore sacs
22. Vientiane country
23. Canadian channel for design aficionados
24. War god, in Scandinavian myth
25. HVAC apparatus
27. "I _____ may . . ."
28. Peruse the paper
29. Eternally ongoing
31. Canadian 800m runner Bishop
33. BC shares a border with this state
35. Chain component
36. Most vile
37. French lullaby: "*Fais* _____"
38. Narrowly spaced
40. Comic follower
43. Scottish city
45. It holds a tie in place
47. Relative of Ramses I
48. Beach substance
49. Percussion instrument
52. Wapiti
53. Eye surgery instruments
56. *Jolly Roger* sailor's chum
57. Baby's toy
59. Airport code for 4-D
60. Potential Juno Award winner
62. Oils anagram
63. Stately trees
65. Chest rattle sound
66. Sirens' snares?
70. Ancient Irish clans
72. Spoiling the eggs?
75. Jokinen who played for the Jets, Leafs and Flames
76. Compulsively collects
78. MacNeil who sang "She's Called Nova Scotia"
79. Pry
80. A Marx brother
82. Insert a comma or a colon
84. Carry on . . . and on . . .
85. Take laundry off the line
87. Threaten: _____ one's head
90. 1990 and 1997 Indy 500 champ Luyendyk
91. Mississauga's Square One
92. Bostonian's favourite plant?
93. East Asian ox
94. Flying formations for Canada geese
95. Blemish
96. Hollywood's Kazan
97. Circular shapes
98. Once, once
99. States further
100. Some provincial politicians (abbr.)
101. Hops drying device

DOWN

1. Dull or boring
2. Ploy
3. Caper
4. Erik Nielsen _____ International Airport
5. Get chummy
6. Like some cookware
7. SPCA pet acquisition process
8. Sib in a family
9. Degree for a doc
10. Takes all the pork chops?
11. She might use an inhaler
12. Taxes
13. Lotharios and Casanovas
14. Main road adjunct
15. Margaret Atwood Giller Prize winner: _____ *Grace*
16. Temporary resident of 58-D (2013–18)
26. 56-D, for example
27. Rouse
30. Some articles in Abitibi
32. Canadian Academy Award winner: _____ *Invasions barbares*
33. Actress Lupino
34. Biographical age info
36. Secure a rope around a rock
38. Bleep over bad words
39. Loose rocks on a slope
41. "_____ be a cold day . . ."
42. Canadian catch: Northern _____
44. Seamstress' swear word?
46. Small knife type
49. Like a male lion
50. Had a meal
51. It's mined in Canada
53. Sodium hydroxide solutions
54. Hot rod rod
55. Saskatoon and Sherbrooke have these musical groups
56. Tennis star Raonic
58. Big Smoke animal attraction
61. Edmonton hotel that opened in 1915
62. Rest and recuperation facilities
64. Most portly
66. Canadian author W.O.
67. Salve for Dame Lynn?
68. Arafat's grp.
69. Drink slowly
71. Egg yolk container
73. Amphetamine or opiate

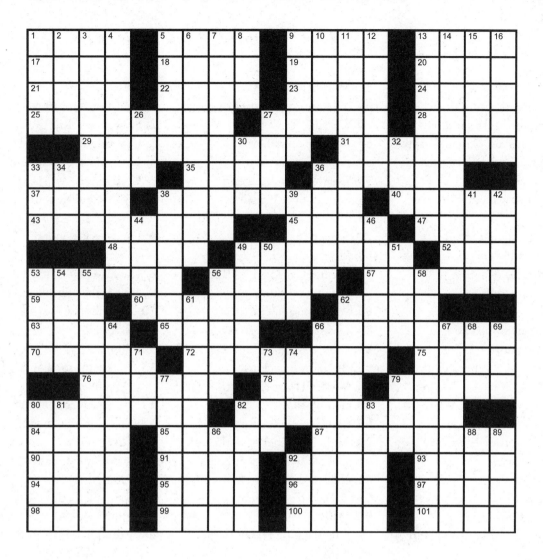

74. Brooklyn Nets point guard Jeremy
77. Sensuous ballroom dance (var.)
79. Down
80. Somber, at the cemetery?

81. More scarce
82. HBC hides, in the early days
83. Forearm bones (var.)
86. Trudge along
88. Recedes, like tides

89. 1979 Neil Young and Crazy Horse LP: _____ *Never Sleeps*
92. She or her, for short

Great Ones of the NHL

Hockey player nicknames

ACROSS

1. *The Lion King* baddy
5. Toward the back, nautically
10. The Canadian National Vimy Memorial is north of this city
15. Asian merganser
19. Strait that separates BC and WA
20. Grand lodgings
21. River with a famous left bank
22. It precedes -Cola
23. Soprano's song
24. Hall
25. Quibble, in the salon?
27. **Bobby Hull**
29. House of Commons tab?
30. Wallop
31. Make over
32. Floral arrangement
33. 1973–74 Tony Musante TV crime drama
34. Happens
37. Federal government body: _____ Canada
39. **Hab and Ranger Geoffrion**
43. Old pal
44. Lincoln or Leicester, in England
45. Thick, like a thicket
46. Sister's sibling, for short
47. Animated show, for short
48. Michael Jackson #1: "You Are Not _____"
49. Corporate stationery
51. Pianist's quick runs of chords
53. 1990s Toyota
54. Famed spy Hari
55. Leave the *Rocky Mountaineer*
56. Fly from Vancouver to Toronto, say
58. Four pecks
60. Similar sort
61. Canadian Olympian Silken Laumann, for one

62. Montblanc or BIC
63. 37-A funds this group: _____ Canada
67. Deprive of authority
68. Enlarges a garment
73. Food thickening agent
74. Sulked, on a Vespa?
75. How hearty partiers behave
77. Gatecrasher
80. Hearty chuckle
81. Former Canadian NHL coaches Quinn and Burns
82. Pollen sheath
83. Greased the wheels, say
84. Curs
85. Black, in Barcelona
86. **Gordie Howe**
88. Bodily trunk
89. Like Seoul residents
90. Little instruments, on Lanai?
91. Golfer's warning word
92. Jack-in-the-pulpit, for example
93. Typewriter component
96. Dark purple fruit
97. **Czech goalie Hasek (with "The")**
102. Atlantic Canada industry trap type
104. Good employee's extra payment
105. Boxer's pre-match garment
106. Rakishly stare at
107. Flies high
108. Not available
109. Metallic element
110. Canada's Milton Acorn: The People's _____
111. Abandoned puppy, say
112. Canadian Armed Forces milieux
113. Crunchy cookie

DOWN

1. 1970s coif or carpet
2. Sweetie, in Sicily
3. Covering for a seed
4. **Long-time Canadien Cournoyer**
5. If you're guilty, you might make these
6. Long-necked guitar
7. Poker pot payment
8. Halifax Citadel, for example
9. Give it the old college effort
10. Help Sidney to score?
11. Respond
12. Brook
13. Nickname for a *Star Wars* Skywalker
14. Free from confinement
15. Sacred beetle, to ancient Egyptians
16. Canadian ice dance champ Scott
17. Raw silk shade
18. Hornet's cousin
26. **Broad Street Bully Schultz (with "The")**
28. Very creepy (var.)
29. Cause to yawn
32. Minute opening
33. Lone Ranger's partner
34. Eightsome
35. Ten million rupees
36. Summarily appoint
37. "Go!"
38. Like some suit fabrics
39. Asian pepper plant
40. Sorcery, in the West Indies
41. Declaim
42. Relating to form
44. Move stealthily
45. Nickname for some WWII British soldiers
48. Adjective for an acrobat

49. Washes oneself
50. _____ *Pinafore*
52. Put on pounds
53. Manhandled, colloquially
57. Four-wheel drive vehicle: Land _____
58. Tree by the sea?
59. "Do _____ others as . . ."
62. Plumbers' ads?
63. Discriminatory hiring practice (var.)
64. Moon related
65. Pirate's eye cover
66. Rage
67. One of Snow White's seven
69. **Long-time Penguin Lemieux**

70. Meryl Streep movie: *August: _____ County*
71. The "U" in UHF
72. Canadian singers Sylvia or Ian
74. Underground agents?
76. Bolt or Volt
78. **Maurice Richard (with "The")**
79. Similarity
80. Bait bass
84. Additional quantity
85. Proper word?
87. Beginning
88. Foot (var.)
89. Canadian NHLers Versteeg and Letang

91. 16-year Kingston-area MP MacDonald
92. Regale
93. Onomatopoeic Alka-Seltzer jingle word
94. 49-A might have one
95. Totally competent
96. Practise boxing
97. Lady of Lisbon
98. Cross to bear, perhaps
99. Barometer pressure unit
100. Woodwind with a double reed
101. Clinton cabinet member
103. Malarkey
104. Baby's covering

ACROSS

1. Drug bust
5. Will be, in Barcelona
9. Emailed an email
13. Go to Home Hardware
17. Ear related
19. Dubai dignitary
20. Die down in intensity
21. Most gory
22. Indulgent behaviour
24. Moose Jaw province
26. Walk feebly
27. Bachman-Turner Overdrive song: "You Ain't Seen Nothing _____"
28. Place to see a memory?
30. Stratford Festival production
34. Protest types
36. Humorous Will Ferguson offering: *Canadian* _____
37. Tot up
40. Hole-boring tool
42. "_____ you would think"
43. Medical tubes
45. City in Switzerland
47. Rocky spots
48. Jann Arden hit: "_____ Is the Only Soldier"
49. Take Cash's boy to court?
50. Old-style servitude
53. Scorn
54. Vigour or vim
55. Prickly rose part
56. "_____-ching!"
57. _____ good faith
60. Decorative enamelware
62. See 20-A
65. Lath strip
66. Winfrey show: *Oprah: Where Are _____ Now?*
67. Too
69. Backyard barbecues
71. Preacher's praise word

73. 24 Sussex resident: _____ minister
74. Second-person pronoun
75. Famous #4 in the NHL
76. Unlocked
78. Not nude
79. Possessing royal authority
81. *Dancing with the Stars* pro Chmerkovskiy
83. 19th-C. Canadian author: _____ Chandler Haliburton
86. Incapable of being reformed
92. Japanese city
94. Capilano Suspension Bridge city
95. Hydrocarbon minus a hydrogen atom
96. Electronic Classroom of Tomorrow (abbr.)
97. They RSVP "yes"
98. TD teller's call
99. Dried out by the sun
100. Old levy, in Lancashire
101. René's mixed-up bird?

DOWN

1. From _____ to riches
2. Mystic's radiance
3. Spring flower
4. This used to be floppy
5. Some Château Laurier accommodations
6. Nova Scotia and British Columbia held these in 2017
7. Poison ivy symptom
8. Eoin Colfer YA sci-fi series: _____ *Fowl*
9. Comfortable cars
10. Revise wording
11. Winnipeg Jet Petan, for short
12. Car dealership transactions
13. Ex-Canucks Henrik or Daniel, for example

14. 1999 Crash Test Dummies album: *Give Yourself a* _____
15. Ago
16. Aristocrat's equal?
18. Modeller's mud
23. Senior member of a group
25. Excessive drinker
29. Trunk tire
30. Buddies
31. Maui gathering
32. Fit of shivering
33. "Owner of a Lonely Heart" band
35. Sawhorses
37. Hand cream ingredient
38. Former Maple Leaf: _____ "Tiger" Williams
39. Newfoundland locale: _____ Lake
41. Black bird
43. Shortened name
44. Bone between the elbow and the wrist
46. Cat's siesta?
47. Sea salts?
51. Cookie brand: Chips _____!
52. Statute, in Saguenay
53. Southwestern Alberta river
54. Flatbread with a pocket
56. National railway acronym (1918–60)
57. Whitish, like the chimney sweep?
58. Winning advertiser's award
59. Tuba anagram
60. Bird's call
61. Unimportant occurrences
62. *Midnight in the Garden of Good and* _____
63. Elevated church platform
64. Raised cattle, say
66. Beats wheat
68. Goblin's kin, in fantasy lit

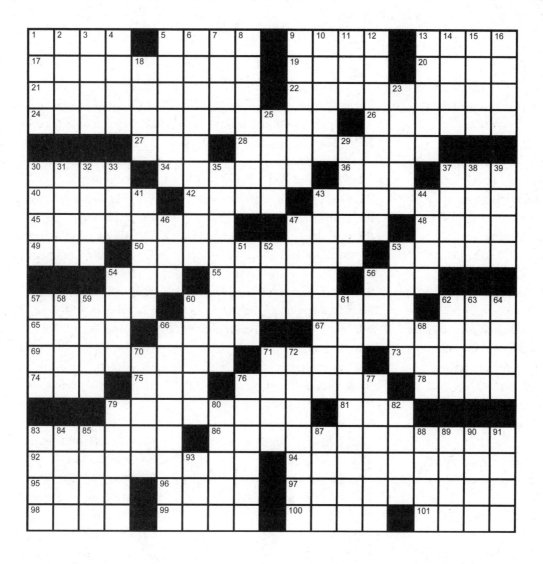

70. South American shrubs
71. He might monkey around?
72. STARS air ambulance service
76. Fancy
77. Canada's Graham Greene starred in this film: _____ *with Wolves*
79. Young salmon

80. Tissue mass (var.)
82. Russian leader Trotsky
83. Holier _____ thou
84. Bring onto the payroll
85. 2003 Atwood novel: _____ *and Crake*
87. Landmark in 94-A: Lions _____ Bridge

88. Crass
89. Say it is so
90. High-schooler
91. Irish or Scottish
93. A temporary Québec City hotel is made of this

ACROSS

1. Put away for a rainy day
6. Extol
10. They served CDA
14. Darlin', in Dulwich
17. Vital bodily vessel
18. Rwandan ethnic group
19. Cruel
21. **Sickly Marine?**
23. Tools for Canadian curler Gushue?
24. Nude, in Nottingham
25. King of Cups deck
27. Make baby booties
28. Social division, in India
29. Brain membrane related
30. Red ink items
31. Push or poke
33. Montréal Expo pavilion: _____ 67
35. 1960s toy: ____ stick
36. Attend a non-credit accounting course?
38. Al MacInnis wore this jersey number for the Flames
39. Parliament Hill has one
43. Ruins a reputation
45. Rainbow shape
47. Bishop's authority area
48. Spicy stew
49. Insignificant numbers?
52. Head wreaths
54. Pearson posting (abbr.)
57. **Locksmith's locks?**
59. Namibia neighbour (abbr.)
60. Some large engines
62. Patch of land for a Canadian bush pilot
64. Four-time Golden Globe winner Laura
65. Astrological sign
67. Traveller's guide
68. Ceremonial English bodyguard

72. Showplace for trees
75. CIBC ATM no.
77. Opposite of everybody
78. 1960s CTV game show: *Double _____ Money*
79. TELUS or Bell
82. One of the deadly sins
83. Hungarian composer Franz
85. Gretzky's Edmonton linemate MacDonald
86. *SCTV* ensemble, et al.
88. Tooth or tummy trouble
89. Musicians' apartments?
90. 1940 Mickey Mouse movie
93. Dirty era?
95. **Toy collector's find?**
97. Most applicable to equestrians?
98. "The Art of Love" poet
99. Excessive drinker (var.)
100. Old-style "in olden days"
101. Newish newts
102. Famed Roman emperor
103. Has the edge in a race

DOWN

1. Settles?
2. Wrongful act, in legalese
3. 416 or 613 in Ontario
4. Unit of solid angle measure
5. Two-time Oscar winner Tom
6. For that reason, once
7. Belonging to us
8. Hopi kin
9. Rebuke to the boy king?
10. Quivers, like a cellphone
11. Sign up at UBC
12. Early Shania Twain single: "What Made You Say _____"
13. Compass point in Pointe-Claire
14. **Bocce player?**
15. In the dark
16. Sleeveless garments
20. Keep one's promise

22. A "Little Woman"
26. Iraqi or Iranian
29. Science display tableau
30. Long-running Canadian kids' show: *Polka _____ Door*
31. Ballet step
32. Piña colada alcohol
34. 1952 film: _____ *Devil*
35. Fully attended meeting
37. Rhetorical figure of speech
40. Inclined, in Ipswich
41. *Desire Under the _____*
42. Tabula _____
44. Like Lesser Slave Lake?
46. You might submit this to Intact
50. Atlas page feature
51. Canadian driver's winter windshield implement
53. Strange, in space?
54. Old Icelandic literary compilation
55. Wedding cake layer
56. **Mr. Darcy's county?**
58. Savoury meat garnish
61. Sleepyheads
63. Pub fixture
66. Survives, on *Survivor*
69. Eggplant-based casserole
70. Years, to Yvan
71. Long-time domain for Roberto Luongo
73. Stuck in a _____
74. Carnivore's preference
76. "Impossible," at Pickering or Darlington?
80. Major Portuguese city
81. Spa treatment, for short
83. Machine in a wood shop
84. Choir anagram
85. Burns poem opener: "There's nane that's _____ of human kind"
87. Rogers Centre theft?

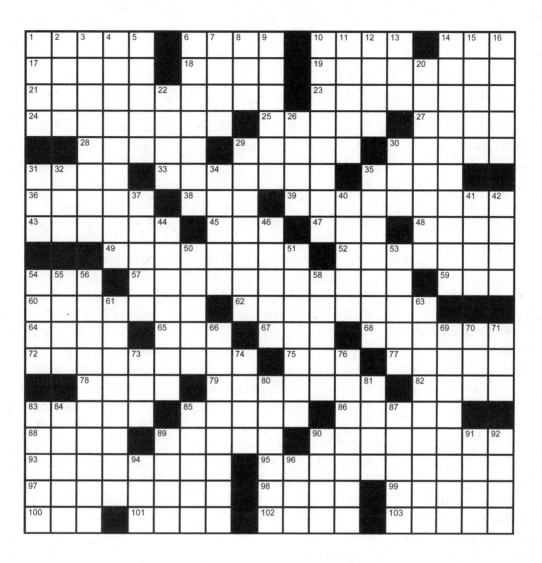

89. Feudal system tract
90. Equitable, at the PNE?

91. Footnote abbreviation
92. Affirmative votes

94. Make a bow
96. Kidlit author Bunting

Canada Cornucopia 4

ACROSS

1. Scots' toppers
5. Niagara-on-the-Lake is known for this: _____ Festival
9. Grab (onto)
13. Alberta's "wild" flower
17. Many places to park?
18. State of deep sleep
19. California valley
20. Articles in Québec
21. Avian pets
23. Honours conferred by the Queen (abbr.)
24. Preliminary race at the track
25. Makes believe
26. Ray Bolger's most famous role
28. Golden Rule preposition
29. Land measurement
30. Short sleep
32. Big work
35. Irish "hush"
37. Snapshot
39. Career path, colloquially
40. National celebration in 2017
43. Loudness measurement units
44. As a whole, to a Québec political party?
46. 2006 Giller winner Vincent
47. Tiny table scrap
49. Description of a desert
50. Overwhelmed the paving crew?
53. Shania's producer ex: _____ Lange
55. Arctic canine
56. Nullifies
61. 24 of 10-D
62. Expediency, say
64. Conical dwelling (var.)
67. Scale note (var.)
69. Sundial numeral
70. In a flowing style, musically
71. Fire
73. Forgotten about

76. Process flax
77. Make changes
78. Parent at the poker table?
79. Orpheus' instrument
80. Grind, say
81. Trudeau might do this to a senator?
84. Area in an abbey
87. Weighing
89. Some protozoa
93. Like a lean body type
94. Colour quality
95. There's one at the Parthenon
96. Nova Scotia landmark: Fort _____
97. European river
98. Long-time *Front Page Challenge* emcee Davis
99. Math branch, for short
100. Untidy dining hall?
101. Loch _____ monster
102. Keeps out of the pub?
103. Ambrosia hit: "Holdin' _____ Yesterday"

DOWN

1. 1998 Order of Canada recipient Gordie
2. Defunct orchard spray
3. Seconds, for Oliver
4. Canadian government ministry: _____ of Women
5. Smell of a penny?
6. 10-year CBC music series: *Country* _____
7. Quantities (abbr.)
8. 2013 Tegan and Sara hit: "I _____ a Fool"
9. Dumplings, Italian style
10. Famous Canadian quaff
11. Musical performance company: Calgary _____
12. Radiation amplifying device

13. German industrial valley
14. Like basketball played by two
15. Oceans are full of it
16. Kitchener clock setting (abbr.)
22. Long-time Canadian media mogul Thomson
26. "Open _____"
27. Edible mushrooms
29. Spanish title for a gentleman
31. Model
32. More than fat
33. Liquid measurements
34. Tashkent citizen
36. Winnie-the-Pooh's greeting
38. Giving a gala
40. Punctuation mark
41. Common crossword word?
42. Gastropod with a pearly interior
45. Turn from church to state?
48. Freshwater reptile
51. Ancient Greek theatre
52. Most sleepy after smoking up?
54. Made plumb
57. Moniker for Canada's Foster Hewitt: _____ of Hockey
58. Journal for a mad housewife?
59. It follows poly
60. Clobbered
63. Making a heap
64. Sun Peaks skier's transport
65. Enlighten?
66. Herringbone and houndstooth
68. Alice Munro protagonists, often
72. Stats for some Blue Jays
74. Some dives
75. Classic Canadian sitcom: _____ *Park Boys*
79. Shed that's aslant?
82. Russian politician Vladimir
83. Text
85. Walks with a heavy gait
86. Transgression
88. "The _____ have it"

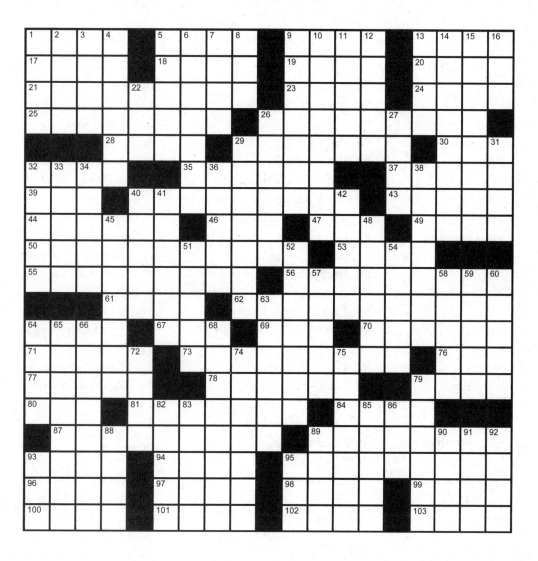

89. Cat who starred on *Iron Chef America*

90. Alberta's Moraine Lake, for one

91. Polish one's writing

92. Utah's state flower

93. *Così fan tutte* composer's monogram

95. Canadian Armed Forces milieu (abbr.)

9 — Where Am I?

Here's the landmark – name the city

ACROSS

1. Desists
6. Eye-shaped windows
11. Average score for Canada's Brooke Henderson
14. Luminous celebrities?
19. Statutory August date in NT, NU and PEI: _____ Holiday
20. Canadian boots brand
21. Common verb
22. Impressive display
23. Ottawa's Canadian Tire Centre, for one
24. Asian capital
25. Like a bump on a _____
26. Chemical weapon agent
27. **St. Joseph's Oratory**
29. Flooring under a futon?
31. Canada signed this international environmental accord
32. Shredded cabbage for Cole?
33. This nut is toxic to dogs
35. Crumpled piece of paper
36. Consumes
39. Artful dodger?
41. Cuts in half
43. Guest of Her Majesty
45. CFL play
47. Gives a jump-start
51. Heart of Motown?
52. Ben Mulroney, vis-à-vis Brian
54. Roman sun god
55. **High Level Bridge**
57. Some calendar components
60. Computing shortcut word
62. Canadian author Klein
63. Store
64. Bartending tool
67. Frolic
68. Plastic pipe type (abbr.)
71. Ontario is Canada's largest producer of this fruit
73. Last Greek letters
75. Cleaning agent
76. Irish word for itself?
78. Eclipse shading
80. Long poem form
82. Pursue in a corn maze?
84. Winnipeg philanthropic group: The _____ Foundation
85. Neurotransmitter related to sleep
90. **Bronte Creek Provincial Park**
92. British band: _____ Zeppelin
94. Acid hit drug, for short
95. Québec MNA Thériault since 2002
96. Like frozen roads
97. Steak selections
99. NHLer Jarome from Alberta
101. Moral uneasiness
104. Cereal type
106. Dine
107. Trig ratio
110. It reflects sunbeams
112. Arm bone
114. Gala or Granny Smith
116. Duck type
117. **Heart Lake Conservation Area**
121. Cantaloupe or Crenshaw
122. Little bit of a thing?
123. Canada's Ryan Gosling, for example
125. Mindless
126. Delete computer files
127. Earlier, in olden days
128. Biblical possessive
129. Social pariah
130. Broody hen?
131. 20-year Canadian NHLer Brind'Amour
132. Like an unkempt garden?
133. Rope a dogie

DOWN

1. Fraudulent scheme
2. Newbie (var.)
3. Kitchen appliance
4. Publicans pull these
5. Hawthorne book: *The _____ Letter*
6. **Parkwood National Historic Site**
7. _____ *Miner's Daughter*
8. Subject of a still life
9. Leggings for little girls
10. Pelvic bone adjective
11. Peer of Charlemagne
12. Bouquets
13. Diet and exercise scheme
14. **Ukrainian Museum of Canada**
15. Salver
16. 1950s Canadian plane: *Avro* _____
17. Yogurt-based dip
18. Church council group
28. Surreptitiously listen in
30. Abacus, for example
33. Chaps
34. Nuclear warhead weapon (abbr.)
36. Sibilant sound
37. Midget buffalo
38. Pornography
40. Turn down a plea
42. Search aid in the sea
44. Maul anagram
46. Tiber city
48. Seat without arms
49. Celebrated Canadian politician Douglas
50. Shoot at a woodcock?
53. Stick-to-your-ribs breakfast serving
55. Irish lough or river
56. They hound you?
58. Dump scavenger

59. Abs strengthening exercise

61. Sleep states from which you can't wake

65. Most attractive

66. Source of chicle

68. Moolah, in Mexico

69. Like important statistics?

70. Marsh bird

72. Historic NL landmark: L'_____ aux Meadows

74. Rummy who drinks too much gin?

77. Santa's staffers

79. Belgian singer/songwriter Jacques

81. Songs for a single singer

83. **Doon Heritage Village**

86. 2003 film: *Anything* _____

87. Number of Blue Jays on the field

88. 1987 Madonna song: "La _____ Bonita"

89. Shipshape

91. Novel from Canada's Robertson Davies: *The _____ of Orpheus*

93. Québec politician's initiative?

97. Topped a levee

98. King _____

100. Saloon

102. Coat to wear in Northern Ireland?

103. Spanish scoundrel

105. **Redwood Park**

107. Humped animal

108. *Rigoletto*, for one

109. Position awkwardly

111. Udders

113. Sleep disorder

115. Come in second

117. Canada Savings _____

118. Memorial Day bugler's piece

119. Defunct Canadian bills that featured Queen Elizabeth

120. Wolfe created by Rex Stout

124. NHL overtime cause

ACROSS

1. Writes in a hurry
5. Hera's son
9. Gulf War missile
13. Puncture
17. Celestial bear
18. Half a provincial name
19. Itch, say
20. It comes before the storm
21. Nickname for Hamilton's newspaper
22. Out for the night?
23. National telecommunications company
24. NYC theatrical award
25. Chemical solution's concentration
27. With no _____ in sight
28. Some legumes, to a Brit
30. Cut, then paste
32. Clumps of hair
34. Affirmative responses (var.)
35. More impoverished
37. Tiara for a noblewoman
39. Worked for Statistics Canada?
41. Jute, for example
45. Young fellows
49. Lab tubes
50. Score instruction for "slow"
51. Ousting from accommodations
53. One who studies abroad (abbr.)
54. Move in an uncontrolled manner
55. Coating a road
56. Units of time (abbr.)
57. Canadian artist Robert
58. They're raised at Kitchener's Oktoberfest
59. Grassy field for livestock
60. Festive December season
61. St. Lawrence River peninsula
62. Siesta or café, for example
64. 1989 Juno Award winner Jordan
65. Dinner scraps
66. People who can't be redeemed
68. Casino visitor, often
69. "Canada's movie website"
74. Seem to be
78. Very pious Jew
80. Vancouver's Pacific Coliseum and Edmonton's Northlands Coliseum
81. Lip blips
83. Hair holder
85. Upstanding?
86. Perch for a mountain goat
87. _____ Webster . . . man of many words
88. Some chandeliers hang here
90. Alberta tourist mecca: _____ Louise
91. Nerves network
92. Environmentalist Al
93. Faux pas at Victoria's Secret?
94. _____ of Wight
95. Dust-ups
96. Developing amphibians
97. Knob on an organ
98. Indian tree

DOWN

1. Canadian singer Bieber
2. Stonecrop plant
3. Blood-sucking fly
4. _____ trust
5. Santa _____ winds
6. Attire for a spa
7. Special spectacle?
8. Foe of a Pharisee
9. Lower layers, in geology
10. Liquid wood preservatives
11. Like the beast, rather than the beauty?
12. Held up
13. Tart fruits
14. Largest instruments in the brass section
15. Skirt style
16. Word heard during grace
26. "Great" Canadian body of water
29. What 68-A does
31. Bowlers' targets
33. Ontario–Minnesota border town
36. Feeling remorse (var.)
38. Early video gaming console, for short
40. Fuel efficiency abbr.
41. Some chapeaux
42. Energy sapping illness
43. Places, for stand-ins
44. Units equal to 1,000 kilograms
45. Releases
46. Embodiment of Canada's James Cameron?
47. Like the worst-case scenario
48. Temporary currencies
50. See 12-D
52. Fork point
54. Volcanic crater
56. Summertime maladies
57. Pop a balloon
59. Get discouraged about a failing fling?
60. 1972 April Wine song: "_____ Could Have Been a Lady"
62. Captain's book
63. Caution
66. Saskatchewan lake or town
67. Foal's father
68. Traditional Newfoundland song: "Jack _____ Every Inch a Sailor"
70. Kitchener's name until 1916
71. Apprehension
72. CFL player's sack
73. Hold in high regard

74. Ghanaian capital
75. Delved into the details
76. Famed student of Socrates

77. Rims
79. Passed out the cards
82. Mansard or gambrel

84. Canada's Rush, for one
89. Solar Power Plant (abbr.)

11 Dual Instrumentalists?

They play both sides

ACROSS

1. Hindu teacher
5. The very top point
9. Body of water in the Rockies
13. Selkirk Mountains ghost town
17. Before long, poetically
18. Scotiabank might give you one
19. Out of the wind, at sea
20. A lot of land?
21. Injure with a dagger
22. Sync a piano
23. **Fisherman's upright instrument?**
24. Meadows
25. Simon & Garfunkel song: "_____ Bound"
27. Doctrine
28. Handkerchief edging material
29. Description of some missiles
31. People lacking skin pigment
33. Type of terrier
36. Paper _____
37. Biochemical solid
38. Karakul lamb's wide pelt?
40. Chi preceder
41. Express your opinion
44. Mulelike?
45. Quartz from Michigan?
47. Form of ether
48. "Our home and native _____!"
49. Dives right in?
51. Electric fish
52. Extraterrestrials
55. UVic grads
56. Oysters' jewels
58. Expel from a group
59. Command
61. Line in a mine
62. 1972 Summit Series team (abbr.)
64. Order at Tim Hortons
65. Consoling words
69. One who robs

71. Tragically Hip drummer Johnny
72. Doctors do this
73. Black drake
75. Sully
76. Nun's nasty no-no?
77. Start using marijuana?
79. Royal Alexandra and Princess of Wales, in Toronto
81. Rave anagram
82. Library classification system
84. Most poor
88. It might have you all tied up?
89. **Brake mechanic's music maker?**
90. Grimm brute
91. Month of Purim
92. Just a single time
93. Pronunciation problem for Sylvester
94. Took off
95. Captain in *Twenty Thousand Leagues Under the Sea*
96. _____-do-well
97. Manitoba, directionally from Saskatchewan
98. Rogers of Canadian telecommunications, et al.
99. Agitated state

DOWN

1. Wound type
2. "Render therefore _____ Caesar . . ."
3. Ramble
4. Like the lightness of being?
5. Christian church table
6. King, queen or jack
7. **Chef's guitar?**
8. Compass pt.
9. Alberta town known for its corn
10. Newfoundland-born singer/ actor Doyle
11. Usher's occasional task

12. Company that manufactures Coffee Crisp
13. **Poetry Muse's keyboard?**
14. *Queen Elizabeth* or *Queen Mary*
15. Austere Athenian judge
16. Those voting in favour
26. Ensemble of instrumentalists
27. Pointy tool's point
30. Feel lousy
32. Bob McKenzie, to Doug, for short
33. *All in the Family* network
34. Fredericton venue: Beaverbrook _____ Gallery
35. Note promising future payment
37. NHLers often get whacked on these
39. Pharynx neighbour
40. *Nom de _____*
42. Former Speaker of the Canadian Senate Kinsella
43. Structural additions
45. **Champagne drinker's woodwind?**
46. Some tents (var.)
49. Aquarium fish
50. Looked for tomorrow?
52. Touch
53. Tie down a sail
54. Refusal to budge, say
55. Essence of rose
57. Some '60s Vietnam-born children
60. Self-serve eatery
61. Provided sanctuary from the storm
63. **Board secretary's instrument?**
65. **Geometrician's percussion piece?**
66. See 27-D
67. Oracle Business Intelligence (abbr.)
68. Soaked

70. Dandy

72. *The Tell-Tale Heart* author

74. Walk like a two-year-old?

75. Wallflowery

77. West African country

78. Sheeplike

79. Bait into bad behaviour?

80. Equipment for 26-D

83. Sissy

85. 1960s TV actress Barbara

86. Long-time Vancouver Canuck player Salo

87. Slow run, around the paddock

90. Frequently, for short

ACROSS

1. Touts
6. Place to enjoy pampering
9. Lettuce variety
12. Crooked
17. Dangerous wave
18. Exhausted
20. Commemorative pillar
21. Reward for Rover
22. Like slightly undercooked orecchiette
23. Ring-tailed animal
24. Very skilled
25. Organisms that share a trait
26. Go after a new job
27. Imp's kin
29. Slice
30. PGA tour stop: RBC Canadian _____
32. Life _____
36. Permanent staffer, say
41. Humorous texting acronym
42. History channel offering: *Ice _____ Truckers*
43. Drills into
44. Toronto Harbourfront boulevard: Queens _____
45. Copied
47. Stared fiercely
49. Long-time Québec children's show: _____-*Partout*
50. Literary adverb
51. Illuminated
52. Signs of life?
53. Thunderstruck
55. German physicist Georg
56. Popular perfume since 1932
57. USSR word
60. Toronto MLB pro
62. "Beware the _____ of March"
66. Country where 43-D practised
67. Cheshire cats, for example
68. Cat food flavour
69. Trident segment
70. Unconcerned by
71. Hive, for example
73. Bit of wit from Tom?
74. Haitian religious cult
76. Not found wanting?
78. Ewes' mates
79. No score, at a soccer match
80. Scotiabank ATM no.
81. Former New Brunswick premier Graham
85. Whist relative
88. Data storage disc
92. Boiled buckwheat cereal
93. More unkempt, like a garden?
94. Sister of Thalia
95. Eastern Christian church member (var.)
96. Pencil toppers
97. Small, in Sherbrooke
98. Quartz type
99. Tennis player's clique?
100. Relative Standard Error (abbr.)
101. Sound of the surf hitting the beach

DOWN

1. Greek salad cheese
2. Cooking fat
3. Architectural arch style
4. Nickname for Don Cherry
5. Early Canada resident
6. Clean a ship's decks
7. RCMP canine
8. Passion for a Canadian?
9. Rabbit type
10. Gushed from
11. Tented one's fingers
12. See 12-A
13. "That's one small _____ for man . . ."
14. 1996 US VP candidate Jack
15. Jewish calendar month
16. Cautious
19. Bottom line, in Brighton
28. Polliwog
31. Overhead Chicago trains
32. Band from Montréal: Simple _____
33. Rock climber's lifeline
34. Famed American general Robert
35. Still in force
36. Jury leaders
37. Canadian territorial capital
38. Rumple
39. Nonchalance
40. Canadian Club whiskies
43. Famed Canadian physician Norman
46. Emptied the tub
48. Opposite of reductionism (var.)
49. Dart players' bar
52. Record of your earnings
54. Former US record label
56. Biblical weeds
57. 1970s Canadian skit show
58. Buckeye State
59. Trattoria serving
60. Foundation garment
61. Birks, et al.
63. Asinine
64. Lone organic compound?
65. Fill to the brim
67. Espies
70. _____ constrictor
72. Arm muscles
75. Like rococo furniture
76. More risky
77. Scheer who became federal PC leader in 2017
79. Auction actions
81. Northern seabird
82. Guess Who song: "_____ on to Your Life"
83. South Korea's continent

84. 2015 Shawn Mendes duet: "I Know _____ You Did Last Summer"

86. Not cluttered

87. Hebrides tongue

89. Lead-in to -tat-tat

90. Elisha who invented the elevator

91. Night flyer

Read All About Him

Bios for the bookish

ACROSS

1. Flue dirt
5. Functions
9. Nimble
13. Great _____ Lake NWT
17. Daughter of Hera
18. Big moment for Carey Price
19. Bread spread
20. Encroachment on an avenue?
23. Loudly opinionated
25. Super Bowl LI entertainer: _____ Gaga
26. Eyelike butterfly markings
27. Like Humpty Dumpty's physique
28. Christopher Plummer's book
31. First Nations governing group: _____ Council
33. Road surfacing material
34. Electric vehicles
35. Hardy succulents
37. Stanley Park art pole
39. Former East German currency
44. Raze
46. Rumour monger
47. Lamb's mom
50. Instrument that gives you a buzz?
51. Canadian businessman and philanthropist Bronfman
54. Ramses I son
55. Temporary hair colouring
57. Quaint place to lodge
58. Women's tennis great Steffi
59. Norwegian land features
61. Atlanta-born *Malcolm X* director
63. Ribbons and ruffles, on dresses
65. Sophocles play: _____ *Rex*
66. Level playing _____
67. Not aboard
72. Not inside
74. Indistinct speaker

75. Hold on tight?
79. Spout off in anger
80. Took a chair
81. Christopher's birds?
82. Sticky baby's syllables?
83. Parental authority?
84. Canadian Wiebe who won wrestling gold in Rio
86. Doe anagram
87. Competitions for yachts
90. Propose a candidate
93. Underwriter, for example
94. Plant stem tissue
96. Lives in a tent
100. Napoli's nation
102. Hippies' hallucinogen
104. Larynx locale
105. Paul Martin's prime ministerial recollections collection
111. Bevelling saw
112. Pupil surround
113. Actor LaBeouf
114. Bad place to be during a quake
116. Made noise at night
117. Loan
118. Canadian DIY outlet
119. Unappetizing fare
120. Court hoops
121. Falco of *The Sopranos*
122. Halt
123. Gels or hardens

DOWN

1. Lynne Truss book: *Eats, _____ & Leaves*
2. Composer's complete works
3. Acquire
4. Proving ground for Sealy?
5. It entertains American GIs
6. Japanese beverage (var.)
7. Gallery opening or gala
8. 1988 INXS hit: "New _____"

9. Arias, usually
10. Nebraska river
11. Cash in coupons
12. Toys on strings
13. Source of renewable energy
14. Forms a sac in the body
15. Warmongering Greek god
16. This can earn an actress a Canadian Screen Award
21. The entire amount
22. *The Count of Monte Cristo* prison: Château _____
24. Major-General Lewis MacKenzie's memoir
29. They play for the Sens and Argos?
30. Ocean bottom
32. South American capital city
36. Most liable to seep
38. Title of several Gretzky biographies
40. Japanese chef's ingredient
41. Impersonator
42. Getting CPP, say
43. Kardashian clan matriarch Jenner
45. *The _____ Ranger*
46. Iron fishing hook
47. Leading *Rogue One* character Jyn
48. Dry with a dishtowel
49. *National Velvet* author Bagnold
52. Whimsically comical
53. Cheap-looking accessories
56. You can do this at Calgary's Canada Olympic Park
59. Tahoma, for example
60. Title of more than one Pierre Trudeau biography
62. Sumptuous
63. Their Santa Claus is called Joulupukki
64. Not at all out of the ordinary

66. Unravel
68. That gal
69. Bestselling Nabisco cookie
70. Tear wide open
71. Celtic language
73. Some ball park stats
74. Husband, in Hull
75. Taj Mahal locale
76. Completes a task
77. Big bikes for pig farmers?
78. Grandson of Abraham
80. Terms at U of T

83. Canadian "Building a Mystery" singer McLachlan
85. "I _____ Stop Loving You"
88. Poem for The Supremes?
89. Foursomes
91. Stew type: _____ podrida
92. Nautical ropes
94. Aahed
95. Sesame paste
97. Streak or blotch
98. 15-year CUPW president Jean-Claude
99. Infuses

101. Thread used for gloves
103. Alcohol retailer in AB and BC: Liquor _____
105. Adele hit: "Rumour _____ It"
106. Coastal bird (var.)
107. Provancher known as Canada's "Father of natural history"
108. Folks' tales?
109. Walk through the surf
110. Torontonian Romano who voiced *The Batman* cartoon
115. _____-de-la-Madeleine QC

Solution on page 211

14 Canada Cornucopia 7

ACROSS

1. Belgrade coins
6. Withdraw from gradually
10. Tibetan priest
14. Shook hands for the first time
17. In flight, say
18. 1967 event in Montréal
19. Oklahoma university city
20. Cooker in the Cotswolds
21. Nunavut cape that shares its name with an Egyptian city
22. Soaks bread in jus
23. Former federal politicians Boudria and Mazankowski
24. Mythological otherworld: _____-nan-Og
25. Electricity unit
27. Fragrant resin
29. Nap or siesta
30. Sarnia-born Masters champ Mike
32. Yellow bird
34. Internet financial transactions
39. 1995 album from Canada's Colin James
43. *The Jungle Book* bear
44. Utah indigenous group (var.)
46. _____ Grove AB
47. Votes in an MLA
49. Struggle to breathe
51. He wrote *The Canadian Establishment*: _____ C. Newman
52. In a hazardous manner
54. Collar a criminal
56. Canadian glam rock band: Sweeney _____
57. Rare basketball play
60. Inflict damage
64. Too much, to Telemann
65. Lost one's temper
70. Taken _____
72. Lout anagram

73. Endeavoured
74. Rutabaga
76. Cylindrical
80. Canadian bookstore chain
81. Most like Superman?
83. Emily Carr was known for this
85. Completely, in *The Wizard of Oz*?
86. Like a naked lady?
87. Shaped like an Easter egg
90. Make a genetic duplicate
92. Financial and insurance company since 1887
98. Sty dweller
99. Like the Duchess of Cambridge, often
100. Egyptian vipers
102. One-_____ victory
103. Hail to Caesar?
104. Canada's fourth-highest mountain: King _____
105. Unaccompanied musical moments
106. Overact
107. Made like the maestro
108. Coffee dispensers
109. Peppard '80s show: _____ -Team
110. Canadian pair skater Moscovitch

DOWN

1. Fill a suitcase
2. Jai _____
3. Churn up sediment
4. Richard Pryor sported one
5. Load cargo
6. Ontario university
7. Film that won best picture at the 1994 Genie Awards
8. Download for a device
9. Plastic surgeon's frequent target
10. Bavarian boy's shorts

11. Lack of moral standards
12. Little lackeys, in the movies?
13. Potential buyers' enticements
14. Partner up?
15. Protection (var.)
16. Promiscuous pastry chef?
26. Sense of wonderment
28. Womanizer
29. Rue
31. Gun the engine
33. Local Authorities Pension Plan (abbr.)
34. Celebrity hairstylist José
35. City in Colombia
36. Cheers for Real Madrid?
37. Spoof
38. Recurring theme
40. Agreement signed in 1965: Canada–US _____ Pact
41. _____ tea
42. Bookish student
45. Dairy industry giant headquartered in Québec
48. One-armed bandit
50. All but Alberta charge these (abbr.)
53. Circular dwelling
54. Ontario town where they like to eat Macs?
55. Macdonald is on these Canadian bills
58. Plant parts for grafting
59. Toothed wheel device
60. Bowlers and boaters
61. Share a border
62. Partially cooked steak description
63. Nova Scotia's 28th premier Stephen
66. Ship's figurehead perch
67. Explorer Marco
68. Happily _____ after
69. Office furniture piece

34

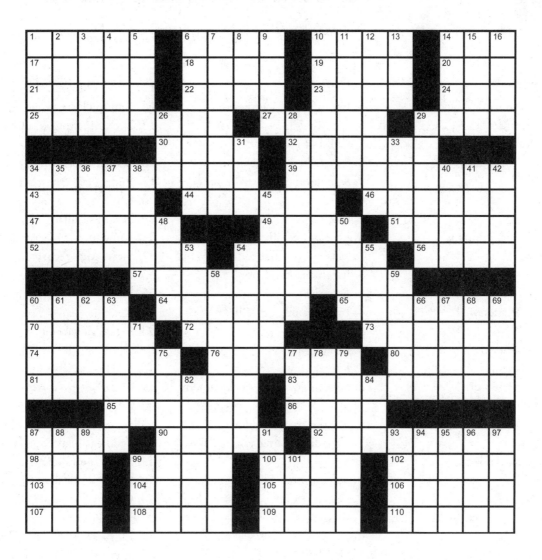

71. Pottery oven

75. Chatham's Fergie Jenkins was one for the Texas Rangers

77. Subside, at the seaside?

78. Run roughshod over

79. Two continents in one

82. Produced by the wind (var.)

84. Ex-NHLer Alfredsson, for 17 yrs.

87. Birthstone for some Libras

88. Famous de Gaulle phrase: "_____ *le Québec libre!*"

89. Grew more mellow

91. Sydney is on this coast of Cape Breton

93. Not new

94. Like some gimlets

95. "Rebel Yell" rocker Billy

96. Greek salad ingredient

97. Ex-prime minister of Britain Anthony

99. Central Processing Unit (abbr.)

101. . . . Fah-_____-lah . . .

You Snooze, You Lose

Don't fall asleep on these nouns

ACROSS

1. Ornamental garden bloomer
7. Money hoarder
12. Sounded like a donkey
18. Places to get perms
19. Smell
20. Created a new version of an old film
21. Mineral that contains magnesium
22. Ankle bone
23. Exact payback
24. Sword for a fencer
25. Snob
27. **Caustic remark**
28. Crayola colour
29. Tilted to one side
30. Discriminatory towards the elderly (var.)
32. **Dirigible**
34. Release a popular book again
38. Consumed
41. Tina of *30 Rock*
42. Painting style that tricks the eye
44. US gun lobby grp.
45. "God keep our land _____ and free"
47. Goes apace
48. Turns sharply
49. Breakfast option
50. Ancient decorative chests
51. You might call "Ahoy!" to him
52. US pipeline co. purchased by TransCanada in 2007
53. **Areas**
54. Revelstoke _____
55. Canadian reno guru McGillivray
58. Former Canadian NHLers Savard and Denis
59. CFB Cold Lake, for example
63. Canadian retailer since 1837: _____ Renfrew

64. Labour Day mos.
65. Like a bucolic setting
66. Quirky
67. Child's tough time?
68. As written, to Caesar
69. Signed on the dotted line
70. Ardour
72. **Cucumber's kin**
75. Like stuffed animals
77. Makes a comparison
78. Israeli-made weapon
81. **Fanatic**
84. Bring shame, to William Shakespeare
86. FBI emp.
87. Fire up, say
88. Federal government document: _____ Paper
89. Middle Eastern language
91. Canadian culinary show: *What's for _____?*
92. Some rounds at the Rogers Cup
93. Canada's Karsh created portraiture with this
94. Jousters' mounts
95. Legislate
96. "_____ no place like home"

DOWN

1. RRSP or RRIF
2. **Rock & Roll Hall of Fame inductee Frank**
3. Flying saucer crew member
4. Individual
5. WSW opposite
6. You don't want to be this at the wheel
7. Afternoon performances
8. Angrily
9. Oblique strokes, in punctuation
10. Big birds that run
11. Jamaican religion disciple
12. Charcoal burners

13. Cover old ground
14. Catkin clusters
15. Masculine force, in Chinese philosophy
16. Beat at the finish line
17. Red _____ AB
26. Child who's sitting with Santa?
29. Not so punitive
31. Some metric measurements
32. **Swiss Alps resort**
33. Hangman's loops
35. Fit of pique
36. Impel
37. Sarah McLachlan song: "Loving You Is _____"
38. Psychoanalysis target
39. Order _____ carte
40. Preschool child
43. Parts of cookware sets
46. Paddler's blade
47. **Some metallic elements**
48. **Ice rink machine**
50. Gulf of California, a.k.a. Sea of _____
51. Ex-PM Paul and *SCTV* star Andrea
53. Uses a microwave, colloquially
54. Grafton mystery novel: _____ for Deadbeat
55. Go to Hudson's Bay
56. Close of some musical compositions
57. Alberta town southwest of 17-D
58. Ways to an end?
59. City in western Germany
60. *Raiders of the Lost _____*
61. Author's submission encl., often
62. Antiquity, poetically
64. Loudmouths?
65. Most fussy about food
67. Flew WestJet?
68. Pelvic nerve name

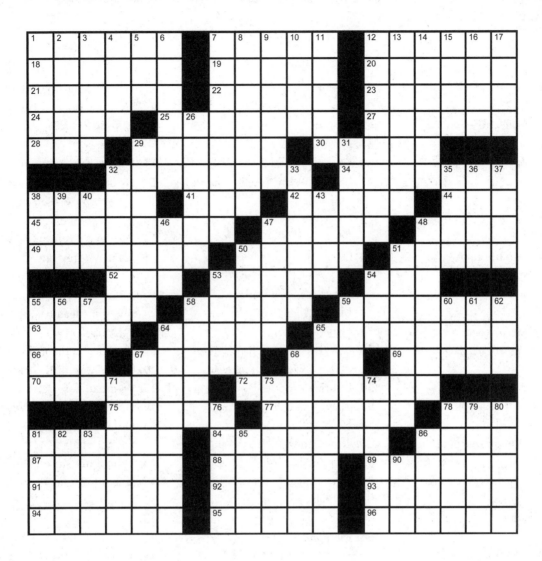

71. Metal or wooden strip
73. Canadian IÖGO yogurt maker
74. Canada's largest property and casualty insurer
76. Opening in the side of a ship
78. Earthy pigment
79. **African country**
80. Machu Picchu people
81. Our last letters
82. Highway 400 off-ramp
83. It might leave pocks
85. Mordecai Richler novel: *Joshua _____ and Now*
86. Boggle or Yahtzee
90. Pep rally word

ACROSS

1. Feudal worker
5. Bend with the knees
10. Mountain valley
13. Stupefied
17. 1972 Summit Series star Henderson
18. Preventative measure?
19. Cry of surprise
20. Mount Pinatubo flow
21. Proactiv target
22. Jason jilted her
23. More expensive
25. Canadian-born Caroline who hosted *The Biggest Loser* (2004–06)
26. Be an accessory
27. Fancy floor covering
28. Damask or denim
31. National organization: Canadian _____ Association
32. Salman Rushdie book: *The _____ Verses*
35. Stick used by a Toronto Rock player
37. Repentigny roads
41. Edible mushroom
42. Recipe instruction
43. Co-star Smythe on 84-D
44. Canadian jeweller that opened in 1879
45. Popular 1930s style: Art _____
46. California place: Palo _____
49. Hamburger holder
50. Old-fashioned knife
51. Former federal politician Monique (1972–1984)
52. Hydrant adjunct
54. Wrapped with rope
56. Fleet
57. Most pert
60. Lose firmness
61. Scruff
65. Network of 53-D
66. Worry excessively
67. Birds at the beach (var.)
68. Cut the grass
69. Get _____ start
71. Canada's Cam Neely wore this number as a Bruin
73. Showed on the convention floor, say
74. 2003 family film: *Finding _____*
75. "Farmer's Song" singer McLauchlan
77. _____ bankrupt
78. Diana Krall Grammy winner: *_____ I Look in Your Eyes*
80. Ovarian output
82. They might carry purses?
86. Fireplace shelves
87. Tastes slowly
91. Extreme bitterness
92. Electronic communication
93. It might be a big one?
94. Significant street in Hamilton?
95. Margaret Trudeau, _____ Sinclair
96. A bride walks down one
97. Former *Canada AM* host Perry
98. Salad or fries
99. Contribute one's two cents
100. Assessed
101. Hot _____ gun

DOWN

1. Pole on a ship
2. A pop, say
3. Early Scandinavian alphabet character
4. Bargain bazaars
5. Corporeal
6. Home province of 25-A
7. 2011 Drake song: "_____ Ground Kings"
8. Component of vinegar
9. You can get one at Davids
10. *Your Show of Shows* comedienne Imogene
11. Fingerprint ridges
12. Former show on 65-A: *Little _____ on the Prairie*
13. Briskly, to a pianist
14. Pace in a pasture
15. Anne Murray hit: "Talk It _____ in the Morning"
16. Saskatchewan-born country singer Fjellgaard
24. Wine cask
27. Conspiracy theorist's narrative?
29. South American cuckoos
30. Pyromaniac's property crime
32. Fox hunt foes, in England
33. Not on board, in the Ozarks
34. Fodder plant
36. Lunenburg sits on this
38. Shield protuberance
39. Big birds
40. "Auld Lang _____"
42. Sire
43. Two-_____ sloth
45. Jam-packed
47. Cars for stars
48. Ensnare
51. Funeral home stand
53. *The National* news anchor Ian
55. Sophie, to Justin
56. Ticker trouble
57. Electronic copy
58. Up to a task
59. Con artist's ruse
60. Impressionist artist Edgar
62. Absent from the barracks
63. Southern Ontario regional municipality
64. "Titan of Twang" guitarist Duane
68. Dad's partner, in Prévost

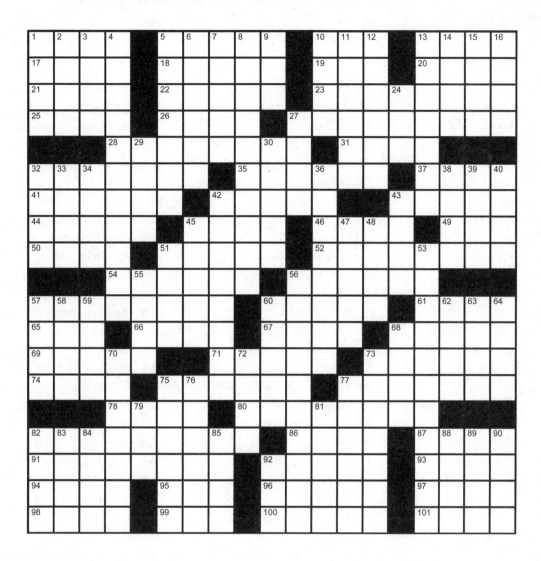

70. Water skier's rope
72. International Real Estate Society (abbr.)
73. Yukon Quest racing vehicle
75. Three-time federal election debates moderator Ann
76. US air carrier
77. On the move in Alabama?

79. Barenaked Ladies hit: "If I _____ $1000000"
81. Chaff the chef?
82. Rubble's loud noises?
83. Brazilian berry
84. Richardson HGTV show: *Sarah Off the* _____
85. Stared at

88. Eva Avila won this CTV reality show: *Canadian* _____
89. Neighbour of Ecuador
90. Absolutely alike
92. Corn serving

Meet the Wilsons

Husband-and-wife entertainers and entrepreneurs

ACROSS

1. Some flavoured coffees
7. Whistler skiers' mover
11. Cozy room in a pub
15. Snow removal machine
19. Remove freight from a hold
20. Field of study
21. Oliva Dionne, to the quints
22. Latvian city
23. Football facilities (var.)
24. Scholastic Canada school events
26. Release radiation, say
27. **Their genre, when they make music**
29. **US soap she appeared on**
31. Van Gogh's avarice?
32. Antlered mammal
34. _____ & Bradstreet Canada
35. Judge or jury
36. Edwardian "earlier"
37. Ringed by an aureole
40. "Armageddon" band from Canada
41. Waste time
42. Swimsuit style
46. Actress Ryan
49. **Their home province**
52. Blue Rodeo hit: "_____ Mine"
53. Frightening
55. *Superman* actor Christopher
56. Decorative wallboard
58. Hindu religious retreat
59. Unit of loudness
60. Fork-tailed ocean bird
61. 2008 Genie winner: *Away from _____*
62. Adjusts
63. Choose
64. Private eye's assignment
65. "_____ Maria"
66. Boys in the 'hood?
67. Singer Hill or actor Aykroyd
69. Beef stew, for example

71. 151, to Octavia
72. Canadian actor Rubinek
73. German shepherd on a famous Canadian TV show
74. Like the immediate past
75. Exhausted from hard labour
77. Sobs
78. Rankin or Bathurst follower, in Canada's North
79. Plate garnishing herb
80. **She is . . .**
82. Where quilters come together
83. Like contagious patients
85. False name
86. Bless, in olden days
87. As red as a beet, for example
89. CRTC's US counterpart
92. Height
95. Trick taker, in euchre
98. He has his own British isle?
99. Ice sheet in the ocean
100. **Their HGTV Canada reno show**
103. **Country where he lived when he met her**
106. Angle, to a botanist
107. Dreadful
109. Bryn Mawr reunion attendee
110. Canadian address necessity: Postal _____
111. US chain in Canada since 1981: _____ Bell
112. *Beetle Bailey* canine
113. Winnipeg CFLer
114. Leg part
115. Rest anagram
116. Former money unit in Peking
117. Drives too fast

DOWN

1. Molson _____
2. Travelling the nation to perform
3. Contract provision

4. Dusty Springfield song: "If It _____ Been For You"
5. Miners' way in and out
6. Scorch
7. Cola can opener
8. Canadian LPGA pro Henderson
9. A billion years (var.)
10. Gathered up the leaves
11. Madrid country
12. Guileless one
13. Raised, old style
14. _____ bypass surgery
15. Tennis tourney early round
16. Restrict the scope of
17. Gothic arch
18. "Bridge over Troubled _____"
25. Winter bug
28. Most cowardly, colourfully?
30. Experiences OCD
33. Myrna of 1930s Hollywood
37. Jackrabbit
38. Boxer Muhammad
39. "Whatcha _____?"
40. Sixteen US ounces of ale
41. **He is . . .**
43. **US city where they renovate houses**
44. She might host a roast
45. 1976 ABC miniseries: *Rich Man, _____ Man*
46. Reduce the price, at Home Outfitters
47. Like a chalkboard or a cassette tape
48. Romper room?
49. Guesstimator's phrase
50. Fabric for a wetsuit
51. Squid's feeler
52. Strident noise
54. Canadian Historical Association (abbr.)
57. Lionel Richie hit: "You _____"
58. Truant

60. As stiff as a board
62. Main railway route
64. Carry on
65. Select group of invitees
66. Piece of gold
68. Offensively curious
70. "Wow!"
71. *Blondie* character Dithers
72. Savoury sauce type
73. **He usually wears these**
74. Spare part of the body?
75. Narrator's yarn
76. Marries

77. Bluff near Balmoral
79. Ursa Minor body
81. Canadian natural resource
84. Notched, like a bread knife
85. Wild Rose province motorists' org.
86. Clement who preceded and followed Churchill
88. Attribute to
89. Fiery cooking technique
90. Scammed
91. Woods for blanket chests
92. Wallop

93. Genus, for example
94. Actor's parenthetical comment
95. Sherlockian phrase: "The game is _____!"
96. Old refrigerant (abbr.)
97. T.S. who wrote "The Waste Land"
99. Slide for a log ride
101. Tolkien characters
102. Titch
104. Snatches
105. Unappetizing food offering
108. Sun, in Spain

18 Canada Cornucopia 9

ACROSS

1. *So You Think You Can _____ Canada*
6. Hiram Walker distillery grain
10. Lang. used by the hearing impaired
13. Sundin's rugs?
17. Chipmunk's munchie
18. Golden Olympic figure skater Kulik
19. Canadian Academy of Engineering (abbr.)
20. Jewish month
21. Position of 2014 CFL most outstanding player Elimimian
23. "_____ bono?"
24. Coins once used in Italy
25. Like a lion on the hunt
26. 2007 Avril Lavigne hit
29. Northern Italy specialty cheese
30. Témiscaming topper?
31. Lithium-_____ battery
32. Emotionally disengaged
35. Played the ham
37. Jean-Paul of French Revolution fame
39. Toronto CFL pro
40. Chop off
41. Pilot training device
44. English actress Miller
47. Ottawa constabulary (abbr.)
49. Vietnamese new year
50. 1993 Stephen King story: *The _____ 'Clock People*
51. Spade for Santa?
52. Reproductive organs
55. 2017 NHL documentary: _____ *the Cup*
57. Trips for vestal virgins?
59. Canadian Gesner who invented kerosene
62. Origins

63. Former Habs coach and GM Gainey
66. Kill a dragon, say
67. Lhasa citizen (abbr.)
69. Astrological sign animal
70. David Suzuki show: *The _____ of Things*
72. Walker's measuring device
75. Long-time US senator Kennedy
77. Couturier Schiaparelli
78. Zinfandel and Syrah
79. Hut by the seaside
81. Strait that separates two eastern provinces
82. *Devious Maids* star Ortiz
83. Some singers
84. Back end?
86. It delivers for the nation?
89. Theatrical intermission
93. Italian wine region
94. "Brains" of a PC
95. Like a well-worn carpet
97. Tormé, et al.
98. Old word?
99. Serengeti nesting place
100. Young eel
101. British withholding tax (abbr.)
102. Illinois city: _____ Plaines
103. Some pasture parents
104. Foul smelling

DOWN

1. Spotted dogs, for short
2. Association canadienne de l'isolation thermique (abbr.)
3. Nada
4. Inventor's idea
5. Together, like a Québec political party?
6. PEI-based celebrity chef Smith
7. Heavy tippler
8. Be untruthful

9. This US retailer missed its mark in Canada
10. Certify
11. _____ Ste. Marie
12. Early Canada explorer Ericsson
13. Improves
14. Unfriends a Martian?
15. Make a left at a light
16. Snowmobile?
22. You might use one at CIBC
27. States of anger
28. Omani money unit
30. Dancing, colloquially
32. Window part
33. Destiny's Child, for example
34. Gothic arch type
36. Two-time Governor General's fiction award winner Brian
37. Radiation, for example
38. Up _____ good
42. Actress Suvari, et al.
43. Newfoundland's "Man of a Thousand Songs" Hynes
45. Biblical animal amasser
46. Flies Pacific Coastal?
48. See 40-A
53. Let in
54. Pianist's pieces
56. City east of Phoenix
57. Egg-based salad dressing
58. It borders the Red Sea
59. Egyptian snake
60. Blustered
61. Brightly
63. Tulip source
64. Ontario Rope Skipping Organization (abbr.)
65. Vanquish
68. Confuses the weatherman?
71. Like perforated paper
73. Beverage in "Beowulf"
74. Some vermin
76. Stitchers who swear?

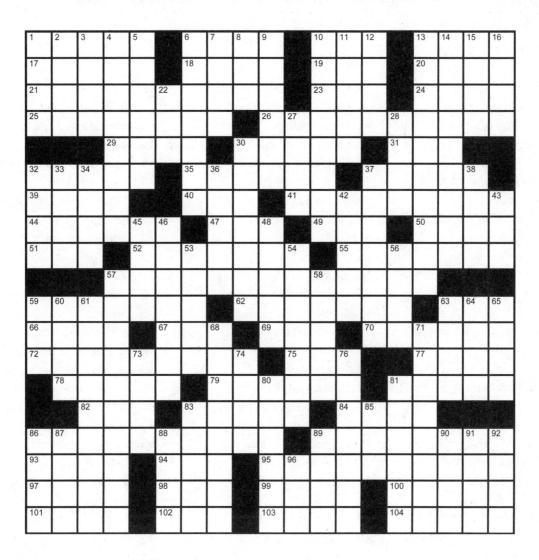

80. Molson stubby, for one

81. ID checker, say

83. Golden Delicious or Gravenstein

85. Airport landing info (abbr.)

86. Bivouac

87. Adrift on the Arabian?

88. Got an A+ on the court?

89. Point Pelee National Park abuts this lake

90. Banff destination: _____ and Basin National Historic Site

91. Lengthy journey

92. Spine-chilling (var.)

96. TV comedy: *Hee* _____

ACROSS

1. Cherokee or Comanche
5. Rambo who played Jack Ewing on *Dallas*
9. Dinty Moore's dish?
13. Coast Mountains lake
17. "Back in the _____"
18. OPEC member country
19. De-icer component
20. Opposite of ecto-
21. Appease a hunger
22. Nova Scotia community: _____ Harbour
23. Slogan about Sanders: "Feel the _____"
24. Céline or Shania
25. Moral depravity
27. Spirit of the times
29. Cell component
31. Childhood malady
32. "Conestoga" vehicle used by Canadian pioneers
34. Rainy day description
36. Spanish surrealist Salvador
37. Ellesmere Island has one
39. Merchant ship
41. Profundity
44. Branch of biology
46. 1978 Bryan Adams song: "_____ Me Take You Dancing"
48. Canadian company that makes Ultimate Maple Crème cookies
49. _____-Japanese War
52. Letters for an environmentalist
54. CN Tower city (abbr.)
55. Hunter
58. These include creamers and sugar bowls
60. How many flew over the cuckoo's nest
61. Old BC fort: _____ Miguel
62. **Play on words**
63. Load freight on a freighter
64. Pot toppers
66. 17th PEI premier Walter
68. Some Asian taxis
72. Character of a culture
74. Bay Street firm employee
78. Swift literary device
79. Structural add-ons
81. Bedroom storage space
83. Gypsy's calling card?
84. Amah or ayah
87. U of T profs, say
89. It measures coil diameter
91. Considered an issue again
94. Norse god of war
95. "Not guilty," for one
96. Kind of agreement
97. Avant-garde
98. Tenant's expense
99. A druggie, for sure?
100. Road Runner's enemy: _____ E. Coyote
101. Number of Canadian provinces pre-1949
102. Saharan landforms
103. Rogers, in the Rockies
104. Handsome horse?
105. Bandy, like George Chuvalo?

DOWN

1. Anne Murray hit: "I _____ Fall in Love Again"
2. Sibling of Jacob, in Genesis
3. Female hormone
4. Do preliminary sorting of data, say
5. *Obiter* _____
6. 2013 Justin Bieber song: "All _____ the World"
7. Volcanic sinkholes
8. Movable pew part
9. Like very cold Canadian winter temperatures
10. Ash or birch
11. Disconcerting
12. Classified section bit
13. Applied more caulking
14. Expect something to happen
15. Typography symbol (var.)
16. Cake variety
26. Winnipeg church consecrated in 1929: St. _____
28. Dalhousie alum
30. Delay on a jet?
32. Old Bailey hairpiece
33. Canadian pilot Billy Bishop, in WWI
35. Yves' fashion house, for short
38. Shaped like a tree cone
40. Dr. Seuss title: _____ *the Turtle and Other Stories*
42. Pony's pace
43. Possessive pronoun
45. Trumpet's cousin
47. Radial patterns
50. **Grey _____**
51. **Topknot**
53. Emits
55. Frigid North or South location
56. Bag of blood in the OR
57. Deceptive device in mysteries
59. Some religious faction members
65. Paintbrush cleaning fluids
67. Part of a circle
68. Past tense (var.)
69. Runway in remote parts of Canada
70. Male mate, colloquially
71. Now-shuttered Canadian retailer: Smart _____
73. Molten metals production waste
75. Listening intently: "I'm _____"
76. You might fawn over her?
77. Funds held by third parties
80. Grab a bargain
82. Nation between Hawaii and Australia

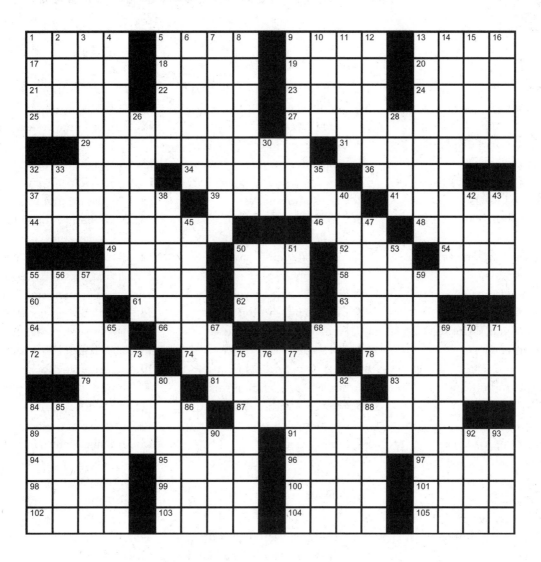

84. Cursed

85. Place to get down?

86. Oklahoma city

88. Annoyed

90. Disco-era band: The Bee _____

92. Active Sicilian spewer

93. Canadian columnist and historian Gwynne

20 Canada Cornucopia 10

ACROSS

1. Cease or desist
5. Ruler of 22-A until 1979
9. Alberta Standardbred Horse Association (abbr.)
13. Glass Tiger vocalist Alan
17. Five-time Governor General's Award-winning author MacLennan
18. "Forbidden" fragrance
19. Wash with a mop
20. Land of leprechauns
21. Adept
22. Canada's Ken Taylor served here
23. Sense of regret
25. Astute
26. NAFTA, and others
28. Jewellery piece for the wrist
29. Source of poi
30. Shapes for Canada's "Armageddon" band?
32. Dies anagram
33. Spy's mammal?
35. Suitcase, in Saguenay
37. One way up at Alberta's Castle Mountain resort
41. Sunflower part
44. US gymnast Simone who won five medals in Rio
45. Concert stage light
47. Cut the shrubs
48. Hamilton OHL player moniker
50. Sailor's hesitations?
51. Nestlé Canada confection
52. Throws
53. Have fondness for
55. Trough for mortar
56. At peace with a situation
58. *The Catcher in the Rye* writer J.D.
60. Blonde's preferred wood?
61. Fish without fins
62. Bigot
63. Montréal NHLers, colloquially
65. Buddhist shrine
67. Certain antennas
69. Marquee event at the Calgary Stampede
70. *Love It or List It* designer Farr
72. Chops into squares
73. Grp. of men in Gatineau?
74. Employee Performance Appraisal Report (abbr.)
75. Smart guys?
77. Hollywood heavyweight Brad
78. End to end, shortly?
80. Fermented milk drinks
82. Fan sound
86. New Brunswick Museum displays a skeleton of this
90. Showered with excessive affection
91. Decorate again
92. Reptile for Canadian poet Lee?
94. Superb review
95. Lola's spicy stew?
96. Hit hard with criticism?
97. PEI's MacLellan who composed "Put Your Hand in the Hand"
98. Colonel Mustard's game
99. Rain heavily
100. Much ado, in the media
101. Mythological love god
102. Regarded
103. Finishes

DOWN

1. Rattle
2. Enjoyed a ride behind a boat
3. See 102-A
4. Amazing occurrence
5. Ceiling finish
6. Capital formerly known as Salisbury
7. Primitive calculators (var.)
8. Muskoka region town
9. Pack animal
10. Variant of 19-A
11. Former Ontario premier Mike
12. Rasps
13. Opening in an inner ear bone
14. Cambodian currency unit
15. Language for an Irish seer?
16. Direction of Alberta vis-à-vis Saskatchewan
24. Slippery stuff
27. Little collectibles?
31. It runs on runners
34. Johnny Bower's jersey number
36. Separates from the others
38. Some Baffin Bay whales
39. It cushions a shock?
40. Swamp plant
41. Mo. that Canadians file taxes
42. Screwdriver type
43. Hawaiian dance, in full
44. McGill campus hall
46. In that case
48. Construct
49. North Bay-raised crime fiction scribe Blunt
52. Subtle shade
54. Cassis and white wine drink
57. Kit and caboodle?
58. Hudson's Bay staffers, say
59. Penned a star's autobiography
60. Tennis great Arthur
62. Pawned
64. High seas call for help
66. Like some Eaton's employees, back in the day
68. Gather fruit that's ripe
69. Soak hemp
71. CFLers strive to gain this
73. Property owner's bad behaviour?
76. Robber during a riot
77. Theatrical trailer (var.)
79. Monopolize a motorbike?
81. "Little" area of Toronto

83. Canadian author Humphreys
84. Ran in neutral
85. Drifts

86. Korean War sitcom
87. America to Canada, say
88. Hit with a hand

89. Faux pas
93. U of A living quarters

Where the Girls Are

Canadian ladies' place names

ACROSS

1. Indonesian island
5. Vocal style for Ella
9. Way in the distance
13. Guys who cheat on you?
19. Opposed to, in dialect
20. **BC place for ex-politician Campagnolo?**
21. Doer anagram
22. Mount Logan climber's tool
23. Like bats and owls
25. Cruise ship's staff
26. Cubic measurement units
27. Dakota dwellings (var.)
28. Bone depository
31. Proclamation
32. Displeased shout from the bleachers
34. Socialite, perhaps
36. *Wheel of Fortune* contestant's buy
37. Lacking vivacity
39. Distinctive atmosphere
41. Most elated
44. Post-it pad piece
45. Boric and amino
47. Blows it
48. Squirm in discomfort
50. _____ in "voice"
53. Window coverings
55. Glow more brightly
57. From C to C or D to D
59. 1966 hit: "_____ Comes Mary"
61. Cow a comedian
63. Medical misfortunes?
64. **AB town for former BC MPP/ activist Brown?**
68. Like a nerd
69. Begin to grow up?
71. Raise
72. **QC spot for *The National* correspondent Crowe?**
73. Gastronome
74. Plagiarize *Peter Pan*?
75. Dupes the court jesters?
76. **MB village for author Laurence?**
77. Easy-Bake _____
78. Tract in Siberia
80. Fabric for a glossy gown
81. General feeling?
83. Taking part in a preferred pastime
85. Like a walrus or rhino
90. Canadian cheese producer: _____ Stelle
91. Sedin who retired from the Canucks in 2018
93. Major-_____
95. Sparkling headpiece
96. Canadian *Party of Five* actress Campbell
97. Graphable curve, for one
100. Rouse
101. Coiled mollusc fossil
105. Yours, in Laval
106. Plummet
108. Coop egg maker
109. Prime rib _____
110. Hit the spot, gastronomically
113. Ruffle
115. Heart malady: _____ fibrillation
117. Ambassador's ability
118. Most gory
122. Issues forth?
123. Range in Russia
124. **ON tour stop for skater Underhill?**
125. James Mason movie: *I _____ Murderer*
126. Housed at The Brick?
127. Technical school, for short
128. A portion of
129. Cameo gem

DOWN

1. National Non-Smoking Week falls in this mo.
2. In a previous era
3. **BC city fit for a queen?**
4. Against
5. Job for a horse farm stud
6. Provide emotional comfort
7. Former *Saturday Night Live* star Gasteyer
8. Baby powder
9. Mysterious
10. Big rides at amusement parks
11. Former British protectorate
12. Spur part
13. It followed the USSR
14. Groups of eight (var.)
15. Film starring Canada's Donald Sutherland: *Eye of the _____*
16. **PEI place for a Dionne quintuplet?**
17. VPs and CFOs
18. Cozy lodgings
24. Market booms
29. Past tense biblical verb
30. Door frame header
32. Meadow sounds
33. "That hurts!"
35. Domain of some peers
38. Fah follower
40. Put two and two together?
42. Canadian retail stalwart: Shoppers _____ Mart
43. Like a wily magician?
46. Aquatic polyp colony
49. Very black
50. Canadian honour: Star of Military _____
51. Enticement
52. Six lines of verse
54. Roofers' tiles
56. **MB destination for *Trailer Park Boys* actress Thompson?**

58. Approximately, in dating antiques
60. Miner's pay dirt
62. Vivacity, in Val-d'Or
64. Share via Facebook
65. Gemini-winning journalist Craig
66. Placid
67. Canadian jazz orchestrator Gil
68. Like a government's foreign policy initiatives
70. Niagara Peninsula hickory
72. Veld hills
73. Food Network Canada airing: *You Gotta _____ Here!*
75. Cashew-based liquor sold only in Goa

76. Molten liquids
79. Core convictions
80. Common Canadian precipitation
82. Lacking teeth
84. That is, in Latin
86. Bro's counterpart
87. AB vacation spot for Ontario premier Wynne?
88. Port Colborne's lake
89. Mend footwear
92. Lewis who hosted CBC's *CounterSpin*
94. Shaped like an egg
96. More intrusive, like a neighbour
98. In an orderly fashion
99. Dress a king for coronation

101. Residents of 11-D
102. Choral work
103. SK stopover for Cowboy Junkies vocalist Timmins?
104. Devour
107. W.O. Mitchell story collection: *Jake and the _____*
111. Source of poi
112. Drops off in intensity
114. Bride's ride to her wedding
116. Limited Slip Differential (abbr.)
119. Southeast Asian language
120. Pigs' domain
121. Goods and Services _____

ACROSS

1. It follows Sunshine, in BC
6. Certain swine
10. Hourly pay
14. Adverb in old poetry
17. Open a gate
18. Over again
19. Wild goat in Asia
20. Canadian bank for over 100 yrs.
21. Smooth to the touch
22. Part for Canada's Ryan Reynolds
23. Trivial pursuit in the House of Commons?
25. Centralized government advocate
27. Treelike, anatomically
29. Crystalline sound
31. Fencing match surface
32. Flowers for a day in May?
35. Ontario CBC Radio host Chen
37. Bat cave dung
39. White House gatekeeper (abbr.)
40. Acid type
41. Long narrative poem
43. All elbows, say
45. Russian carriage
46. Up-and-coming Canadian tennis star Shapovalov
48. Like a passé relationship?
49. CBC News Network or Bravo
50. Toddlers' TV fare: _____ Street
52. Brief Second Cup order?
53. He designed 50+ churches in London
54. Geological Society of America (abbr.)
55. Theatrical displays?
59. Twelfth mo., on a calendar
62. Coins formerly spent in Florence
63. Monarch in a Steve Martin song

64. Sexy Cuban dance (var.)
68. CANDU power generator
70. Creed anagram
72. Pine for
73. Military uniform brassard
74. Merrymaker?
76. Canada's Triumph, for one
77. Mocked (var.)
78. US cardiac health org.
79. Lacking moisture
81. Montréal goalie great Dryden
82. Anagram for Ares
83. Former BC premier Christy
85. Become wider, like pupils
87. Forced from active duty
90. Canadian parliamentarian
93. Hospital visitors' gathering places
95. "_____ digress"
97. Share a conjecture
98. Russian royals' Fabergé collectible
99. Rim
100. GI's firepower
101. Swiss chocolatier since 1845
102. Stag and _____ party
103. Goes from blonde to brunette
104. Red farm building
105. Toronto CFL players

DOWN

1. Swear a blue streak
2. "Step _____!"
3. Tissue removals in the OR
4. Hindu female embodiment
5. These times can test your patience?
6. World's longest covered bridge, in New Brunswick
7. Mrs. Lennon #2
8. Neuter, on the horse farm
9. Use a besom
10. Canada's southernmost city

11. Cancels a space shuttle liftoff
12. Former name of a Canadian cinematic prize
13. Highway 401 off-ramp
14. Clouding a view
15. This bird doesn't get off the ground
16. Eggs from fish
24. Raging wind in African deserts
26. Auk's brethren
28. Rechargeable battery type, for short
30. Phrase spoken on 31-A
33. Canadian actor Myers, et al.
34. Milan landmark: La _____
35. Gets married mid-week?
36. Weapon used on 31-A
38. North Carolina adjunct: _____ Banks
40. See 27-A
42. Thailand's previous name
44. Heir or heiress
45. Madonna movie: A League of _____ Own
47. Extracted metals through heating
49. Toronto's Raptors play on this (abbr.)
51. Ex-NHL goalie Darren from Milton
53. Put the hose on the garden
56. Stephen Brunt book: Searching for Bobby _____
57. Gastropod genus
58. Animal fat
59. Tedious car races?
60. Out of this world?
61. Ontario place for William and Kate?
65. Leon's engages in this
66. Cracker topper
67. Ever and _____
69. Scrubs or scours

70. Swiss _____
71. Scorn
74. Furniture for loungers?
75. Cause annoyance: _____ up
78. Make a claim
80. Western Canada crop

83. Fairway worker at Glen Abbey
84. Shish _____
86. Snouted herbivorous mammal
88. Aspired to win
89. Russian parliament
91. Japanese folk music style

92. Softens flax in water
93. Twin or double furniture piece
94. Narcissist's ideal?
96. Texting abbr. for the day after today

Solution on page 213

O Canada Crosswords Book 19 ■ *51*

Doppelgängers
Oscar-winning roles

ACROSS

1. Central American bean tree
6. Belts for kimonos
10. Louisiana stew staple
14. Stash
19. Squash type
20. _____ Minor
21. Bluish-green duck?
22. Goodbye, in Granby
23. **Barbra Streisand shone as this Fanny**
24. Clock or watch
26. He goes to court?
27. Showing good judgment
29. Of excellent quality
30. They pair with crossbones
31. Info sheets for Toronto NHLers?
34. Canada's Stephen Leacock, eg.
36. **Jamie Foxx starred as this entertaining Ray**
40. Bury a casket
42. "Grapes" Cherry
43. Migraine preceder
44. Dance in the ballroom
46. Lengthens
52. Covered with goo, in *Ghostbusters*
55. Animals' farm home
56. Parched
57. Benedict XVI or Francis
58. Ate
59. City in Spain
61. Mixed veggies veggie
62. Asian antelope
63. List thesis references
64. Turns topsy-turvy
66. Annual Toronto event: Santa Claus _____
67. **Colin Firth clinched this royal performance**
71. Dvořák work: *Symphony No. 9 _____ minor*
72. **Meryl Streep mimicked this Margaret**

74. *Canadian _____ Dictionary*
75. Topeka state
78. Montréal Expos manager Felipe (1992–2001)
79. Playfully harass
80. Asian place: _____ Kong
81. Stephanie Labbé, on our Rio bronze soccer team
83. Friend for Joey?
86. Crones
87. Québec political figure Lévesque
88. Juno-winning Jann Arden song: "Could I Be Your _____"
89. Ominously
91. Like the most stoic Stelco employee?
93. Michael Ondaatje Giller Prize winner: _____ *Ghost*
95. Pakistan neighbour
96. Institute of Technology Development of Canada (abbr.)
97. _____ Barbara
99. **Cate Blanchett soared as this Katherine**
102. Fair play?
107. Second Commandment breaker
109. Capers
110. Can of "Who" this taken by The Grinch
112. Symbol of Ontario and Alberta
117. Final stage of insect development
118. Like an irate sniper?
121. **Nicole Kidman won as this writer**
122. Alberta place: High _____
123. Goad into action
124. Canadian country music legend Snow
125. Star-studded event attendees
126. US radio personality Howard
127. Positive responses
128. Cake ingredients

129. Umpires enforce these

DOWN

1. Taxis
2. Cabbage patch?
3. Loonie or toonie
4. Bow shapes
5. *The Iceman Cometh* playwright Eugene
6. Goal for *Survivor* contestants
7. Short legal document?
8. Information Security Management (abbr.)
9. Society of Automotive Engineers (abbr.)
10. Serving no purpose
11. Avid
12. Off to the _____
13. Pub patron's drink
14. **Eddie Redmayne played this physicist**
15. Aroma
16. Zesty mayo
17. Country dances
18. Robert who was the subject of *The Jinx*
25. **George C. Scott commanded as this general**
28. Show on Canada's Comedy Network: *Full Frontal with Samantha _____*
30. 1993 Governor General's Award winner: *The _____ Diaries*
32. Printer's concern, per page
33. Plaque preparer's task
35. Bedeck
36. **Reese Witherspoon scored as this C&W singer**
37. Waikiki "wiggle"
38. See 56-A
39. Meadow male
41. Adjust a clock for DST
45. Rhyme scheme letters

47. Opposite of most
48. Outline
49. Hebrew scripture compilation
50. Horatian poem form
51. Where rats reside
53. Political refugee
54. Passé
60. Bulgarian money unit
61. Make a surreptitious entry
62. Zen enlightenment stage
63. Calgary Roughneck's stick
65. Navy one-striper (abbr.)
66. Grew ashen
67. Early Teutonic people
68. Leave of absence from Eton
69. Coming _____
70. Eastern church art pieces (var.)
73. Chance

76. Dill seeds
77. It precedes killer or number
80. Pays attention to advice
82. Extension to a home
83. South American country on the Pacific
84. Old apple spray
85. **Sissy Spacek emulated this coal miner's daughter**
87. Ceremonial occasions
88. **Ben Kingsley acted as this Indian leader**
90. Chest bone
92. **Daniel Day-Lewis played this president**
94. Yiddish comedian's bits?
98. Theatre passageways
100. After sunset, poetically

101. 1913 description
102. Locks up
103. Like unfulfilled aspirations
104. Ward (off)
105. CFL competitor: Hamilton _____-Cats
106. Percentage of a pot, say
108. Copying
111. Pond surface bit
113. Fragrant balsam resin
114. Vex
115. Additionally
116. Small salamanders
118. US retailer in Canada: Best _____
119. Sarah McLachlan *Toy Story 2* song: "When _____ Loved Me"
120. Kids' game

ACROSS

1. A colour on Canada's flag
6. Dowdy dressers, say
12. 2017 HGTV Canada series: *Buy It _____*
17. 2017 Grey Cup half-time performer (with 94-A)
18. They're ostracized by society
19. Kind of message, in computing
20. Sci-fi author Jules, et al.
21. Gives consent
22. Get _____ out of
23. Making loan payments, say
24. Cozy kitchen corners
25. Blue?
26. Pull an all-nighter, say
27. Wild plums
28. Spiritedness
29. Classified sales ad abbr.
31. Cloth for cleaning
33. A Canadian files this in Apr.
34. Haulers' work
38. 1970s BC premier (with 71-D)
40. Homes for High Park hatchlings
42. Headless Washington Irving character
43. Creative nuggets
45. Utmost, to a mathematician
46. They're honoured in May
47. Loblaws counter
48. Mother, for example
50. Star of 12-A Mike
52. Famed Canadian rower Hanlan
53. They commune with the dearly departed
56. Schuss at BC's Silver Star Mountain Resort
59. Long-time tool company
60. Added on
64. _____-*majesté*
66. Rose part that's prickly
67. It comes in sticks (abbr.)
68. Room type at Calgary's Palliser Hotel
69. Sheds for beehives
71. Foretells
73. Nicholas II, for one
74. Subtraction figure
75. Panama or pillbox
76. Employee Assistance Program (abbr.)
78. Canadian sports lovers' channel (abbr.)
79. 1961 Nobel Prize winner Hammarskjöld
80. Type, in Témiscaming
82. Like most Pizza 73 orders
84. Fossil resins
87. Tiny facial openings
88. Often poisonous plant
91. A Canterbury pilgrim
92. Mackenzie and Liard, in the NWT
93. Factory's work period
94. See 17-A
95. Summer beverage (var.)
96. Peyote
97. Pivoted (var.)
98. Dough for a pie
99. Old Indo–European

DOWN

1. Mulroney and Reagan sang this in 1985: "_____ Irish Eyes are Smiling"
2. Book that's difficult to read?
3. Empress Hotel locale: _____ Harbour
4. Clasp for a cravat
5. Memphrémagog municipality in Québec
6. Fruity desserts
7. Bedrock covering
8. Relocates a plant?
9. Long-time *Hockey Night in Canada* analyst Howie
10. Manitobans' paper: *Winnipeg Free _____*
11. US draft org.
12. Orange juicers
13. Forcibly entered
14. House of Commons Liberal, colloquially
15. Steven Sabados, on CBC's *The Goods*
16. It tops a deuce
17. Reporting mark of the Southern Railway of Vancouver Island (abbr.)
25. Most scanty
29. Frigg's spouse, in Norse mythology
30. Grammy-winning singer Erykah
32. Produced power, at Pickering
34. Parliament Hill working group
35. Preacher's final word
36. Strong wind
37. Lady of Arthurian legends
39. Has dinner
41. Skunks' markings
42. Ontario place: _____ Landing
44. See 39-D
46. Bygone bird
49. Steps in a hair-colouring process
50. Attila the _____
51. Depots (abbr.)
54. Former Hab and Flame Kostopoulos
55. Bunny's back end
56. Bang a door
57. Flat-topped military hat
58. The proof _____ pudding
61. Website about our country's past: _____ Canada
62. YWG postings, for short
63. *Coming Home* actor Bruce

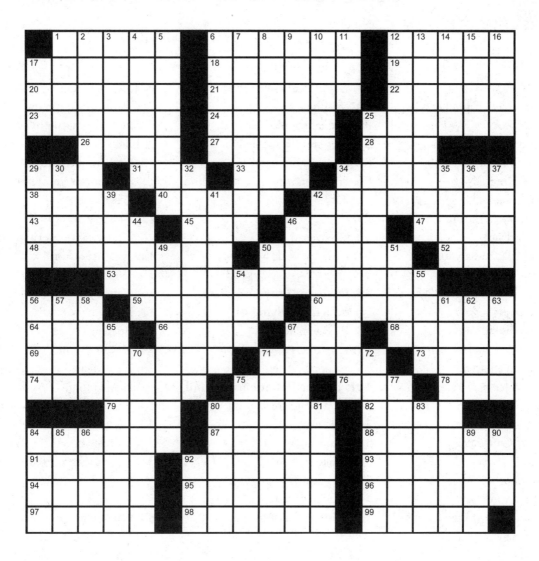

65. French brandy
67. Toddler who's unsteady on his pins
70. Behind?
71. See 38-A
72. Mandarin orange variety
75. Ungulates' feet

77. Balloon buster
80. Orthopaedic splint
81. English class assignment
83. Daring
84. Ottawa building: National _____ Centre
85. Weakly cry

86. Beautiful, in Baie-Comeau
89. US federal gov. operative
90. It might seek shelter in a lee?
92. Letters seen on tombstones

This Land is Your Land

Find the letter pattern

ACROSS

1. When doubled, capital of a US Pacific territory
5. Raptors and Redblacks
10. Earlier, to a golfer?
15. Alaskan King _____
19. "What a shame!"
20. 2009 *Survivor* setting
21. Butter tart nut
22. Novel by Canadian author Martel: _____ *of Pi*
23. **BC Strait of Georgia place**
26. Plot of land
27. Hindu religious teacher
28. Family tree females
29. Blast from a barrel
31. Christian feasts
34. Viper
35. Psyche loved this god
36. South of Canada country
39. Deface
41. More adept
43. Some scale notes
46. **Red Deer shopping centre**
48. Beaver's kin
50. Canadian award for athletic excellence: Lou _____ Trophy
52. Eye part
53. Not at all
55. Paternity test material
57. California city or valley
58. Screech upon seeing a mouse
59. _____ donna
61. Leave out a vowel
63. Sign of bad things to come
64. Sheltered, at sea
65. Old-style copper alloy
68. Give directions in Japan?
70. **Nova Scotia national park**
74. FBI word
75. Transferred software from one computer to another
76. Jemima or Em
77. Credit card company, for short
78. Michigan city
80. Surrealism pioneer Max
82. He's crazy for cashews?
85. Mystical old letter
86. Fisherman's foe, on the Grand Banks
87. Drupe
90. Go over in detail
91. Unimpressed
93. Threw together a salad?
95. **Dinosaur Provincial Park milieu in Alberta**
98. Bro's female kin
99. Canadian sports journalist and author Stephen
101. Former Toronto mayor Ford
103. Eradicate corruption, say
104. Doves' whisperings
105. Iron or Bronze
107. Take to heart?
109. It's added to gasoline
112. Russian currency (var.)
114. Topper for Miss Universe Canada
118. Ergo
119. **Place to stay in Edmonton**
123. Pepsi or Coke
124. Completely
125. Sault Ste. _____
126. Bother
127. Québec city opposite Ottawa
128. Perimeters
129. City on the Ruhr
130. Western Canadian restaurant chain: White _____

DOWN

1. Kicking Horse _____
2. "There oughta be _____!"
3. Apple grown in Ontario
4. East Germans spent these
5. Baking powder amt.
6. Teacup handle
7. Chemical compound
8. Singular philosophy?
9. Like 27-A
10. Cathedral components
11. Aluminum silicate (var.)
12. Wood sorrel
13. **Calgary Stampede chuckwagon derby name**
14. Weather a storm
15. U of T lecture
16. Canadian impressionist Little
17. Bushy hairdo
18. Borscht veggie
24. Occult symbol
25. He drowned in the Aegean after a failed flight
30. Canadian comedian Macdonald
32. Obamacare acronym
33. Bicycle basket
36. ". . . blackbirds baked in _____"
37. Foal's parent
38. Canadian alpine racer Guay
40. Black cuckoo
42. Lying in wait, say
43. Planted untrue evidence
44. Tall, trembling trees
45. Old style contraction
47. _____ Pérignon
49. Cut molars, like an infant
51. Designate a religious successor?
54. Surname of TV's John-Boy
56. Greek mythology keeper of the winds
59. Defendant's entreaty?
60. Ward off
62. Dutch birthplace of Rembrandt
64. Highest points
66. Vital arteries
67. Blasting crew's substance
69. Fiery diatribe
70. Some clouds

71. Centre Bell and MTS Centre
72. Inferior imitator (var.)
73. Record of Parliament Hill debates
74. Canadian figure skater Underhill, et al.
79. BC nickname
81. Chafe against
82. Taboo
83. Language spoken in Pakistan
84. Canadian band: Crash _____ Dummies
88. Austere cactus?
89. Two words from a groom

90. Super Bowl LI champs
92. Blake's black
94. Shock and awe?
96. Female antelope
97. Reluctant to
100. Rohypnol tablet
102. Feminist Abzug and model Hadid
104. Rideau _____
106. They're scored in 71-D
108. Closes in on
109. Carve
110. First word of most Commandments

111. It hath no fury like a woman scorned
113. 1986 coming-of-age drama: *Stand* _____
115. At the summit
116. Overhaul
117. Multitude
120. Paddock elder
121. Never, in Munich
122. CBC reality show: *Dragons'* _____

ACROSS

1. National _____ of Canada
7. Soak in the tub
12. Acting Tom
18. Spiny lizard
19. Six-time Juno winner Lavigne
20. They're built in Alliston, Ontario
21. Segment of BC's Highway 99: George Massey _____
22. Sleep Country mattress brand
23. Incite to evildoing
24. Ye shall find if you do this
25. Asian civets
28. Aussie actress Swinton
29. Ontario Science Centre city (abbr.)
30. Type of turtle
32. _____ continuum
37. Seafood serving: Sole _____
41. One of Canada's Great Lakes
42. Triplet, in genetics
45. Ex-Reform Party of Canada leader Manning
46. Indigenous Alaskan
48. Christmas seasons
50. Actress Ullmann
51. Some Canadian critters
52. Make amends
53. Goofy
55. Aggravate
56. Large river in 43-D
57. Filbert or pecan
58. Hatfields and McCoys
61. Happy cats' sounds
62. Most stressed
66. Haul
67. Vietnamese city
68. So far
69. Wifely
72. Romeo, for example
74. Very cold
75. Glossy garden bloomers
77. Wayne Gretzky's birthplace
79. They're scanned by Loblaws cashiers
82. Initial scale notes
83. Poplar variety
86. Like cloisonné pieces (var.)
88. Abhor
92. Angry looks
94. Winged, in biology
95. Lady in peril
97. Shake a snake?
98. Not worldly
99. Succeeds with a spreadsheet software?
100. "_____, Captain!"
101. Squares for Scrabble players
102. Second-hand car lot transaction

DOWN

1. Little drill parts?
2. Malaria symptom
3. Crescent shape
4. Rangy
5. Moose Jaw-to-Regina dir.
6. *Love It or List It Vancouver* realtor
7. Species of catfish
8. Turned aside trouble
9. Vestige
10. Like a scar on a seed
11. Beetles' wing coverings
12. Canadian Hydrographic Service (abbr.)
13. Habitual, to the gymnast?
14. Removes twine
15. Kelly Clarkson, for one?
16. Carnelian
17. Economics Society of Northern Alberta (abbr.)
26. Canadian actresses Luttrell and Durance
27. Swatch or sip
29. Some outdoor enthusiasts
31. Averages at Glen Abbey
32. Bell competitor
33. Softly whine
34. Length x width
35. 1985 Canadian film: *My American _____*
36. My, in Memphrémagog
38. "_____ never work!"
39. Bit of fibre
40. A deadly sin
43. Province of 77-A
44. Middays
47. Classification
49. Conclude
52. Cupid's dart
53. Summertime head protectors
54. Third-person pronoun
56. *Annie Get Your _____*
57. Domain for Connor Hellebuyck
58. 1980s Canadian band: Parachute _____
59. Elegant
60. Wide-eyed
61. Former Dieppe NB amusement centre: Crystal _____
62. Harangue
63. Thus
64. Blend batter
65. First name of 6-D
67. It grows on you?
68. That lady
70. Canada's first female astronaut Bondar
71. In a foolish manner
73. See 93-D
76. Voiced
78. One who dozes off
80. One of five Canadian honorary citizens: _____ Lama
81. Cellphone communication
83. Taj Mahal city
84. Do in the dragon, say
85. Hors d'oeuvre item

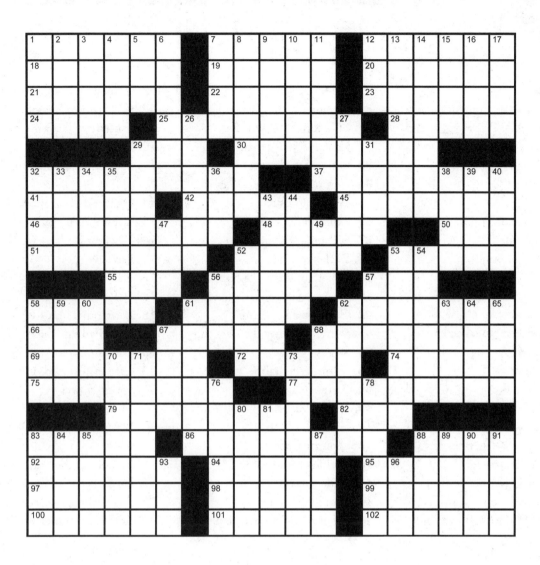

87. Janitors' strong soaps

88. Royal Canadian Navy ship designation

89. Adrift on the Atlantic?

90. 1988 single from Canada's Sass Jordan: "_____ Somebody"

91. Otherwise

93. Glimpse

96. Terminate a logger?

Presidential Nicknames

Oval Office monikers

ACROSS

1. International landmark between BC and WA: Peace _____ Park
5. Chefs' starch
9. Winnipeg NHL team
13. Flubbed
19. **Coolidge**
21. Like Canada's prairies
22. Reverse one's past
23. Lysine, for example
24. Guess Who member Jim
25. Former Soviet Union leader
26. Liveliness
27. Swiss Chalet chicken entree
29. **Clinton**
31. Silk sorts?
32. Anagram for 43-A
34. Zenith's opposite
35. Reddish-yellow colour
38. Gala for gardeners?
42. Dakar country (abbr.)
43. Confucian principle
46. Complimentary words
48. Tincture for treating bruises
49. Paying attention to
51. Assists
52. Court's calendar
54. Arena level
56. 1992 Barenaked Ladies song
57. **Johnson**
58. Ratty informants?
59. Pet store purchase: _____ Mix
60. Not the present, in Papineau
61. *Corner Gas* star Brent
62. An ermine, in summer
64. Move unsteadily
65. **A Roosevelt**
69. Popeye, for example
71. Book's odd-numbered page
72. Light and breezy
73. Holy table
74. Cargo moving vehicles
75. Grain husks

77. See 65-A
80. Like many margaritas
81. BC's Johnston who was Canada's first female premier
82. Classroom absentee
84. Company that sells Wagon Wheels in Canada
85. Childhood illness
87. Souvenir with a slogan
89. Rocketed
91. Canadian literary figure: _____-Marie MacDonald
92. Computer key (abbr.)
93. Satirical literary device
95. Steeps
96. Shimmering fabric
98. Formula _____
99. _____ Major
101. **Nixon**
105. Southpaw (var.)
108. Bride's keywords
111. Antenna
112. Bangkok native
114. Genre for Québec pianist Marc-André Hamelin
116. Curly might play a prank on him?
117. Name, _____ and serial number
118. **Lincoln**
119. Knew, in the Highlands
120. Blade that's blunted
121. Withdraws, with "out"
122. Just okay

DOWN

1. "Stat!"
2. Winter windows coating
3. Paper holder
4. Lobster mama
5. Austere
6. A way in
7. Mother of Cronus

8. Carmaker founded in 1897: _____ Motor Vehicle Co.
9. **Kennedy**
10. Rubber band
11. Head and shoulders above the rest?
12. Oktoberfest attendee's mug
13. Central Asia animal
14. Disentangle
15. Panache
16. Plug in?
17. Nefarious doings
18. Refuse to admit
20. Dukes and duchesses
28. One-thousand kilograms
30. Crescent-shaped nut
31. Spring flower
33. Miners' passageway
35. BC precious gem mine operator: _____ Resources Canada
36. Baby's bed
37. Pilgrimage to Mecca (var.)
39. Breach computer servers, say
40. Bothers
41. Cake, in Cowansville
43. Christmas tree icicles
44. Liqueur flavouring
45. American poet Nash
47. *Toronto Star* employee
50. It can precede "beloved" or "departed"
53. 1971 Guess Who hit: "Hang _____ Your Life"
55. Tiny amount, in Alexandroupoli?
58. Uproar
59. Personal magnetism
60. Canada's Duhamel & Radford, et al.
61. Secures a rope for rock climbing
62. Enclosures for eggs
63. Explosive abbr.

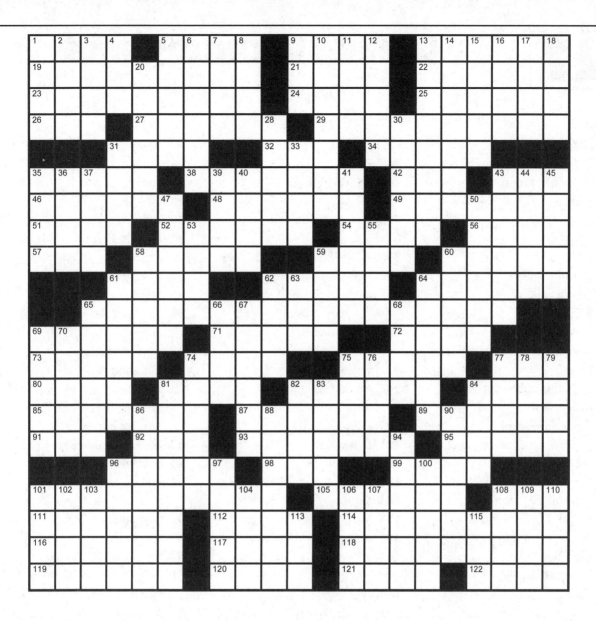

64. Floral fabric

65. Nickname of Canadian wrestler Hart

66. Campus grp. for guys

67. Canadian parliament body

68. Round bread

69. *From Dawn till Dusk* actress Hayek

70. Unfamiliar, on a UFO?

74. Like a sticky liquid

75. Canadian-born actor Raymond

76. It follows "Pro" in a Latin phrase

77. Renown

78. One of Canada's Property Brothers

79. Cerise and cherry

81. Designed anew

82. Slender

83. Bright star in Orion

84. Children's TV series: _____ *the Explorer*

86. Discharge

88. Washington state city

90. Become overly concerned with

94. *Teenage _____ Ninja Turtles*

96. PEI's Robert Ghiz, to Joe

97. Fertilizer ingredient

100. Hemingway book: *The Sun Also _____*

101. Chore

102. Plexus, for example

103. Laundry room appliance

104. Fellow

106. Jilted Greek nymph

107. Do poorly at the box office

108. UN air safety agency (abbr.)

109. Touches on?

110. Spread for bread

113. **Eisenhower**

115. 2005 Michael Bublé CD: _____ *Time*

ACROSS

1. Fans' Hollywood favourite
5. Plaza for Pythagoras
10. Highlander's hat
13. Not _____ snuff
17. _____ *That Tune*
18. Wept
19. 2016 Drake hit: "_____ Dance"
20. Angel's aura?
21. Canadian garment manufacturing company since 1856
23. Colourful tuber
24. Lesser Slave _____
25. Sharp flavour
26. Northeastern Italy mountain range
28. Nitre anagram
29. Lady of Las Cruces
30. Prepare potatoes
33. Religious splinter groups
35. Blythe in *Anne of Green Gables*
40. Join the Canadian Armed Forces
43. Songs for a pair of singers
45. Muscle disorder
46. Suffering from lack of energy (var.)
48. Canada Post might deliver one to you
50. Bollard
51. Signs of oldest life on earth were found here in 2017
53. Bird on a Canadian coin
54. Appraises
55. Knot again
57. Brooklynese for "Y'all"
59. Dye
63. Canadian Citizenship _____
65. More punctual
70. _____ Office
71. Derived from lime

73. Qatar, for example
74. Separate from
76. Pago Pago place
78. Ribbed cotton fabric
79. Okanagan Valley town
81. Fit of anger
83. Nova Scotia natural resource
84. Deeply investigated?
86. Some Canadian Opera Company singers (var.)
89. TTC commuters' vehicle
93. Sent again by boat?
97. It's a knockout?
98. Drunk, colloquially
99. 18th-C. instrument
100. Qom country
101. Dine at The Keg
102. Just beat out
103. Ruminants' regurgitations
104. Skillets
105. Stallone's nickname
106. Moosehead libations
107. 1966 film feline heroine

DOWN

1. Researchers' workplace (abbr.)
2. _____ processing
3. Muscat is its capital
4. More prolonged
5. Blackberry drupes
6. Spinach and Swiss chard
7. Peanut or canola
8. You wouldn't wash these with whites
9. Magazine revenue source
10. Pacific Northwest shrub
11. Like non-digital timepieces
12. Ottawa landmark: National War _____
13. Jamaican tangelo
14. Town map
15. Puff
16. Has a loan from Scotiabank

22. West Coast tree: Douglas _____
26. Ruin
27. Soda fountain offering
29. Purloin
30. White Spot entree
31. Food Network Canada show: *Bake with _____ Olson*
32. Chunk of marble
34. It follows Grey or Stanley
36. The Who song: "_____ O'Riley"
37. QEII off-ramp
38. Ceremonial event
39. Body art, for short
41. Ottawa-born 20th-C. poet and novelist Elizabeth
42. Bay of Fundy motion
44. Journalist's ice cream serving?
47. Halton Hills park: Terra _____ Conservation Area
49. Get used to (var.)
52. Cambodian currency units
54. Send in a bill payment
56. Houdini, from his Chinese Water Torture Cell
58. 1985 Power Station hit: "_____ Like it Hot"
59. List header
60. American folksinger Burl
61. Canada is one of 29 members of this (abbr.)
62. French Open playing surface
64. Shy
66. Steep cliff
67. Pacific islands tuber
68. Antarctic island
69. Highlands fling?
71. Softly laughs
72. BC's Highway 5, colloquially
75. Handle a hardship
77. French country inn
80. Friendly, on Internet media?

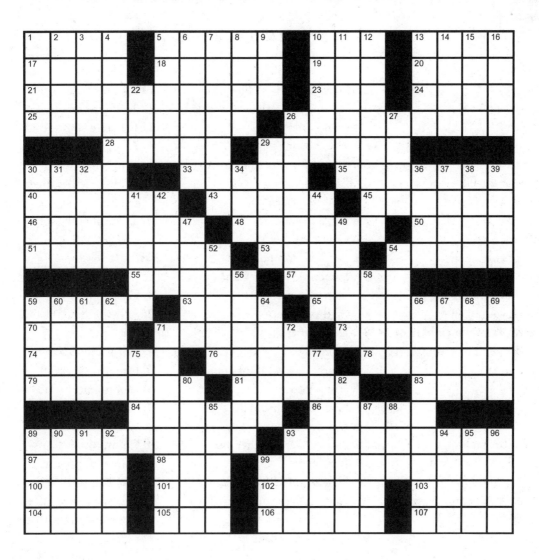

82. Important spring day for Christians

85. Like a crazy chiropterologist?

87. Outbuildings

88. A bit of liquid

89. Lighthouse drummer Prokop

90. Scarlett's homestead

91. Vancouver-born *Deadpool* actor Reynolds

92. Geological time spans

93. Took a trolley

94. Coffey who played for the Oilers in the '80s

95. Finales

96. Indian pancake

99. Black History mo. in Canada

For Their Service

A nation says thank you

ACROSS

1. Clump of banknotes
4. Thick piece
8. Went to the bottom
12. Hip hop kin
15. Member of the US Congress (abbr.)
18. Whitesnake song: "Here _____ Again"
19. A story of two cities?
20. Creative flash
21. Scratch out a living, say
22. Fire truck equipment
23. **Medal for family members of those who died in action**
26. Venezuelan city
28. Netted?
29. Rival
30. Via, to Ruth?
32. Some U of A buildings
33. Court order
34. _____ profundo
36. Underhill's ice skating partner
38. TV chef Martin who got his start in Calgary
39. Trunk for treasures
41. Bridle part
43. Illicit cigarette
46. Divert, on the tracks
47. Jewish month
48. Dodge for a sheep farmer?
49. 1996 Johnny Cash cover: "_____ Been Everywhere"
50. Most cozy
53. Mary Pickford moniker: _____ Sweetheart
55. Open _____ of worms
56. Acts of contrition
57. Arabic VIPs
58. Follower
60. Bliss Carman poem: "Low _____ on Grand Pré"
61. Like a white rat

63. Decibel isotropic (abbr.)
64. "Losing My Religion" music group
65. YYC posting
66. **Award for acts of heroism**
69. Fairy tale being
72. Half of a facial pair
74. Sun anagram
75. Gentle stroke
76. *Garfield* strip pooch
77. Sometime job for Canada's James Cameron
80. Bath powders
81. Landowner's land
83. Clods
84. Source of wealth for young aristocrats?
86. Gathered gastropods?
87. Licorice bit
88. 2007 Giller Prize winner Elizabeth
89. Hale, Jr. of *Gilligan's Island*
90. Clara Peller's complaints?
91. Implant deeply
93. Got 100 per cent
94. Mount Ida is this island's highest point
95. Stat for a pitcher
98. Wormwood
100. Eschew
102. Fine-tunes one's skills
104. Lifeboat lowering device
106. Bird with a long bill
108. Six-season show: _____ *Pilots NWT*
109. Sugar paste confection
110. Former
112. **See 66-A**
115. Lillehammer nation (abbr.)
116. Saskatchewan place: Fond-du-_____
117. Small amount
118. Prevaricates

119. Long-jawed fish
120. Whatever amount
121. Potato sprout bud
122. "Double Stuf" Nabisco offering
123. Historic BC town north of Hope
124. Naval rank (abbr.)

DOWN

1. Dorothy L. Sayers detective: Lord Peter _____
2. AGM order of business
3. Ruler's realm
4. Got ready to work out
5. Installed tile, say
6. Montgomery state (abbr.)
7. *Titanic* was built here
8. Stable papas
9. Commotion
10. Home for herons
11. Northern Pakistan language
12. Happen once more
13. Wanted poster letters
14. Daily living allowance
15. **Decoration for Canadian Forces members**
16. Midterm or final
17. "Untouchable" lawman
24. Literary monster
25. Price
27. Outstanding
31. Operated
34. Not straight
35. **Exceptional contribution award since 1967**
37. Garbage
40. Hungarian cavalry member
42. Rabbits have large ones
44. Canadian media personality Solomon
45. Monthly expense for some
46. _____ *qua non*

47. Acid found in proteins
48. You listen to CBC on these
50. Dislike a lot
51. Fail to include
52. **See 66-A**
53. Something that's as good as a mile?
54. TELUS wires?
55. 1957 hit: "Chances _____"
57. Ridiculous
59. It's human to do this
62. Without friends
63. Canadian history figure: Thomas _____ McGee
66. Computer's data processing unit (abbr.)
67. *Babylon 5* character
68. Online news group
70. Lo-fat, in ads
71. Provide with sustenance
73. Conventioneers' badges, for short
76. Blues singer Rush
77. Cornbread
78. Pour
79. Kinkajou's kin
80. Enamelled metalware
82. Lodgings for a protected witness
85. Hombre's pride?
86. Johnny planted an apple one?
88. Unfriendly
90. Succinctly, to an attorney?
92. Funereal write-up
93. Provincial financial institution since 1938 (abbr.)
94. French fashion designer Chanel
95. Interlock, like gears
96. US president when Mulroney was prime minister
97. Michaelmas daisies, for example
99. Family female
101. Small songbird
103. 1867 song: "_____ Dominion"
104. Spanish lady's honorific
105. Unknown author's appellation?
107. See 9-D
109. "The First _____"
111. Canadian statutory holiday month
113. Took the cake?
114. Tom Clancy novel theme (abbr.)

Solution on page 215

30 Canada Cornucopia 15

ACROSS

1. Basra nation
5. See your sweetie on a Saturday night
9. "_____ I care!"
13. "_____ pigs fly!"
17. Main button on a remote
18. Cheese tray cheese
19. Award won 24 times by Anne Murray
20. Former boxer Oscar De La _____
21. Plant with a soothing gel
22. 1960 golden Canadian pair skater Wagner, for short
23. Appealing to emotions, rather than reason
25. Canadian "We'll Sing in the Sunshine" singer Garnett
26. Old Greeks gathered here
28. Put away for a rainy day
29. Pair of pullers in the pasture
30. Type of oil or bagel
32. Calgary's Saddledome, to the Flames
33. Fr. holy women
35. Make morose
37. Gets the most out of
41. National park in Alberta
44. Large-headed match (var.)
45. Whirl like a dervish
47. Brock University is named for him
48. Ontario's capital city
50. Of a certain metallic element
51. Ethiopian currency unit
52. Seductress who gives you a warning?
53. Linen colour
55. House builder's site
56. Commence hostilities
58. Global crime-fighting agency
60. 100 lbs., American style
61. Canada's Patrick Chan often landed a triple one
62. Coming up, at the pub?
63. Wander around on the range
65. Long-time Canadian furniture giant
67. Made a choice
69. Nasal membranes
70. Local idioms
72. Alone, in stage directions
73. Responded flippantly
74. Tori's Canadian-born mate McDermott
75. Problems for pretenders?
77. Shelter for sheep
78. Zorro might leave you with one
80. CBC's *Mr. D*, for one
82. Toronto pop quartet since 1950: The Four _____
86. Mental deterioration
90. Fruit for Don Cherry?
91. Currency used across the pond
92. Trouble in the atmosphere
94. Division word
95. Ocean Spray offering: _____-Apple juice
96. *The Lord of the Rings* characters
97. Zest
98. Arabian Peninsula place
99. Bangladesh bread
100. Construct
101. Withered
102. Apollo's instrument
103. Homophone of 101-A

DOWN

1. Insect development stage
2. Take a break
3. Arboreal lizard
4. Legislature locale in 48-A
5. One who humiliates
6. Saws and axioms
7. Edible tubers
8. Battlement slots
9. Bestselling Steely Dan album
10. Bathtub bubbles
11. "Is there an echo _____?"
12. Security, for the shoemaker?
13. Cat's facial hairs
14. _____ *soit qui mal y pense*
15. Ogled
16. Entitle
24. 1988 Leonard Cohen single: "I'm Your _____"
27. South American rainforest
31. Ontario ski resort: Glen _____
34. Pulp fiction sleuth, for short
36. Diplomatic stand-downs
38. BC city
39. Weaken or stunt
40. Breakaway religious group
41. Sail type
42. So to speak
43. California city
44. Lacking a distinctive shape
46. Groucho's series: *You Bet _____ Life*
48. Out of gas
49. Canada's women's eight rowers, for one
52. Jazz combo woodwind
54. Congressman, for short
57. Québec, directionally from Ontario
58. Loft's design style, say
59. Opts for early
60. Covered up?
62. Alberta drilling device
64. Furious
66. Balderdash
68. British runner Sebastian, et al.
69. Took a load off
71. Floral bracts
73. 2011 Adele smash: "_____ Like You"
76. Bird from Baltimore?

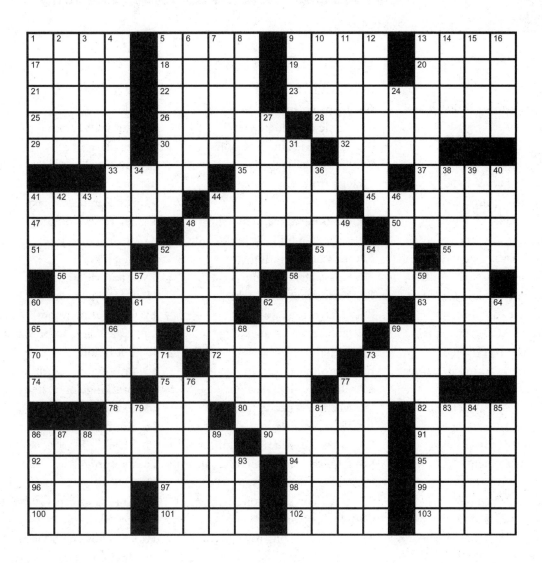

77. Whirlybird
79. Annual Aug. event, in 48-A
81. John who played *SCTV*'s Johnny LaRue
83. Halos (var.)

84. Canadian rap star
85. Salvaging aid at sea
86. Disastrous destiny
87. Canadian Levant who founded *The Rebel Media*

88. Spoof
89. Banned chemical spray
93. One way the wind might blow (abbr.)

ACROSS

1. Canadian actors Cavanagh and Jackson
5. Vancouver _____ Gallery
8. Pile of papers
13. Took a lecherous look
19. Sandwich of sorts
20. Corp. honcho
21. Busch Gardens city
22. Central Asian sheep
23. Noble, in Neustadt
24. Officer at Calgary's Canada Olympic Park?
25. Undisguised
26. **French brandy?**
27. They spearhead social upheavals
31. "Me too"
32. Magistrates in ancient Rome (var.)
33. _____ colony
34. Attire for an identical?
36. Radios in semis
37. Winnipeg's Arvid Loewen did this across Canada in 2011
38. Electrical plug component
39. **New Yorker's cocktail?**
43. Full of courage
45. As _____ as a fiddle
48. Wicker worker's willow
49. Louis of the Red River Rebellion
51. Smidgen
52. Yowl of pain
53. Sows and hogs
54. Madagascar animal
56. Newish newt
57. **French fruit?**
58. "Kum Ba _____"
59. Rogers Arena mascot
60. Biggest desert in the world
62. Structural support
63. Famed Canadian aviator Max, et al.
65. TD ATM no.
66. Torment, in the schoolyard
68. Circle of influence?
71. It's intoxicating to tabbies
74. Greek letters
75. Cat from *Cats*: Rum _____ Tugger
78. **Japanese agreement?**
79. Canadian military rank (abbr.)
80. Hawaiian greetings
82. Chase after a rabbit?
83. Sore god of love?
84. Heart valve locale
86. Cheese for a dame?
87. Fixes
88. Get hitched
89. Flick up a light switch
90. **Mexican's petite pet?**
92. Peels potatoes
93. One's true self, in Hinduism
96. English Language Development (abbr.)
97. U of T presentation
100. Pivots (var.)
101. Common bugloss: _____ *officinalis*
105. Signalling (var.)
106. Ocean liners' frameworks
109. **Irishman's coat?**
111. Disfiguring facial marks
112. 1996 C&W #1 from Alberta's Paul Brandt
113. Insect ova
114. Newly decorated
115. Overly affectionate parent, perhaps
116. Obi anagram
117. Jodie Foster film: *Little Man* _____
118. Ices a cake
119. Gives permission
120. Absorb liquid
121. Wee dram of whisky

DOWN

1. Jerk
2. National honour: _____ of Canada
3. Novelist Binchey
4. Rorschach's spots?
5. Spellbound, to Shakespeare?
6. Alex Haley's origins?
7. African antelope
8. On a high?
9. **Cuban cigar?**
10. Green gemstones
11. Fundraising month for the Canadian Cancer Society
12. Lot in life
13. Huron, to a Quebecer
14. Breaking down, like a levee
15. Defacing 91-D?
16. Bombasts
17. Thrill
18. Flowering plant classification
28. Type of pneumonia
29. Annual Rogers Centre events for the Jays
30. Like a by-the-book disciplinarian
35. Policy _____
37. Analgesic's target
38. Ready-made?
39. Morose (var.)
40. India's continent
41. Near, in old poetry
42. The general drift?
44. She might mimic a monkey?
45. Honshu Island volcano
46. Terry Fox, to many Canadians
47. Heavy?
50. Jumped
52. 1970 Neil Young hit: "_____ Love Can Break Your Heart"
54. Long-time retailer: Canadian _____
55. **Beijing dinnerware?**

57. Falls ill
59. Popular 1800s card game
61. Like a feeble old female
62. In addition
63. Soaks
64. Treats contemptuously
67. Savoury, in Japanese cuisine
68. Distort data, say
69. Funereal rite platform
70. Urban gang's turf
72. Anne Murray's range
73. CBC Radio offering
75. Trig function
76. Karachi tongue

77. Neighbour of Phoenix
79. Apple pie makers' gadgets
81. 1944 chemistry Nobel Prize winner Otto
82. Seeks brainy potential employees?
84. That certain glow?
85. Literary work excerpts (var.)
87. Swindle
89. Go off on a _____
91. Farm building for birds
92. Ill-famed recalled Ford cars
94. Ankara bird?
95. Grp. of gentlemen

97. Skin surface flakes
98. 18th-C. Swiss mathematician
99. Err
100. Scare a ghost?
101. Sound
102. Dickens' humble Heep
103. Bench-clearing brawl, say
104. GIC or RRSP
107. Beehive or bun
108. Meal choice at The Keg
110. Renewable Energy Source (abbr.)

ACROSS

1. Archipelago bit
6. Circle in the centre of a shield
10. Peanut-free Canadian candy bar name
14. Dusty Springfield hit: "_____ of a Preacher Man"
17. Toronto-born "Treat You Better" singer (with 10-D)
18. You might dip this in dal
19. Improve an essay, say
20. Parrot a primate?
21. Currency control advocate
23. Canada joined this org. in 1949
24. Street, in Saguenay
25. Witnesses, while playing poker?
26. Word list word
27. Early Celtic religion
29. Nation's capital newspaper: Ottawa _____
30. Altar locale
32. Superior card sharp?
33. Embarrassing episode
38. Notable Toronto waterfront street: The _____
43. Canadian food and lifestyle channel
44. Orphans
46. Stream sediment
47. Computer user's return button
49. Motorsport series since 1957: Canadian _____ Championship
51. Lions' lairs
52. Sidestepped
53. Desert beast
54. Show aired on 43-A: Martha and Snoop's Potluck Dinner _____
55. Enterprise Europe Network (abbr.)
56. Made rattan furniture
57. Fish catcher
58. Mustard type
61. Plays at a SkyTrain station
62. Slews
66. Responsibility
67. They meet up with tibiae
68. Empress Hotel city
69. To whom it may _____
71. Auspices
73. Dye-yielding shrubs
74. Most snobby
76. Retaliatory actions
78. Senator Wallin, for short
79. North African streambed that's only wet when it pours
81. Springsteen hit: "Born to ____"
82. Leafs match in Montréal, say
86. Coniferous tree secretion
88. Cause the ruination of
92. Pride or envy
93. Pierre Berton children's book: The Battle of Lake _____
94. Like artsy innovators
96. Tourists' lodgings
97. Diatribe
98. 1980s Calgary Flame Nilsson
99. Woodworkers' tools
100. Newfoundland band: Great Big _____
101. Completes
102. Work units
103. Big bangs

DOWN

1. Distinct doctrines
2. Toronto venue: Bata _____ Museum
3. Superman role for Canada's Margot Kidder
4. They bleat
5. 1976 AC/DC hit
6. Like lapsed Chatelaine subscriptions
7. Cause harm
8. Rice type
9. One way to serve Molson Canadian
10. See 17-A
11. Purim month
12. In a ceremonial manner
13. Showing little if any reaction
14. Hindu lady's wrap
15. Soup anagram
16. Indian subcontinent tree type
22. U of M reunion attendee
28. Revealing moments?
29. Hem
31. Some seeds
33. Grows older
34. Half of a bed set
35. Sparkling wine: _____ Spumante
36. 3-D imagery
37. House of Commons "no" vote
39. Gloomy atmosphere
40. Strongly state your opinion
41. Old-style blow
42. Terri Clark US/Canada #1 hit: "You're _____ on the Eyes"
45. 2017 CBC TV mystery series (with 80-D)
48. Sault Ste. Marie-born artist Danby
50. Conducted the orchestra
53. Fruity ice cream
54. Apply (to)
56. Scoundrel's dog?
57. MoMA locale
58. Vets and Ph.Ds
59. Get _____ a good thing
60. Fan Choice Award won by 17-A in 2017
61. Cause of a downfall
62. Publisher's rejects?
63. Piece for Canadian opera star Wall

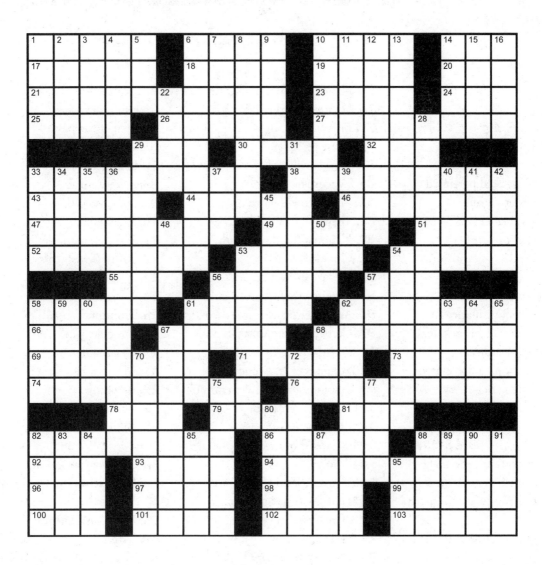

64. Canadian potato chip flavour: _____ pickle

65. Lippy response

67. Three-hulled boat

68. Go for the gold

70. Bric-a-brac shelf

72. One who's mourning

75. Laura Secord treats?

77. Pipsqueak

80. See 45-D

82. Final sale caveat

83. Okanagan or Niagara product

84. CBC news host and correspondent, _____ Maria Tremonti

85. You might change yours

87. Emulated Jann Arden

88. Wall panel

89. Tiny pasta type

90. The same, to Hadrian

91. Loch _____

95. Yatter

33 | Watch Your Qs (but not your Ps)

Canadian place names

ACROSS

1. Phony
6. No ifs, ands or _____
10. Derelict, in duty
16. NHLer Steve from PEI
19. Yellow-flowered perennial
20. Army troops' group
21. US record label (1974–2011)
22. Surname for Jane?
23. Deflect
24. Spaghetti sauce brand
25. Some medicinal plants
26. Former Saturn model
27. Excuse for bad behaviour?
28. **Provincial capital**
30. Sean Lennon's middle name
31. Antioxidant-rich berry
33. Lambs' sounds
34. Glittery garment bit
37. In 1991, this caused $400+ million of damage in Calgary
40. First letters?
43. Applies a product improperly, say
44. Justin Bieber, to some girls
45. Mosses
46. Hawaiian house adjunct
47. Too portly
48. Always, to a bard
49. Not many
50. Arm bone adjective
54. Baghdad country
56. Bear in the night sky
58. "Finally," to Etta?
61. Theatre patrons' box
62. Where future American ensigns train (abbr.)
64. Leaves the terminal
66. Held dear
68. **Former name of Haida Gwaii**
73. *Animal Farm* author George
74. Lindsay Wagner TV show: *The _____ Woman*
75. National emblem of Wales
76. Hammerhead end
77. Burps
79. Cease
81. _____ Selkirk MB
85. Draconian
87. WWII intelligence org.
88. They come before mis
89. National holiday month, in Canada
90. Greyish-brown colour
92. It follows South and North
96. Assist
97. Comedic TV stuntman Super Dave
100. Quebecer Jean-Luc who won moguls gold at Lillehammer
101. _____ meridiem
102. Bombshell's shade?
103. "Taps" horn
104. "Sorry, my mistake"
106. Cover ground?
107. **Nunavut national park**
111. Crosswise, to a sailor
115. Original sinner
116. Mame, for example
117. Drive-_____ window
118. Mantel
119. Mattress annoyance
120. Glib talk
121. Single
122. Canada's Andre De Grasse won a silver one in Rio
123. Caribbean island music genre
124. Toolbox tool
125. Once, old style
126. Sow's sound

DOWN

1. Throw _____ loop
2. Canadian skater Stojko excelled at this jump
3. Ceremonial French military hat
4. Look at, like the ophthalmologist?
5. Piece of the past?
6. Ladies' swimsuit that covers all
7. Rainforest canopy critter
8. Andrews of *The Mod Squad*
9. More blunted
10. Rapscallions
11. Builds a barn, say
12. Petite British cars
13. "_____ It a Pity"
14. Doesn't go out
15. Scandinavian Airlines (abbr.)
16. Disgusting
17. Canadian coin
18. Mortise insertions
29. Pizzazz
32. Be indisposed
35. Biblical brothers: Jacob and _____
36. **"Goose Capital of Saskatchewan"**
37. You could play LPs on this
38. Month of Purim
39. Letter that comes after theta
41. Treats with a cold pack
42. Emotional outburst, at the Royal Alexandra?
43. Large mouths
46. Rent out
49. Arrow makers
51. Canada, say
52. Grew up
53. Warren Beatty movie
55. **United Empire Loyalists settled here**
56. Long-running CTV kids' show: _____ *Bobby*
57. Cheerleading cheer component
58. Neural transmitters
59. Long-haired monkey
60. Panasonic product

63. Canada's Dan Aykroyd starred on this show in the '70s (abbr.)
65. Opposite of 49-A
67. Product of Nova Scotia's Alexander Keith's brewery
68. Hebrew letter
69. _____ formaldehyde
70. Jug with a spout
71. Bad treatment
72. _____ at ease
78. You need this to skip
80. Where Russia is
82. "Praise the Lord!" phrase
83. BC landmark: _____ Spring Island
84. Genre
86. Canadian-owned beverage producer: Mike's _____ Lemonade Co.
88. Move to a new place
91. Like a not fair share
92. Debaters
93. Neighbour of Senegal
94. Mallet and hoops game
95. Fuss
96. Faded star
97. Become compulsive
98. Bratislava citizen
99. Hispanic shop
100. Having less leisure time
103. Picture _____ AB
105. Hand parts
108. _____-hero
109. Norse mythology god
110. Buffet coffee pots
112. Type of tuber
113. Petri dish gel
114. Thaw
116. iPhone download

ACROSS

1. Canadian Club 100% _____
4. ABC dramedy that starred Canadians Katic and Fillion
10. Fabled creature
13. Agitate
17. Canadian "Big League" group: Tom Cochrane and _____ Rider
18. Roseanne Barr, by birth
19. Affectionate murmur
20. Bathgate who notched 17 seasons in the NHL
21. In a sorrowful state
22. Find new nouns, say
23. *Canada's Worst Driver* legal expert Woolley
24. It's 6,853 kilometres long
25. Declares
27. Provincial parks rent out these
29. Songs you sing at Notre-Dame Basilica in Montréal
30. JFK-era "renaissance"
31. Canadian car parts retailer: Princess _____
34. Excel, as a traveller?
36. Possessed, say
40. Makes impolite noises at dinner
43. Desert wanderer
45. Beach hut
46. Star in Scorpius
48. Bigot
50. Seeks information
51. Canadian children's author who created Franklin (with 87-A)
53. Rave's partner
54. Grind one's teeth
55. West African republic
58. US singer Joan, et al.
62. "All You _____ Is Love"
63. Soaks
68. Winnipeg Symphony Orchestra instrument

69. Canadian women won Olympic bronze in 2012 and 2016 in this
71. Canadien "Rocket" Richard
72. Jump on a trampoline
74. The Pentateuch
76. The mind
77. Canadian debit card network
79. Free from worries, say
81. Sacred religious image (var.)
82. Poem with three stanzas
84. African country
87. See 51-A
90. Powerful abilities?
94. a.k.a. word
95. *Batman Forever* star Kilmer
96. Digging deep?
97. Like Willie Winkie
98. In stead of
99. Barely get by
100. Rate
101. Irish independence grp. formed in 1917
102. Minus
103. Hippies tripped on this
104. _____ hound
105. Sir John A. Macdonald appears on this Canadian bill

DOWN

1. Canadian's investment option (abbr.)
2. Calendar span
3. Caribbean taro
4. Like a pig's tail
5. Elite '80s TV group?
6. Making logs
7. 20th-C. Canadian artist Tom
8. Metallica member Ulrich
9. At your wits' _____
10. English philosopher: William of _____
11. Roved

12. Interweave, old style
13. 20-A, for example
14. "You can bank _____"
15. Monty Python member Eric
16. Some cleansers
26. Like 29-A
27. African wildcat
28. Hindu mythology god
30. Friendship
31. Rapidly (abbr.)
32. Luna's arm bone?
33. Royal Winnipeg Ballet member's skirt
35. Bryan Adams hit: "(Everything I Do) I Do It _____ You"
37. Former employer of Canada's Marc Garneau
38. Signs in pen?
39. Toonies and loonies
41. National news source: Canadian _____
42. First segment of a tennis match
44. Ate supper
47. Kind of clerk
49. 1985 Luba hit: "_____ Before the Calm"
52. Build up?
54. Taxonomic group
56. Independent Canadian label: True North _____
57. Pane anagram
58. Long-time Ford slogan: "Quality is _____"
59. Deep black, to Donne
60. _____ *de suite*
61. Dark and gloomy
64. 1987 k.d. lang duet with Roy Orbison
65. Yokel
66. 2014 dramatic movie: _____ *Park*
67. W.O. Mitchell CanLit classic: *Who Has _____ the Wind?*

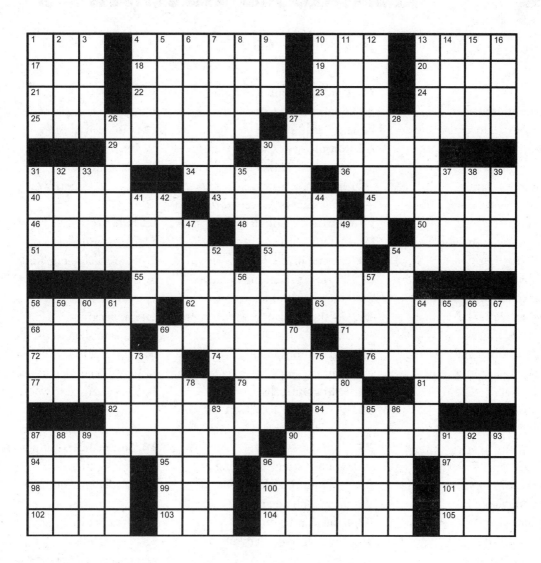

69. Some of New Orleans is below this

70. Room heater, for short

73. Rugged outcrop

75. Brand name on Canada's Hickory Sticks

78. Flowing outer garments

80. Mythological vengeance goddesses

83. Felt sick

85. Thick in the head?

86. Feeling of dread

87. Newfoundland's 13th premier Dwight

88. William Joyce children's book: *Big Time* _____

89. Manipulates

90. Former Chicago Cub Sammy

91. Numbskull

92. 2011 Avril Lavigne song: "Wish You Were _____"

93. Great Big Sea singer McCann

96. Montréal Canadien, colloquially

You Gotta Have Heart

Songs from Ann and Nancy Wilson's band

ACROSS

1. Sami, previously
6. Still under the duvet?
10. Tempo
14. Masses of hair, say
18. Rabbitlike rodent
20. Evil, in a way?
21. _____ Nui
22. 2002 Céline Dion album: _____ *Day Has Come*
23. **1986 ballad on which Nancy, rather than Ann, sang lead**
25. Canadian rockers: Bachman-Turner _____
27. Southern Alberta city: Medicine _____
28. Ogles
29. Prodded a pig?
31. Ascends
32. UBC lecture
33. See 28-A
34. Kokanee container
35. Of a vertebrate
38. More facile
40. Like a docile dog
44. Make bigger
46. **It hit #1 on Canada's charts in 1977**
48. Collagen injection site
49. Hollywood star Cameron
50. Not in favour of playing poker?
52. Past, to a bard
53. You might do this at the Royal Bank?
54. US award won by Canada's Shatner and Sutherland
55. You might visit an oasis here
58. Canadian *Pineapple Express* screenwriter Goldberg
59. The red oak is PEI's official this
60. Give a plant fresh soil
62. Mound atop old tombs
64. Affectionate stroke

66. Lymphatic bumps
68. Singer Adam Cohen, to Leonard
69. Toronto's Air Canada Centre was renamed this in 2018: Scotiabank _____
71. Input data for a second time
74. Cartilage cushions
76. Gully
80. Eclectic medley
81. Mexican's spending money
84. Not subject to taxes, say
86. Unemployed Brit's government cheque
87. Old Trafford's football club, for short
88. Telling untruths
90. Anagram for René who didn't do well?
91. Command to Fido
92. Property Transfer Tax (abbr.)
93. **1978 hard rock single**
96. Scott Joplin genre
98. Some stanzas
100. Ancient Egyptian king
102. Hags
103. Helm heading (abbr.)
104. Macedonians' neighbours
105. Hit from 25-A: "_____ Care of Business"
107. Reject
110. Burton Cummings song: "I Will _____ Rhapsody"
111. As _____ as a rock
112. It regulates US broadcasters (abbr.)
115. Having nothing to do with ethnicity
117. **Led Zeppelin cover that's a concert favourite**
120. Type of flute or sax
121. Intersecting network of blood vessels

122. Paste
123. *Titanic* star Stuart
124. In need of funds
125. Software company client, say
126. Casino ratios
127. _____ a positive note

DOWN

1. _____ and plaster
2. Kurdish chieftain's title (var.)
3. Canada's Milton Acorn, for example
4. Sup anagram
5. Outstanding, to the astronomer?
6. Reluctant
7. Dressmaker's prejudice?
8. 1821 Constable work: *Study of an _____ Tree*
9. "All hope is lost" state
10. Stock traders' employers
11. Roof gutters
12. Made like a gorilla?
13. Goopy substance
14. Marc Jordan hit: "_____ del Rey"
15. Tropical birds
16. Glacier component
17. Certain sheep
19. Theoretical molecule matter
24. Place to live at Carleton
26. Genre of many CBC programs
30. Milieu for a mezzo-soprano
32. **Debut American single released in 1976**
33. Glasgow School of Art (abbr.)
34. See 10-A
35. Ceremonial Jewish dinner
36. Spirited, in Saguenay
37. Vise device
39. Crosswise, on a ship
40. Albacore
41. Klaxon blat
42. Alice Munro collection: _____ *of Girls and Women*

43. Piste weapons
45. Related through mom
47. Gastown municipal abbr.
51. So
53. **1978 North American Top 20 single**
56. Deceptive manoeuvre
57. **#1 power ballad released in 1987**
61. Peak
63. Windows alternative, in computing
65. Half-Canadian comedy duo: Cheech _____ Chong
67. Exhaust resources
69. See 61-D
70. More mature, on the vine
71. Cavorts

72. Make happy
73. Temporary hair treatments
74. Hochelaga resident
75. Have a gut feeling
77. Relationship
78. Tim Hortons additive in Québec
79. Putters aim for these
82. Hatchling in a hawk's nest
83. _____ John A. Macdonald
85. Pursuing prey
89. Uncomfortably bright, when you're driving
93. Mehndi paste ingredient
94. Trade barrier
95. Sound of a leaky balloon
97. Pancake-making appliance
99. Overwhelming fear

101. Feeds the fire
104. Roster of candidates
106. _____ carte
107. Canadians often weather this: Cold _____
108. Marco's game?
109. Long-time CBS show: *Lamp _____ My Feet*
110. Pumpkin-filled desserts
111. Gulf War weapon type
112. Oakville car plant
113. History Muse
114. Family group
116. Vineyard in Provence
118. Yukon community north of the Arctic Circle: _____ Crow
119. Canadian comic James

Solution on page 216

36 Canada Cornucopia 18

ACROSS

1. Shed feathers
6. Draper's loot?
10. 1970 Jackson Five hit
13. Annexes
17. *Schitt's Creek* actress Murphy
18. Mama's partner
19. Scrooge interjection
20. Onion's cousin
21. Avant-garde artists
23. Caribbean music genre
24. Host of 11-D Dan
25. Improve your finances?
26. Sept-Îles sweet spot?
29. Canadian history moment: _____ of 1812
31. Wonky
33. He fills stockings
34. Angry cat's sound
36. _____ good example
37. Hamilton CFL team
42. Goodbye, in Gran Canaria
44. He deals in old clothes
46. Sickening feeling?
47. Sketched again
49. Put your house in order
51. 1972 Neil Young song: "A Man _____ a Maid"
52. J. Trudeau cabinet minister Chrystia
54. Done with, once and for all
56. 1980s Canadian game show: *The Mad* _____
57. Big do?
58. _____ et nunc
59. Crown corporation: _____ Rail
61. Charity, in Dickens' time
65. *Front Page Challenge* inquisitors, for example
67. Ottawa university
72. The Blue Bombers play here: Investors Group _____
74. Government department: _____ Canada
76. Jupiter moon
77. Film genre
79. Quran language
81. Small shops
82. Try again
84. Sailor's greeting
86. Rotisserie
87. Overdramatize
88. They often accompany regulations
90. Aloof
91. Bringing happiness and joy
96. Winged (var.)
98. Part for Canada's Ryan Gosling
99. Mopey
100. Receiving a legacy
104. 2016 Bryan Adams single: "Don't _____ Try"
105. Lethbridge College caregivers' prog.
106. Bounder
107. Proportion
108. Disco brothers: The Bee _____
109. Ocean liner's call for aid
110. You might arrange one at BMO
111. In a crafty manner

DOWN

1. Whitechapel parent
2. Yoko's dismayed expression?
3. It's down below?
4. Bank holding
5. _____ firma
6. More zesty
7. Victorian-era furniture piece
8. Renter's unit (abbr.)
9. Sharp intake of breath
10. Eschewed alcohol
11. CBC TV 2017 premiere: *The Great Canadian* _____ *Show*
12. Censure
13. She, in Baie-Saint-Paul
14. Lewd look
15. Stampeder named most outstanding CFLer in 2016: Bo _____ Mitchell
16. Actress Ione
22. Jodie Foster film: _____ *Island*
27. Unstable, in physics
28. Kitchen wrap
29. Richmond BC attraction: Fisherman's _____
30. To assist, in Abitibi
32. Guru's herb?
35. Angry about an ache?
38. Signalled a pool shark?
39. Between ports
40. Koppel and Danson
41. Miss Universe Canada's ribbon
43. "To thine own _____ be true"
45. *Anne of Green Gables* Cuthbert
48. Skew
50. Truro province: _____ Scotia
53. Lexicographer Webster
55. Grammy-winning Montréal band: Arcade _____
58. Encourage the cardiologist?
60. Grad from U of A
61. Off in the distance
62. Scalp vermin
63. Will Rogers quote: "I never _____ man I didn't like"
64. Open an envelope
66. Ocean motions
67. Short-haired dog breed
68. Sear anagram
69. Lack of vigour
70. Related to sight
71. Like a mean girl
73. Showered with love

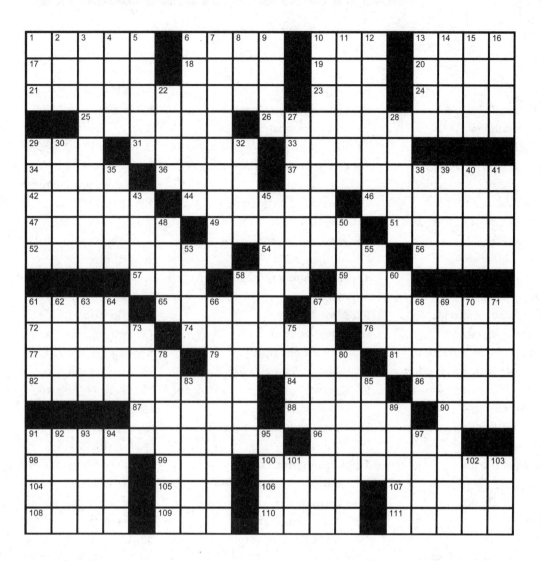

75. Alberta's Marmot Basin installed one in 1974
78. Unbeatable enemies
80. Dewhurst who portrayed 45-D
83. Prince Albert's domain
85. 1976 Al Stewart single: "_____ of the Cat"
89. Rouses

91. Blue Rodeo member Keelor
92. Alice Munro Giller winner: *The _____ of a Good Woman*
93. Sheltered from the wind
94. Lions' lodgings
95. Céline Dion song: "Always Be Your _____"
97. Bibliography abbr.

101. Naval Oceanographic Office (abbr.)
102. Nada, in a Newcastle match
103. *Royal Canadian Air Farce* star Luba

ACROSS

1. Pillowcase
5. Hoboes' haunches?
9. Supreme Hindu god (var.)
13. Blue Bugle, for example
18. Complete and _____ failure
20. Paying close attention to a task
21. Halifax Stanfield International Airport postings (abbr.)
22. Species subdivision
23. Savvy
24. Cat-o'-_____-tails
25. NHLer Sundin who played for three Canadian teams
26. Abhors
27. **Downtown Toronto market**
29. Bones in the hips
30. Ouzo flavouring
31. NBC news personality Lester
32. Emulated Michael J. Fox
33. Legally permissible
35. Litmus _____
36. Stevie Wonder hit: "_____ Ground"
38. *Sine* _____ *non*
39. Its neighbours are Draco and Cygnus
41. Earning, say
44. Certain Muslim
46. Highway 401 incident, for example
50. Pub order
51. Beach bug
53. **Winnipeg market**
55. Japanese writing system
57. More ethereal (var.)
58. Drivers' permits, in Pittsburgh
59. 40-year CBC staple: *The Fifth* _____
61. _____ *Yankees*
62. Cooking pot for a cantina
63. Time zone for TO
64. Deaden, at the dental clinic

66. Digs for doves
68. Bygone Russian royal
71. Group of whales
74. Former *Hockey Night in Canada* cartoon character: Peter _____
76. Bon mot
78. You'll need to go here?
82. In a discordant way, musically
85. They harmonize pianos
87. Marijuana butt
88. **Eponymous Ontario town market**
89. Most hirsute
91. However, informally
92. Big grin description
93. Goes on the road, like Rush
95. A writer might use this figure of speech
97. Tennis tournament exemptions
99. Opposite of post-
100. Opera great Enrico
101. CBC news correspondent Petricic
104. *SCTV* star Harold
106. 1948 Pulitzer-winning poet W.H.
107. A grand amount, for short?
111. Spring bloomer
113. *The Fountainhead* author Ayn
114. **Calgary market landmark**
116. Nimble
117. Song for 77-D
118. _____ best friend
119. Ammonia compound
120. Golden Fleece myth princess
121. Like the scent of Christmas trees (var.)
122. Ne'er anagram
123. Boot for an angler
124. Exploits (with "on")
125. Some U of C grads
126. South China and Salish
127. Autos

DOWN

1. Cache of cash?
2. _____ *Succeed in Business Without Really Trying*
3. To any degree
4. Indo–Aryan language
5. Orthopaedic surgeon's dishes?
6. Like some consequences
7. Kitchen tool
8. Warhorse
9. Shaped like a half moon
10. Nationality of 100-A
11. Like 86-D
12. Tear into
13. Old Turkish title (var.)
14. **Montréal** *marché*
15. Loosen a ribbon
16. "American Woman" band: The _____ Who
17. Canada Savings Bond, once
19. *All Quiet on the Western Front* actor Ayres
28. Hip hop/reggae offshoot
34. Pigeonhole a stenographer?
37. Undisturbed (Lat.)
38. **Saint John shopper's destination**
40. Prevalent
41. Bryan Adams' first single: "Let Me _____ You Dancing"
42. Expression of regret
43. BC Fraser Valley district
44. Green goo, say
45. "_____ do you good"
47. Language spoken in Ireland of old
48. HI guitars
49. Quiet attention-getter
52. Former New Brunswick premier McKenna
54. Haft or handle
56. Weedless Wednesday occurs in this mo. in Canada

60. Your boss
62. Dogwood variety
65. Source of 111-A
67. Mediterranean port city
69. Major arteries
70. Canada's Penny Oleksiak won Olympic gold here
71. Time gone by
72. Holy Roman emperor (962–73)
73. Martial arts training facility
75. Bump under the skin
77. First lady of opera?
79. Strip of wood
80. Lover of Narcissus
81. Thunderous god
83. **Vancouver shopping spot**
84. Hurting
85. Nights on which NBC featured sitcoms for 20+ years
86. Women who look to the future?
90. Overwhelms
94. Expressing one's opinion
96. River that flows through DC
98. Mexican man's shawl (var.)
100. Arrow poison
101. Calgary CFLer
102. Winter fishing tool
103. Park chute
105. County north of San Francisco
106. They're at the top?
108. BC landmark: _____ Gwaii
109. More unusual
110. Drug addicts
112. Round, green veggies
115. Like carrots before cooking

ACROSS

1. 1974 Guess Who hit: "_____ Baby"
5. Folklore creature
10. Direction to one Canadian coast
14. You work up a sweat here
17. Luau dance
18. *Being Erica* actor Michael
19. International military alliance (abbr.)
20. Lobster eggs
21. Sometimes
23. Tools for Canada's Kelly Jay?
25. Ontario tri-cities area: Kitchener-Cambridge-_____
26. Percussion instruments
28. _____ and potatoes
29. Gourd family member
30. Beginning of the _____
31. Red Rose tea type
34. Ribs
36. Calgary mayor Naheed
39. Flower or eye part
40. Law enforcement series aired on Canada's Action station
41. Arizona landforms
43. Montréal suburb: Sainte-Marthe-sur-le-_____
44. *Candid* _____
46. Rower's blade
48. Barfly
49. Ocean predator
50. 1995 Tom Cochrane album: *Ragged _____ Road*
51. Diviners
54. CFL offensive position
56. Podiatrist's favourite plant?
58. NDP leader selected in 2017 (with 81-A)
61. Polyurethane, for example
62. Bikini part
65. Australian birds

66. Alberta city: _____ Deer
68. LPGA tour player Michelle
69. Sea near Crete
71. "Defending Liberty, Pursuing Justice" US org.
72. Glass-polishing powder
74. Business transaction
76. Long and lean in stature
77. So-so
79. Lies in wait
81. See 58-A
82. _____-splitting
83. Like rose stems
84. Hewed
86. You can Roll Up the Rim to Win here
89. Arts and culture government department: Canadian _____
93. Butchers' building
94. Like a stale idea
96. No score, in a Montréal Impact game
97. Rodgers and Hart classic: "_____ It Romantic?"
98. Semi-aquatic amphibians
99. 23-year Pittsburgh Steelers coach Chuck
100. US gov. org.
101. Butterfly catchers
102. Common Canadian birds
103. Wicked wind

DOWN

1. It's aired on Gusto: *Great Canadian Food _____*
2. Feline food flavour
3. Scads
4. Clustered flowers description
5. Start of a musical refrain
6. Rice dish
7. Hodgepodge
8. Emmy- and Oscar-winning actress Melissa

9. Some Canadian wildcats (var.)
10. Pens in
11. Windsor-born NHLer Ekblad
12. "_____! In the Name of Love"
13. Some finches
14. Gabriela Dabrowski is the first Canadian woman to win this type of tennis title
15. Yesteryear
16. Disorderliness
22. Canadian First Nation
24. German city
27. Big Bang theory substance
29. Indian cuisine spice mixtures
31. Typography unit
32. Some Rogers Centre stats
33. CBC TV comedy: _____ *Convenience*
35. Geological time span
36. CN word
37. Maori chant or dance
38. Coin anagram
40. Rose to the top of one's profession?
42. Singer's syllables
45. Tom Kirkman, for Canada's Kiefer Sutherland
47. Order more *Canadian Living*
49. Greeted for the first time
52. More pertinent
53. In a sombre manner
55. Staff symbol
56. European river
57. Aerodynamic
58. Former Governor General Michaëlle
59. Ancient church dais
60. Central American country
62. Rowan Atkinson character: Mr. _____
63. Phoned, in Portsmouth
64. Cross that's looped at the top

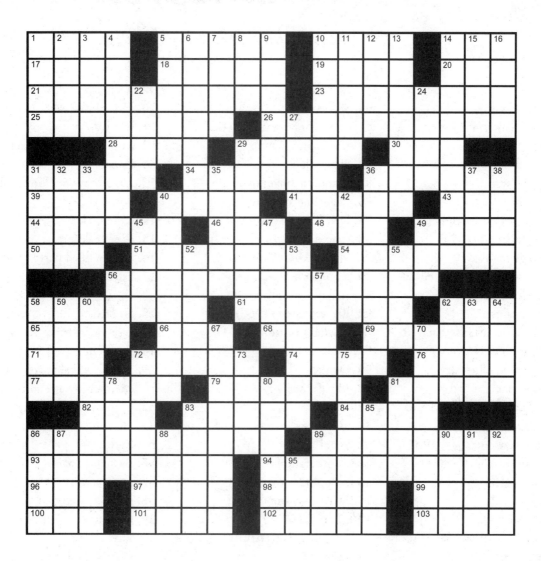

67. Plays a boisterous game of hockey?
70. Sparkling
72. Vitamin A source (var.)
73. Analogous
75. States with conviction
78. Thailand money

80. Like some heroes?
81. Guzzle a Kokanee, say
83. Eke out
85. Get up
86. Zesty beverage mix?
87. Long-legged wading bird
88. Flower for the God of Love?

89. Hockey legend Gordie
90. Indonesian animal
91. Effrontery
92. Lachine lady's magazine?
95. Mila Mulroney, _____ Pivnicki

39

To the Top, x2

Songs that reached #1 twice

ACROSS

1. Rifle attachments
7. Port city in ancient Rome
12. Pindar poem stanza
19. Chemical salt
20. _____ of war
22. More wary
23. **Little Eva (1962) and Grand Funk Railroad (1974)**
25. Like plywood, say
26. Not good, but not bad, either
27. In excellent shape
28. Religious doctrine
30. Yielded a donation?
31. Kitchen utensils
36. Ongoing, in olden days
37. Hit the spot
38. **The Marvelettes (1961) and The Carpenters (1975)**
42. Fitness workout: _____ Bo
43. ID number issued by the GC
44. Former Bulgarian rulers
45. Goa garment
46. Roof projection
49. Margaret Atwood collection: *Bluebeard's* _____
50. Indigenous group in Japan
51. Canadian golf great Norman
54. CTV milieu
55. Some studs go here
57. Like some garments in the washer
59. Rest anagram
60. Administrative aide
63. Crosby or Gretzky position
64. Supreme Greek god
66. **Shocking Blue (1970) and Bananarama (1986)**
67. Pipes bent at right angles
68. Prepares oneself, at Dofasco?
71. Washed or dried?
73. Middle Eastern religion VIP
77. Plant found near the paddock?
79. Auditory
80. Shade of grey
81. Long-running CBC series: *The Passionate* _____
82. Happy face?
83. Marketing promos
85. Old-fangled ladies' cape
87. Den for cubs
88. Canada's Victor Garber starred in this ABC drama
90. It comes after Cancer
91. Rail line beam
92. **Percy Sledge (1966) and Michael Bolton (1991)**
97. TD Canada _____
98. Donkey
99. Move a bench?
100. Sweet potatoes
101. Ontario-born NHLer Fisher, et al.
103. Botheration
104. Trouble with a tap
108. Crucially important
110. **Labelle (1975) and Christina Aguilera/Lil' Kim/Mya/Pink (2001)**
115. Harp on
116. Sonata component
117. Bumpy
118. Barrel-_____
119. Run out, like a subscription
120. Most cheerful, old style

DOWN

1. Is in session, like the House of Commons
2. Salmon you might catch in BC
3. Poetic works from Keats
4. Hairy
5. Executive District Officer (abbr.)
6. Wine bottle word
7. Heavy metal
8. Illuminated, on stage
9. Bit of tater?
10. Ten minus seven, to Caesar
11. Plenty
12. Multiple _____ Society of Canada
13. 2004 Wayson Choy Giller Prize nominee: *All _____ Matters*
14. Cote male
15. Paper folding art
16. Candy-filled party plaything
17. Loverboy soundtrack song: "_____ in Your Eyes"
18. Goofed
21. Disdainful expressions
24. Frequency
29. 1980s federal government energy program (abbr.)
32. Ottoman Empire bigwig
33. Thailand's continent
34. Rates
35. Bachelor's party
37. Fruity pastry
38. Pathway slab
39. City in West Yorkshire
40. Physics unit
41. Parsley family plant
42. Bulky book
47. Some swanky hotels
48. This flows through the TransCanada Pipeline
50. 1960s TV cartoon character: Atom _____
51. Clever word used in Québec?
52. Toronto-based band: _____ Lady Peace
53. Québec in *juin, juillet et août*
56. Senator to a Canadien, say
57. Mini map, in an atlas
58. Store grain
60. Mozart's birth country
61. Explosive for Wile E. Coyote
62. Word processing function
65. Classy

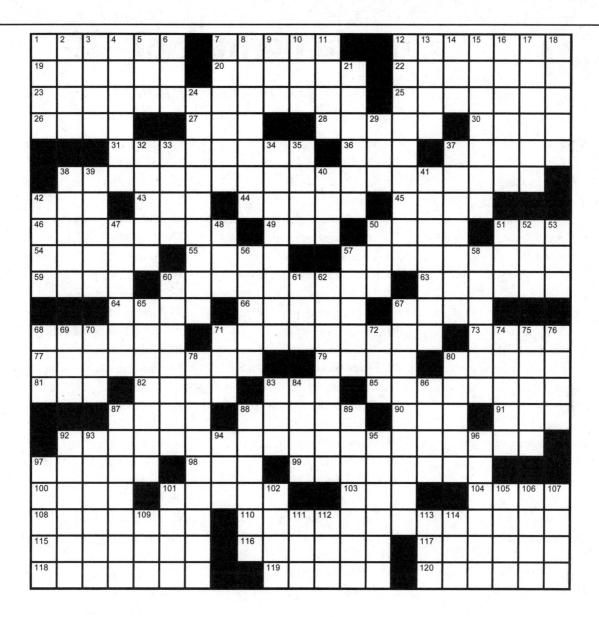

67. It takes you up when you're down?
68. "Every Little Thing _____ Does Is Magic"
69. Old Cracker Jack box bonus
70. Ubiquitous crossword palindrome
71. No. you use at 97-A
72. Game played with matchsticks
74. Mediterranean country
75. Had a home-cooked meal
76. Distribute (with "out")
78. Sent via WestJet?
80. Footrest

83. Nelly Furtado hit: "_____ Good Things (Come to an End)"
84. Christian of fashion fame
86. Former US presidential candidate Gingrich
87. Landlords
88. Scholasticism founder
89. Some bun seeds
92. Apparition
93. Multi-purpose military vehicle
94. 2002 Avril Lavigne track: "Too Much to _____"
95. Prepare a patient for surgery

96. Combo of songs
97. Conforming, for short
101. Link up for life?
102. Go by yacht
105. Over-the-top review
106. _____ of March
107. Cooped (up)
109. Create lace
111. Your genetic fingerprint
112. "Yes," slangily
113. You might use one at Coffee Time
114. Ex-women's tennis star Ivanovic

40

Canada Cornucopia 20

ACROSS

1. Sec
5. Physiques, in slang
9. Machine teeth
13. Emailers hit this button
17. Important Arabic personage
18. "Paradise Lost," for example
19. Canada's largest lead-zinc mine, once
20. Manitoba First Nations group
21. Bargain time, at Roots
22. Crime scene worker, for short
23. Major Western Canada river
25. Look at Lego?
26. Amusing action
28. Least factual
29. Christmas, in Chicoutimi
30. Grim spectre?
32. Acquires
33. Partly open
35. Flatware maker, say
37. Ewes and mares
41. See 1-D
44. German nation state
45. Wheel on a pulley
47. Belch
48. Pertaining to an eye part
50. To this point in time
51. 1-D or 41-D
52. Berehowsky who played for the Leafs, Oilers and Canucks
53. Lomond or Ness
55. Doctor's office employee (abbr.)
56. Sing to one's sweetie
58. Sleeper train car in Europe
60. Soap unit
61. Thin coat of paint
62. Vancouver Island place
63. Old Roman poet of note
65. Demean
67. Cause of cheers at Rogers Centre
69. Personal philosophy, say

70. Sanctuary tables
72. Cinnamon and Spice?
73. San Diego MLBers
74. Feel like
75. Threw like a CFL quarterback
77. Indigenous language in Brazil
78. Suffix with psych-
80. Ransom note writer
82. Civil wrong
86. Concert residency city of 27-D
90. Sri Lankan primate
91. Mixed bag, say
92. Dinosaur type
94. Fabric ridge
95. Travel document issued by the Government of Canada
96. BC-born *Ironside* actor Raymond
97. Antler point
98. Veer anagram
99. Nights before some holidays
100. Observes
101. Food starch
102. Cincinnati baseballers
103. Lease

DOWN

1. Alberta UCP leader (with 41-A)
2. Idealization, in psychology
3. Girl, in Gaspé
4. Writer who works for nothing?
5. Electron stream
6. It follows can or home
7. Courtroom pronouncements
8. Stocky dog originally bred in Europe
9. Banned refrigerant (abbr.)
10. Honolulu island
11. Music for the unclean masses?
12. Organizers
13. Skis at Whistler
14. The Niagara River flows from this lake

15. 1962 Hockey Hall of Fame inductee Stewart
16. Bodybuilder's big muscle, for short
24. Old PC component
27. Québec-born chanteuse Dion
31. Yukon Quest, for example
34. Air Canada aircraft
36. Grey matter mass
38. Northwest Territories town
39. Late afternoon, to the poet
40. Stiff hair, in zoology
41. Canadian Taylor who served in Iran
42. Like whiteboards
43. Count
44. Parkway pigs?
46. American violinist Hilary
48. Sound of a collision?
49. Get Web access
52. 22-A might gather this
54. Hudson Bay island
57. Still-life painting jug
58. Dominant nation
59. Bully a baron?
60. Bleats from sheep
62. Shreddies or Cheerios
64. Computer operating system acronym
66. Russian tea urns
68. 91-A abbr.
69. Topper for a Blue Jay
71. Faucets
73. Shipboard personnel
76. Wolfville university
77. Worked hard
79. Number of Canadian provinces
81. Construction crossbeam
83. Popeye's gal pal
84. Up and about
85. Breakfast food
86. Trudeau, et al.
87. Shivering fever

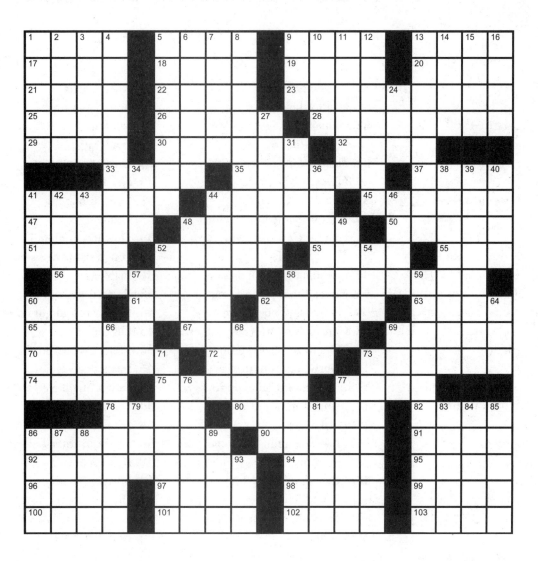

88. Totally positive

89. Murray McLauchlan wrote one about a farmer?

93. Popular part for Canada's Keanu Reeves

Provincial arboreal symbols

ACROSS

1. "Legal" lead-in
5. 1960s decorative fad
13. Dummies
18. Persian Gulf country
19. Froze
20. Vancouver venue: Rogers _____
21. **Alberta**
23. Secretes
24. Enjoyed a run at Sun Peaks
25. Sought political office
26. Sue Grafton mystery: _____ *for Silence*
27. Processes of cell disintegration
28. _____ grinder
30. Brag
32. iPad download
33. Like creamier custard
35. *For Me and My* _____
37. Suggestive look
39. Knock
41. Ripped apart
42. _____ tunnel syndrome
45. Rehearsals
47. Tors
49. CBC's *Schitt's Creek*, for one
51. Responds
52. Turn up a cuff
53. Chooses one over the other
55. Australian marsupial
57. A coast of Canada
58. **Manitoba**
61. Pulpit platform
65. Lowest deck on a liner
66. Puffed and huffed
67. Passports can serve as these (abbr.)
70. Entice
72. Sign up for Concordia classes (var.)
74. Languor
76. Gene sequence related
78. Most certain
80. Highly excited
81. Call for help at sea
82. Genie-winning 1988 film: _____ *Ringers*
84. *Hawaii Five-O* network
85. Newly
87. Morse code word
89. Famous name in fine china
91. Popular Canadian whisky: _____ Royal
92. Canadian _____ Forces
94. Mineral that contains metal
95. _____ way you slice it
97. Canadian prairies crop
100. Organized crime group
101. **Northwest Territories**
104. Important Dubai personages
105. With a mind open to learning
106. Dalai _____
107. Like winter in many parts of the country
108. Canadian Gerry who won World Championship downhill gold in 1982
109. Whole lot

DOWN

1. Dippers and Grits, say
2. Out of order?
3. Wireless message
4. Making mad
5. Guff
6. Oak tree fruit
7. Southern hemisphere constellation
8. Red Sea gulf
9. Take a cut?
10. French military boat
11. Like a lowly worker's labour
12. Ironed
13. *Charlie and the Chocolate Factory* scribe
14. Some East Indians
15. **Nova Scotia**
16. Boyhood attire
17. See 5-D
22. Lead, say
29. Crescent shape
30. **Newfoundland**
31. Central BC city
33. Carve
34. Downtown Hamilton park
35. Tough tissue in a steak
36. Liable to
38. Bread type
40. Letters you might whisper
43. On the move
44. Roller coaster thrill
46. Like salad veggies
48. Parent of a piglet
50. You might lose these?
54. Fake Shaw staffers?
56. They can come before storms
59. Billions of years
60. Meadow merino
61. "So sad"
62. Extravagant play, say
63. **New Brunswick**
64. Doe anagram
67. Usually, to a top army staffer?
68. Tegan and Sara, et al.
69. Soft gasp
71. Venerable
73. Circular shape
75. You might see these in Baffin Bay
77. Coats for early Canadians
79. La Brea _____ Pits
83. Mythical place: El _____
86. Domesticated bird
88. Will proceeds recipients
90. Raise scruples
91. Pedal like Canada's Clara Hughes
92. Asian nursemaid
93. Quick run

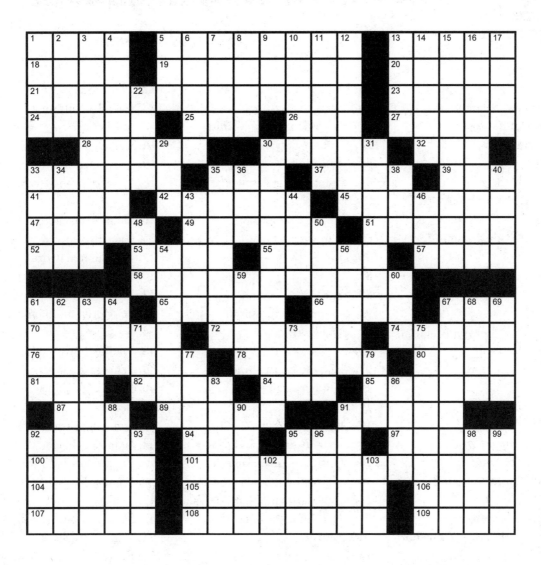

95. Cable-patterned sweater

96. Captures

98. Peak point

99. Unfreeze

102. Frequent serve from Serena

103. Canadians Danby or Dryden

ACROSS

1. Muslim title of honour (var.)
5. Mendelssohn carol opener
9. Foals' illness (abbr.)
12. Stunt
17. Byron's black
18. River that runs through six states
19. Way below the Mason-Dixon line
21. Little litter member
22. Bleacher level
23. Lacking know-how
24. Complex carbohydrate
26. Sheds that slant?
28. Swiss Chalet entree: _____ Chicken Dinner
29. Large volumes?
31. Province of 81-A + 89-A
33. Cigar leavings
35. Author's offering
37. Middle Eastern ethnic group member
38. Ups and downs?
43. Toronto NHL player, for short
45. Old Dutch fishing vessels
47. Sporting match loss
48. Overwhelming fear
50. Squeezed water from a towel
51. It might come with fame
52. Fine Young Cannibals hit: "_____ Drives Me Crazy"
54. Ski mask openings
56. Bar band's collection?
57. New Brunswick city
61. Magazine that went online only in 2017: Canadian _____
63. Pie _____ mode
64. Unlawfully enter
68. It tests the water?
69. Beirut country
71. Reed instruments
73. Nova Scotia celebration: _____ Day
77. Norwegian currency units
78. Minuses' opposites (var.)
80. Rock climber's gear item
81. Western Canada town (with 89-A)
82. Circumcision rite
83. Chair for an MP?
85. Tiny, in Troon
86. Yelled
89. See 81-A
91. Metropolit who was a Canadiens centre
95. Totalled
97. Whacked on the head
100. Church services
102. Calculus or algebra
104. Gratify with grub
105. Data dissectors, in Dorset
106. Gusto, in Guadalajara
107. Elbow–wrist connector
108. Canada's highest falls, in BC
109. Hair salon product
110. Warp results
111. 1960s Lotus car name

DOWN

1. Towel word
2. Lie next to
3. Winnipeg-born NHL star Toews
4. Abbreviated onset?
5. Perspiring firebrand?
6. Tuna type
7. Manitoba Métis leader Louis
8. Canada's Carolyn Waldo won two Olympic golds in this country
9. Duke who launched a Canadian youth awards program in 1963
10. HVAC techs who gripe?
11. Belleville ON store: Sam the _____ Man
12. Cleopatra's killer
13. Canadian author and broadcaster: _____ Richler
14. Canadian Brass brass
15. "_____ all end in tears"
16. Culinary reality show: Top _____ Canada
20. Grammatical tense
25. Canadian specialty channel
27. Unsaturated hydrocarbon
30. School zone speed
32. Feeling of intense dislike
33. St. Moritz mountain
34. Salish or Labrador, for example
36. Wading birds
39. Petite salamander
40. Reduce, _____, Recycle
41. Bêtes noires
42. Some proofreaders' marks
44. Salmon or sole
46. Royal Canadians bandleader Lombardo
47. Old-style second-person verb
49. Spicy condiments
51. Winter malady
53. See the _____ of one's ways
55. Take too much to heart
57. Refuses to obey orders
58. On one's guard
59. Unacceptable, socially
60. Quebecer Serge Joyal was named one in 1997 (abbr.)
62. Close
65. Manners, in Magog
66. Took drugs too often
67. 1975 hit from ABBA
70. Three-time Lou Marsh Trophy winner: Barbara _____ Scott
72. Permeate
74. Provincial government stakeholders' forum
75. Gorilla
76. American author Harper

78. Excessive modesty
79. Jump for Patrick Chan
82. Able-_____
84. Chinese philosophy concept
87. Fairy tale baddies
88. Makes easy: _____ down

90. Distribute copies of *Chatelaine*?
91. Happy
92. Bar come-on
93. And others, in brief
94. _____ and void
96. Banff National _____

98. Neat volcano?
99. McAmmond who played for the Flames, Sens and Oilers
101. Mat for Mats' home
103. 2–2, say

43 Letter-perfect Presents

. . . from Greeks bearing gifts

ACROSS

1. Florida coast city
6. On, in Outremont
9. Scribble a note
12. Short scouting mission?
17. Stewed meat medleys
18. **Collectibles shelf**
20. Canadian actor/comedian Graham
21. _____ cavity
22. Andorra's official language
23. Seed structure
24. **Ford vehicle**
26. Photos of moonshiners?
27. Arrears
28. Crisp or clean
30. _____ down the law
31. Peso anagram
33. It connects storeys
37. Transported by Coach Canada
39. Montréal Canadien Doug Harvey wore this jersey number
42. Several millennia (var.)
43. Less thick
45. Male sheep
47. Japanese comics
49. Quick coffee?
51. Hangman's rope
52. Prior to, to Matthew Prior
53. Landlocked Asian country
55. Detailed workings, colloquially
57. Awesome
58. _____ Aline Chrétien
59. National retailer: Shoppers Drug _____
60. She fires up relationships?
64. Type of lily
65. Novel by Canada's Nino Ricci: *Where _____ Has Gone*
68. Nebraska city named for a Native group
69. Assail
71. Post on 33-A

73. Sometime Stratford Festival star Sir Derek
75. More speedy
77. Molls and misses
78. Beatle bride
79. Canada's Walk of Fame induction ceremony, for example
81. Matador's dance?
83. Canada's Gowan joined this US band in 1999
84. Get a move on, quickly
86. Wear for a rani
87. Bushy hairdos
90. Nipple surround
93. **Seafood serving**
97. Grassland, in South America
98. Becoming oxidized
100. Country shaped like a boot
101. Lost, in Montréal?
102. **Wine for dinner**
103. Kuwaiti currency
104. Clean up at the Oscars?
105. Store doors info
106. Nightfall, to a poet
107. Segment of a script

DOWN

1. The bulk
2. Parts of the pelvis
3. Hokkaido Natives
4. Grieving
5. Magazine producer, say
6. Wine classification
7. Actress Hagen, et al.
8. Noisy snakes?
9. Colourful candies
10. _____ history
11. Present and future, in grammar
12. **Backyard bloomer**
13. These hang around your house?
14. Bar stock: Canadian _____
15. Early European

16. Early Guess Who hit: "These _____"
19. "Earthy" Greek goddess
25. Amniotic enclosures
29. Some puddings
32. Bench in a church
33. Track on Joni Mitchell's *Court and Spark*: "_____ Situation"
34. Salty drop
35. Four-star, say
36. Without, to a Quebecer
38. Big vases
39. Biblical pronoun
40. BC milieu: _____ Coast
41. Mind finds
44. Horse rider's foot holder
46. Honk your horn
48. **Kids' lunch serving**
50. Docile demeanour
54. Archer's talent
56. Old horse
57. Reverberation
58. Transposition of sounds, in grammar
60. Personal pizzazz, say
61. "I need to see _____ about a horse"
62. Chip for salsa dipping
63. He wrote *Show Boat*
64. It follows cream or club
65. Q-tip
66. Calgary Stampede event, informally: Half-mile of _____
67. 1959 Eddie Cochran hit: "Somethin' _____"
70. TransCanada _____
72. Self-serving
74. Plant in all provinces but Newfoundland: Poison _____
76. Gad
80. Eastern Orthodox Church bishop
82. Ancient Celtic priests

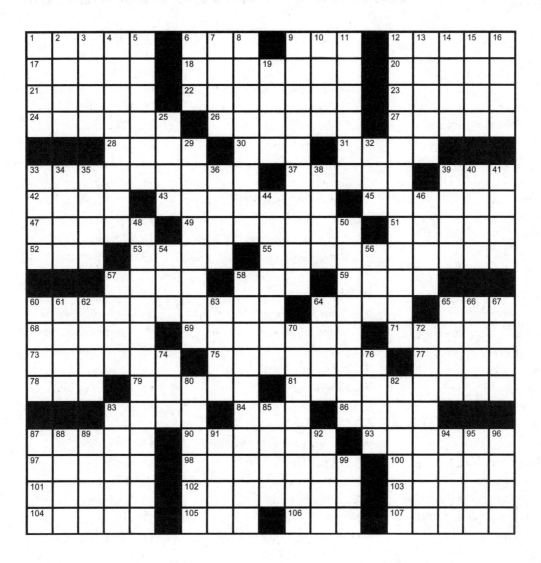

83. Meteorological measuring device

85. Barely detectable amount

87. Peak place in Europe?

88. Went by WestJet

89. Like pink steak

91. Region in northwest Germany

92. Chips for the poker pot

94. All there?

95. Liveliness

96. Instrument in ancient Greece

99. Rummy game

44 Canada Cornucopia 22

ACROSS

1. Cease, through the court?
6. Inundated, at the laundromat?
11. Tim Hortons speciality
17. Chaplet
19. Abdominal trouble: Diastasis _____
20. Like a temperamental hen?
21. Rinomato who hosted 25-A (2006–11)
22. Compound used in glass polishing
23. Walked with purpose
24. Scrambled _____
25. Canadian realty show: _____ *Virgins*
28. Group of eight
29. Infectious illness
30. Canada Savings Bonds, prior to 2017
32. Process of preening
36. Secured a load
40. She sings with Lunch At Allen's and Quartette (with 53-D)
41. Third canonical hour
44. Stretchy
45. Flattered obsequiously
47. Hemmed and _____
49. Fasten a shoelace
50. Mended a seam again
51. Canadian discount store: Giant _____
52. Yellow pigment, in Pittsburgh
54. _____ Francisco
55. *Corner Gas* actress Wright
56. Palindromic interjection
57. Full of flavour
60. Indonesian island
61. Aged
65. Employee Related Expenses (abbr.)
66. It gives you the beat
67. Brotherhood member in Québec?
68. Digital currency
71. Ohio city
73. Ontario place once known as "Leathertown"
74. Not yet processed into leather
76. Fills the coffers?
78. Business gatherings
81. The Queen bestows this honour (abbr.)
82. Shoelace end
85. A Toronto factory makes 3.5 billion of these every year
87. Blemish
91. Former European coin
93. King in *The Iliad*
94. 1985 Canadian charity song: "Tears Are Not _____"
96. Jet's nose cone, for example
97. Former Greek coins
98. Company that produces 85-A
99. Foreshadowed
100. Ontario town or county name
101. Building supplies retailer absorbed by RONA

DOWN

1. Lessen discomfort
2. Unexpected obstacle
3. Taste sensation
4. Bookies give these
5. For each rep?
6. With the bow, on a score
7. More tearful
8. Farming tracts
9. Provokes the pot?
10. Respite from hernia pain?
11. *NCIS* network
12. European cuisine bird
13. Delivery room tool
14. Put your best _____ forward
15. Classic Icelandic literary work
16. Green-_____ monster
18. Symbolic Canadian tree
26. Like a bumpy road
27. Gossipy chat
29. Like unmanageable hair
31. Born and _____
32. 1989 Rush track: "Red _____"
33. Great responsibility
34. Most inactive
35. 1950 Art Ross Trophy winner Lindsay
37. Essence
38. Ngoyi of the 2015 Grey Cup-winning Eskimos
39. Farley Mowat's first book: *People of the _____*
40. Audi or Acura
42. Southern Alberta weather phenomenon
43. Gung-ho
46. George Armstrong wore this Leafs number for 21 years
48. Sopping
51. Florida Gulf Coast city
52. Disconcert the portrait painter?
53. See 40-A
55. Blue Rodeo singer/guitarist Cuddy
56. *Stars Wars* pilot Solo
57. Indian ox
58. Canadian-born operatic soprano Wall
59. Paving stone
60. Core beliefs
61. American icon Marilyn
62. Bodily network
63. Cupid
64. Group of Scouts
66. It gets right to the point?
67. Hoodwink a hustler?
69. Kapuskasing-born *Titanic* director James
70. Has-been?

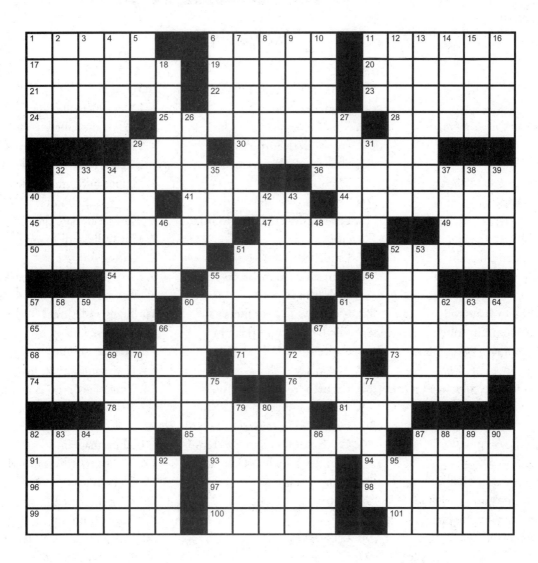

72. Say "Wisconsin" again?
75. Cute facial feature
77. *Peer Gynt* dramatist Henrik
79. Nasal openings
80. Holds a stagehand's hand?
82. Coif for curly-haired folks

83. Style for some '70s rock stars
84. Miners' trove
86. Canadian-created big screen technology
87. Good, but not great
88. Golf green stroke

89. Stare
90. Those folks
92. American actor Beatty
95. Bottom line earnings description

Who Am I? 1

Name this actor

ACROSS

1. Dossier
5. Dominican Order member
10. Corroded or eroded
14. Moving about
19. River that ends at the Caspian Sea
20. Slowly, to a pianist
21. Cellist Ma
22. Latin American plain
23. **2006 film for which he received a nomination for 52-A**
25. Mouthful of tobacco
26. Dining room furniture piece
27. Medical clinic worker (abbr.)
28. Exhaust one's supplies
29. **Russell Crowe co-starred with him in this 2016 film**
31. Mel Gibson cinematic series: _____ *Weapon*
33. Moult
34. Nation of 102-D (abbr.)
35. They can be green or yellow
37. Canadian history figure: _____ de Champlain
39. Canadian Keanu who played John Wick in a 2017 film
44. Tear open
45. Some figures of speech
47. Sully
48. Hoary
49. Pink slip issuers
50. _____ Canada
52. **Acting award he's been nominated for twice**
53. Tropical waters fish
54. **Actress Eva who is the mother of his daughters**
57. Point on a pitchfork
58. Hounds without homes, say
61. Inner ear component
62. Short grandmother?
63. Touchfree electronic instrument
66. Parliamentarians' rules of conduct (abbr.)
67. Sap of energy
70. Post-WWII European org.
71. Slow musical movements
73. More authentic
74. Caresses
76. **His southwest Ontario birth city**
77. Unlocked a safe
80. **Actress Emma who co-starred with him in 3-D**
82. Chaney of horror films
83. Moved back and forth in a breeze
84. Arrest, say
87. German irises, for example
89. Fatuous smiler
92. Bean used to make miso (var.)
93. Golden 2000 Olympics tennis doubles Canadian Daniel
94. Near the tail
95. Chums
96. Twist-_____
98. Clasped
99. Collateral _____
101. **Acting award he won in 2017**
106. Step up?
107. *Top Gear* broadcaster (abbr.)
110. Willow
111. Currency for an Italian vacation
112. **He dropped out of this to pursue acting**
114. Incense oleoresin
115. Polar regions bird
116. Peak points
117. Parks of civil rights fame
118. _____ boom
119. Exam
120. Insolent
121. Domed beehive

DOWN

1. Oilers ex-goalie Grant
2. Mashhad country
3. **He played a jazz pianist in this 2016 critics' favourite**
4. Helper in Santa's workshop
5. _____ and blood
6. They let inmates go
7. Fills walls with foam
8. Resting on
9. MacLean who came back to *Hockey Night in Canada* in 2016
10. British Isles tree
11. Gasped with glee
12. **His first name**
13. Like some situations
14. Best friend who gets inside your head?
15. Stelco waste
16. Abut anagram
17. Not outwardly, old style
18. Some bucks
24. Filbert fanatics?
29. Plural pronoun
30. Centre of a CANDU reactor
32. Final chapter, say
33. Ottawa and Edmonton newspaper names
35. Sister's sib
36. Conger
38. Seconds, say
40. Bygone days
41. Close by, in your neigbourhood
42. Come from
43. More peaceful
45. Filled with vapours
46. Compos mentis
47. 1930s Canadian child star of Hollywood Bobby
49. Canadian literary critic Northrop
51. Doing nothing
53. Battle between nations

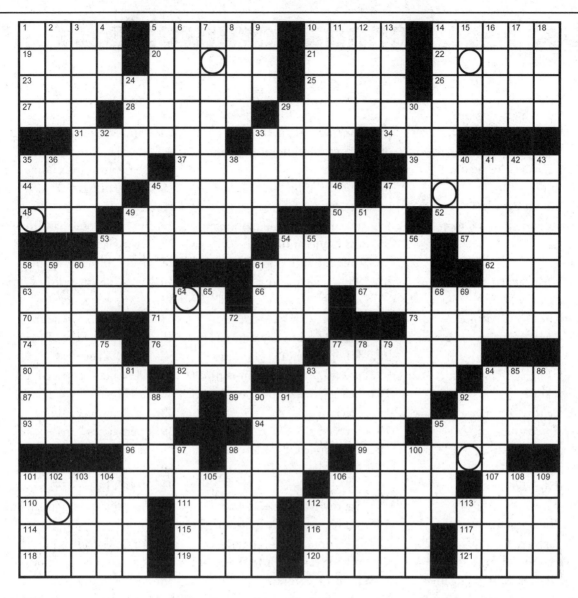

54. Numbskull
55. Seth's first son
56. More severe
58. Second marriage male relative
59. Coquitlam venue: Molson Canadian _____
60. Some church officials
61. Vivacity, in Venice
64. Fans adore them
65. Prefix that means "one-billionth"
68. 1960s Saskatchewan Roughriders star running back George
69. Brit nursing services grp. during the World Wars
72. Victoria's Butchart, et al. (abbr.)
75. Angry shaver's lather?
77. Had debts
78. Ideal examples

79. Mascara goes on these
81. Like obscure information
83. Tater
84. **His 2004 romance film blockbuster (with "The")**
85. "Yes," to a sailor
86. Some degrees from UBC
88. *Dancing with the Stars* co-host Andrews
90. Craft for some Canadian wintertime sportsmen
91. Manly?
92. Give way to gravity
95. Juno-winning vocalist Jordan
97. Expel
98. Falcon-headed Egyptian god
100. Not at all tidy
101. Heads out the door

102. Winter Olympics city, in 1952
103. Legal claim
104. Ballerina's position: _____-pointe
105. **His role in *The Place Beyond the Pines***
106. Costa _____
108. Audio speakers brand name
109. Hit from Canada's Beau-Marks: "_____ Your Hands"
112. Eats
113. 60 min. increments

Use the circled letters to unscramble his surname:

_ _ _ _ _ _ _

Solution on page 219

46 Canada Cornucopia 23

ACROSS

1. Newfoundland science facility: _____ Bay Marine Station
6. Ran, in the wash
10. It connects car wheels
14. Palindromic expression of surprise
17. Girder
18. Canadian singer–songwriter Frost
19. Caribbean and Mediterranean
20. 2016 Margaret Atwood novel: _____-Seed
21. Daunting
23. Lie against
24. Unhealthy
25. Join forces, politically
26. More secure
28. Mouselike rodent
29. Land depression
31. Tame
33. Pencil honing device
38. Playing musical chairs, perhaps?
42. Roman Forum wear
43. Group of three rhyming lines
45. Crowd rabble-rouser
46. Expressed one's view
48. "Don't bet _____!"
50. Look into closely
51. Mario Lemieux was one for two decades
53. Bridge bid
55. Murder
56. Show that airs on 82-A
59. "Money _____ everything"
63. Towers on cathedrals
64. Steep stretch of the Coq
69. Got up when the judge came in
71. Scene between sous-chefs?
72. 1979 Anne Murray hit: "I Just Fall _____ Again"
73. Shut down a PC
75. CBC news blog: _____ Politics
79. Courtroom rapper?
80. Fabergé creation for Russian royals
82. Canadian cable specialty channel
84. Ancient tombstone monuments
85. Bear found in Italy?
86. Montréal-born pop singer Kim
89. 1980 movie starring Dom DeLuise
91. Pekoe brewing gadgets
97. Romanian currency unit
98. Monopoly card: _____ jail
99. Picked a perp from a lineup
101. Petro-Canada pump purchase
102. Place to dock
103. Scented powder
104. Long-time CBC journalist Milewski
105. _____ Gallery of Southwestern Manitoba
106. Vehicles made by Ransom?
107. 2006 Juno Awards new artist of the year nominee Sweetnam
108. Historic Toronto neighbourhood: The _____

DOWN

1. Back to the Future trilogy character Tannen
2. Clarinet's orchestra companion
3. Misfit who loves math?
4. 2016 Kiefer Sutherland country song: "Calling Out Your _____"
5. Middle Eastern title
6. Obvious
7. Defamed person
8. 45-inch English measurement, historically
9. Anil and indigo
10. Indian cuisine powder (var.)
11. Three-masted trading ships
12. Waterloo university
13. Kapuskasing clock setting (abbr.)
14. Neil Armstrong's home state
15. Monty or Massey
16. Lego anagram
22. BC-born comedian Broadfoot
27. Some glands
28. Oval Office prerogatives
30. _____ on the side of caution
32. Set the table, say
33. 2011 Avril Lavigne track: "_____ Standing There"
34. Fraser Valley town
35. L'il Abner's "opposed to"
36. Pealed
37. Nom de plume (abbr.)
39. International Trade Law Library (abbr.)
40. St. Petersburg river
41. The CFL's cup is this colour?
44. The police, colloquially
47. Buenos _____
49. Purple Canadian bills
52. Nabisco product: Cheese _____
53. Hypodermics
54. Competition round, for short
57. Courtroom combatants
58. Air Canada subsidiary (2001–04)
59. Capri, for example
60. Greek portico
61. Egg-based beverages
62. Little piggy place (var.)
65. Eastern European
66. Hoisted, in sailor-speak
67. To the end of time
68. Lean on for support
70. 1985 Bryan Adams/Tina Turner type of tune
74. Girl Guides of Canada adult group: _____ Guild
76. Single guy's final phrase?
77. In a messy manner

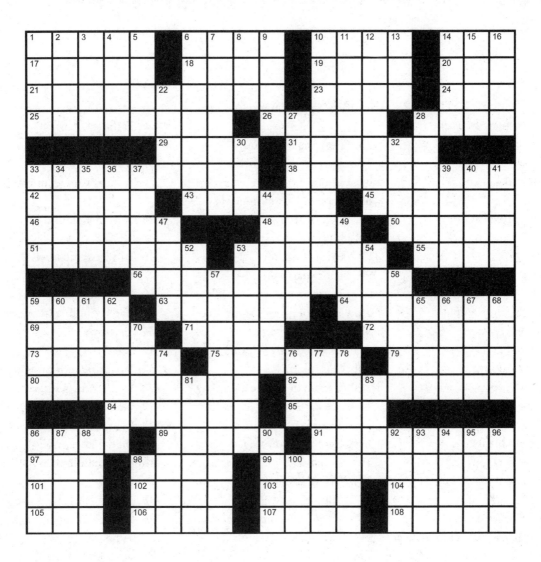

78. Aroma
81. On cloud nine
83. Red Serge, for one
86. Pool organism
87. Come closer to

88. Queen classic: "Another One Bites the _____"
90. Settles on
92. It precedes gamma
93. Dane anagram
94. Hopeless, old style

95. Entice
96. River of Hades
98. Rural mail pickup place (abbr.)
100. Area adjacent to Victoria: _____ Bay

47 Anagram Unscramble

Hint: It's nouns you seek

ACROSS

1. Bum from
6. Month on a Jewish calendar
10. 133.32 pascals
14. _____-fi
17. Bee related
18. Sole
19. Calgary Philharmonic Orchestra instrument
20. Ad _____
21. **SEBNA**
22. Raw numbers, say
23. Eardrum, for example
25. Thermometer type
26. Set down laws
28. Canadian "Nova Heart" band: The _____
29. Croup sound
31. Secretly wed
33. Chopper's blade
35. Pasta strainers
37. 100 per cent
38. "Quiet!"
41. Taro
42. Electromagnetism pioneer Nikola
44. Collections for Eugenie Bouchard?
45. Forcible overthrow
47. **ORHES**
49. New Age composer and pianist John
51. Retired supersonic jet, for short
52. Seductive charm
54. Kennedy, et al.
56. Sherbrooke summers
58. Complain about stomach pain?
60. Strong statement
65. Last spouse of Henry VIII
66. Bombardier _____ 8
68. Band's crew member
69. PC's "insides"
72. Render speechless

74. **HRTON**
76. Region in Ontario: Nickel _____
77. Humerus neighbour
79. Live in the real world?
81. Basmati or brown
83. Shape of a certain letter?
84. Book of Jewish laws
86. Jet's runway approach
89. Feminist author Gertrude
90. Pic or snap
91. Desert shrub
95. Cream of _____
97. Cigarette lighter?
99. Fall while on vacation?
100. Skin ulcers
102. Canadian cookie company
103. **See 21-A**
104. Wrath
105. Keel anagram
106. Prima donnas' problems
107. Come about
108. Hippie's acid
109. *The Best Years of Our Lives* actor Andrews
110. Stitches a quilt
111. Fifth canonical hour

DOWN

1. Mexican resort destination: Los _____
2. In pieces
3. **NDIAR**
4. The Rankins sometimes sing in this
5. USN rank
6. Fabled city on the Amazon
7. Truck's cargo
8. Loosened laces
9. Passed out pamphlets
10. Canadian singer Cochrane
11. Too heavy
12. Cavort

13. Like some Christianity converts
14. Stan Rogers' "Barrett's Privateers," et al.
15. Prince Philip and the Queen Mother
16. Annual Canadian tour: Stars on _____
24. National clothing retailer since 1973
26. Icily unsympathetic?
27. Olden days
30. Forest female
32. Barely audible interjection
34. Take five
36. **See 74-A**
37. Port Elizabeth province
38. Strikebreaker's lesion?
39. Golfer's cup?
40. "The Golden Jet" Bobby
43. Meriwether's dregs?
46. Canadian industry: _____ and paper
48. Pip
50. Canada's Paul Henderson, in 1972
53. Stockholm carpets
55. Ribbon for a pageant participant
57. Wound with a knife
59. Essence of the matter?
61. **See 47-A**
62. Thought, in Témiscaming
63. Some paints
64. Fishing gear
67. Feelings and beliefs
69. Bryan Adams hit: "_____ Like a Knife"
70. Party trays
71. Like most Petro-Canada gas
73. Near, to a poet
75. Fruit's maturation point
78. Middle Eastern VIPs
80. Neatnik's opposite

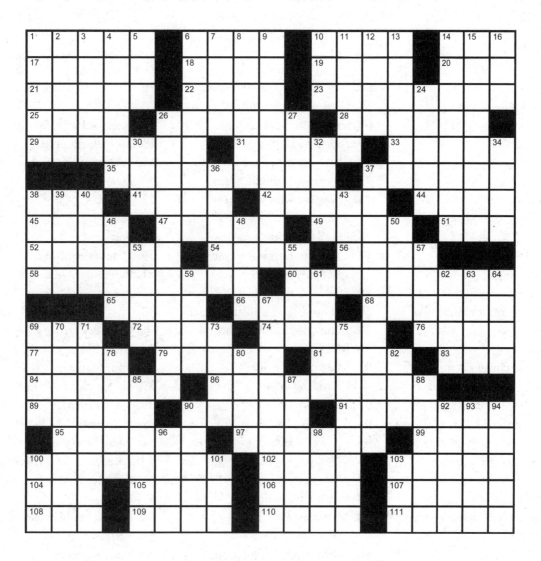

82. Addis Ababa nation (abbr.)

85. Like countless stories of the ER?

87. Senility

88. Straight, in sexuality

90. Gussy up

92. See 3-D

93. Temporary hair tint

94. Sanctuary sections

96. Spacious location?

98. "Pretty maids all in _____"

100. *The Family Circus* cartoonist Keane

101. Calypso relative

103. Forbid

Bonus clue: Unscramble a third anagram for 3-D and 92-D (NDIAR):

— — — — —

ACROSS

1. Calgary CFLer's postage purchase?
6. Priests' garb
10. Sign on a staff
14. Subside, like a tide
17. Tops of mushrooms
18. Amazing accomplishment
19. Loathe
20. Prefix with Georgian
21. In single file
23. Qatar and Kuwait
25. 1973 Elton John track: "I'm Gonna Be a _____ Idol"
26. Winnipeg _____
28. Novi Sad citizens
30. Some animals live in this
31. Cause of physical discomfort
35. 2017 National Ballet of Canada production: _____ *Lake*
36. Transplanting a plant
40. Pile of rock rubble
42. Mystical board
44. Palindromic Ottoman Empire title
45. _____ the line
46. Anne Murray classic
48. West African country: _____ Coast
50. Grammy Hall of Fame Award winner Simone
51. 1,000 per cent increase description
52. Slumbered
53. More sage
54. Tattoo shop liquid
55. New Brunswick cascade: _____ Kitchen Falls
56. Go for the gold?
57. Down in the dumps
60. Legendary Himalayan creatures
61. South African spear
65. _____ *Well That Ends Well*

66. Serving of tea, in Shropshire
67. Gardening gadgets
68. Irish actor Stephen
69. Southern US state (abbr.)
70. Desktop receptacle
72. Toronto hospital: Mount _____
73. Canadian who wrote *The Book of Eve*: _____ Beresford-Howe
76. Like a big budget movie?
78. Canadian business supplies company since 1976
79. 10-year Calgary Flame Roberts
80. LSD user, colloquially
83. Impressive intimidation
86. Recreational walker
91. McDonald's game: Canada Coast To Coast _____
92. Kentucky city
94. *The Lord of the Rings* creature
95. Approximately
96. Behold the man: _____ homo
97. Not suitable
98. Canadian singer Amy
99. Monahan who joined the Flames in 2013
100. Boxing refs' stoppage decisions
101. Crowded

DOWN

1. Canadian restaurant chain founded in 1928: White _____
2. Nite anagram
3. On the safe side, at sea
4. Nasty
5. Filled flatbreads
6. Epilogue
7. Luau necklace
8. Bologna babies
9. Inscribed marker
10. Québec Oka, for example
11. Dominion Archivist of Canada (1948–68): William Kaye _____

12. Cause of medical conditions
13. See 10-A
14. Intestinal inflammation
15. Moosehead product
16. Former W Network show: *Undercover _____ Canada*
22. "Rock of _____"
24. Some
27. Frays
29. Data transmission speed rate
31. Barely audible hiss
32. Pimply outbreak
33. _____ Ore Company of Canada
34. Some Screech drinkers, informally
37. Segment of the whole
38. Sister's zilch?
39. Equipment
41. Piano key wood
43. *Love It or List It Vancouver* designer Harris
47. Kind
49. Ontario Public Service (abbr.)
50. Skittles target
52. Stage scenery item?
53. Stinging insects
55. Cool
56. It follows chi
57. Québec's shortest-serving premier: Pierre-_____ Johnson
58. Butter substitute
59. Sonority
60. Chinese currency unit
61. Dreadful emotions?
62. MacLellan who wrote 46-A
63. Saudi or Omani
64. Egyptian goddess
66. Scottish sword
67. Second-yr. college student
69. One of the three Fates
71. Sleeper's footwear

74. Security And Stability Operations (abbr.)
75. Johnston or Marble, in the Rockies
77. Train components
81. Cay, for example
82. Former Governor General Johnston

83. Eight-time Grammy nominee Tori
84. Retailer name until 2012 rebranding: Mark's _____ Wearhouse
85. *The Private Life of Henry VIII* actress Lanchester

87. Blue Rodeo hit: "Diamond _____"
88. CPP word
89. Some record types (abbr.)
90. Tree anagram
93. University of Central Oklahoma (abbr.)

A Literary Legend

Books by Alice Munro

ACROSS

1. Gate fastener
5. Edmonton and Calgary papers
9. Domed church part
13. Singer Taylor and satirist Jonathan
19. Festive December candle type
20. _____ chowder
21. Country formerly known as Persia
22. Illinois city
23. **1986 Governor General's Award winner (with "*The*")**
26. You might do this in addition to hemming
27. Dine at Earls
28. Type of valve
29. Avoidance of alcohol
31. Tome anagram
32. Scot's tongue
34. Days of yesteryear
35. Canadian export
36. Characteristic
39. Go back over one's steps
42. Musical trill
44. BTO hit: "Let It _____"
45. Jacket badges
46. _____ *en scène*
47. **1994 Governor General's Award nominee**
51. Like some softball teams
53. Original Wiggles member Jeff
57. 1981 film: _____ *Boot*
58. Give authority to
59. Pasture male
60. Photographer's problem?
61. 1970s Cree artist Ray
62. Dwelling
64. Astronomer's solar system model
65. **1998 Giller Prize winner**
70. Hardy's comedy movie mate
71. Pinball penalties
72. Small hotels
73. "Enigma Variations" composer
74. Divided into stripes, in heraldry
75. Ice-cold shower?
77. Type of tub
80. Consider
81. Cry weakly
82. ***Hateship, Friendship, Courtship, Loveship, Marriage* was republished as this**
85. Let _____ a secret
87. French Impressionist painter
89. Nonpareil
90. Kidney stones, for example
93. One expressing disdain
95. BC CFL team
96. Oklahoma City University (abbr.)
97. *Driving _____ Daisy*
99. Kiln for hops
100. Xeric
102. Tenor clarinet
105. London's river
107. Norwegian "Take On Me" band
110. Be in accordance with the rules
111. **1992 Governor General's Award nominee (with "*The*")**
114. Spleen related
115. Top of the very top
116. Assayers analyze these
117. Wrong, in the eyes of the law
118. In a caustic manner
119. Scottish island
120. 06/06/17, for example
121. Very limber

DOWN

1. Sensational publicity
2. Angel's ambience
3. Opening for a coin
4. Cribbage player's counter
5. Lavender or lilac
6. Irish province
7. Former employer of Canada's Chris Hadfield
8. Southern US flowering shrub
9. Bulb of garlic
10. Old Canadian reality show: *To Serve and _____*
11. You might do this at BMO?
12. Battlefield foe
13. Circular shape
14. Models, for example
15. Corn Belt State
16. Festival name in several Canadian cities
17. Container for Campbell's
18. Most wise
24. Crowd's brawl
25. Search out a small mammal?
30. "Horse" for Canada's Kyle Shewfelt
31. Demeanour
33. Cheeky response
36. Stepped on
37. US morning show host Kelly
38. Juicy drinks
40. Pantyhose shade
41. Former currency unit of Portugal
43. Misshapes
48. Container for canned peaches
49. Sign up at U of C
50. 455, to a Roman
52. Yellow-tinted bread spread
54. Out on the ocean
55. Bird seen at the beach
56. 2004 Nelly Furtado hit
59. Marshes
60. Immediately
61. Tile type
62. "If I could be _____ on the wall . . ."
63. Blue Jay's slugger

64. Business proprietor, often
65. Atwood book-to-TV drama: *The Handmaid's* _____
66. Really big
67. Latin abbr. that ends a list
68. In 2017, these AB NHLers made the playoffs for the first time in a decade
69. 1960s Canadian prime minister, for short
70. Guided the troops
74. Dispense discipline
75. Beatified status
76. Kin of a harp
77. "Skedaddle!"

78. Magical stage act: _____ & Teller
79. Mythological god
81. In a mannerly manner
82. Indonesian dwarf buffalo
83. Most awful outcomes
84. Motel employee
86. One, two or three?
88. Issue addressed at federal election debates
90. See 35-A
91. The Maritimes, earlier
92. More luxuriant
94. Aircraft propulsion device
95. Have a pronunciation problem

98. Cell bodies
101. An environmental "R"
103. Posted an envelope
104. BC place: White _____
106. East Coast organization: Atlantic Formula Racing Association (abbr.)
107. Above
108. Frau's partner
109. Quite pretentious
112. Jacqueline Kennedy, _____ Bouvier
113. Michael Bublé hit: "_____ a Beautiful Day"

ACROSS

1. Casino freebie, for example
5. Long-time CBC Radio show: _____ *Happens*
9. Edmonton-born *Law & Order* actress Hennessy
13. Canadian Golf Hall of Fame inductee Coe-Jones
17. _____-TASS
18. Blood fluids
19. Garnier hair colour brand
20. UN civil aviation agency (abbr.)
21. Sicily sight: Mount _____
22. Links snare?
23. Birds' bills
24. Leave flabbergasted
25. Breeders' group: Canadian Texas _____ Association
27. Vocabulary
28. Structural support column
29. Athabasca Glacier landforms
31. Thaw
33. Precious gem weight unit
36. New Mexico arts community
37. Canadian specialty channel: _____TV
38. Not as much
39. Ontario city
41. Avoid
44. Banjolike Japanese instruments (var.)
46. Currency for 7-D
48. Old-style black
49. M.G. Vassanji Giller nominee: *The Assassin's* _____
50. Eugene Levy *SCTV* character Sammy
53. "Put a _____ on it!"
54. Coach Scotty who notched the most NHL wins
57. Spear and Bonavista, in Newfoundland
58. University in 39-A
60. Tropical black bird
61. Takes back one's testimony
63. Chinese-born Canadian fashion designer Alfred
64. Former Canadian NHLers Daneyko and Hodge
66. Bringing up the rear
67. Duos
71. Prevent, like poets?
73. Sailor
76. Use a mobile
77. Constructs a structure
79. Winnipeg ensemble: _____ Gentlemen's Choir
80. Vivacious
81. She hosted 5-A (with 74-D)
83. Banda Aceh resident
85. Stewpot
86. Black tea type
88. Looks into?
92. Excessive amount
93. Lab vessel
94. Yours and mine
95. Lacking good manners
96. Canadian charitable org. founded in 1900
97. Lip
98. Guitar part
99. Soothes a sprain
100. 1989 Jeff Healey Band hit: "Angel _____"
101. Famed Scottish loch
102. CRA employees, for example
103. Talk online?

DOWN

1. Sky, in Sherbrooke
2. Australian actress Miranda
3. Donald who helped build Canadian Northern Railway
4. Level-headed person's philosophy?
5. *Titanic* character John Jacob
6. Making jagged cuts
7. Tehran residents
8. You might get Labatt Blue on this
9. Jennifer who led the Canadian women's curling team to Sochi gold
10. Holly type
11. Frisky?
12. Glasgow girls
13. Debunk a hypothesis
14. Potentially libellous
15. High-pitched whines
16. Supreme Court of Canada group, for example
26. BC place: Radium _____ Springs
27. More or _____
30. Seasonal quaff
32. Old interjection of disgust
33. Canadian Aids Society (abbr.)
34. US lawyers' org.
35. See 97-A
37. Cancels
39. Dogs' shelter
40. Makes plumb
42. Ruin
43. To the _____ of the earth
45. Fly high
47. LCBO word
50. Large tropical ray
51. Rental ad word
52. Montréal-based religious group: Grey _____
54. Make cookies
55. First numbers
56. Annual Ottawa/Gatineau February festival
57. Attorneys' attachés?
59. Self-obsessed
62. Throw off the boat?
63. Broiled, in the Big Smoke

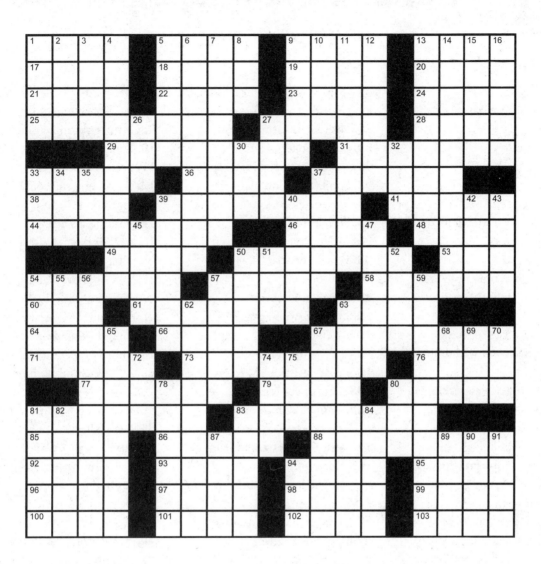

65. Food preservatives: Potassium
_____

67. Robert Louis Stevenson classic:
_____ *Island*

68. Pharmacist Awareness mo. in
Canada

69. Antlered animals

70. Sneaky like Stallone?

72. A princess slept on one

74. See 81-A

75. Direction for Mia?

78. Lacking courage

80. Solo dance performance: _____
seul

81. Hollywood Humphrey's
nickname

82. Commixed metal

83. Canadian Tire revenue source

84. Takes time out

87. Droops

89. Cry of pain

90. "What's the big _____?"

91. Diagnostic procedure

94. CBC Radio host Carol

51 Band (Members) on the Run

They left at the peak of success

ACROSS

1. Latin ballroom dance
6. Annoy
10. Health resorts
14. Still
19. "Get _____ of yourself!"
20. Toast topper
21. The "L" in L.M. Montgomery
22. You can see one at 5-D
23. Flaring stars
24. Prime-time time slot
25. Arabian Peninsula nation
26. Leading the pack
27. Optometrist's social skill?
29. **Geri Halliwell withdrew from . . .**
31. _____-high to a grasshopper
32. Per person
34. Campsite bed
35. New hawk
38. Like a grumpy greyhound?
40. Trig term
43. Press down on
47. Edited for publication
49. Medium's building tool?
52. Metrical feet, in poetry (var.)
53. Performance for Blue Rodeo
55. New Testament book
56. Spiel
57. Some are Alaskan kings
58. Olfactory offensiveness
60. Popular Campbell's soup
62. Lyricist Gershwin
63. One of Canada's McGarrigle sisters
64. **Steve Perry pulled out of . . .**
66. Cold symptom
68. Principle of Chinese philosophy
70. Japanese cooking wine
72. Buddy
73. Angler's angry spouse?
78. **Peter Gabriel got out of . . .**
81. Curling team's conclusions?
85. "Gross!"
86. Old-style revolutionary
88. Positive investment result
89. Salon looker?
90. Cover yourself with a cape?
92. Subject in a law class
94. Spot or Fido
95. New York state city
96. Jockey's preferred seasoning?
98. Present paper
100. Lushes
101. Spaniards' cheers
102. Bodily swelling (var.)
105. New Canadians' pledge: _____ of Citizenship
106. Alias letters
108. Pear or apple
109. Iranian Community Association of Ontario (abbr.)
111. **Axl Rose retreated from . . .**
117. Torontonians Robinson and Toyne invented this
122. Develop
123. Cherry flavoured drink
124. Specific space
125. Wedding reception host
126. Mental disorder
127. Ovule sheath
128. Hitchhiker's hope?
129. One who dubs
130. Spiral-horned antelope
131. Baseball line
132. Deal (out)
133. Sour, for short

DOWN

1. Horse's crowning glory?
2. Shipmate's greeting
3. 1974 Gino Vannelli classic: "People Gotta _____"
4. **Ozzy Osbourne opted out of . . .**
5. Cineplex _____
6. Adriatic Sea country
7. Pelvis parts
8. Combatant on a piste
9. Of the unborn (var.)
10. Spill
11. You do this at Petro-Canada
12. Berry for a smoothie
13. Harmonious: In _____
14. Post pupa stage
15. 2/9/90 Blue Jays record book moment
16. 1995 Bryan Adams hit: "Have You _____ Really Loved a Woman?"
17. Currency used in 25-A
18. Singer Nugent, et al.
28. 1988 Gemini nominee: *A _____ of Singing Birds*
30. Genuine, to a German
33. See 102-A
35. Erin Karpluk played the lead on this CBC series: *Being _____*
36. Long (for)
37. Fellow jingle writer?
39. Quebecer's farewell
40. Brother of Marlon and Michael
41. Jack-in-the-pulpits, for example
42. Month that comes after Adar
44. To no _____
45. It's just over a yard, in Canada
46. Courtroom entreaties?
48. Sue Grafton mystery: _____ *for Corpse*
50. Having compassion for
51. Natural fibre sponge (var.)
54. Beginning of an idea
59. Galahad, et al.
61. Bettor's tidbits
64. Unite
65. Yeats poem line: "_____ Time transfigured me"
67. **Lindsey Buckingham beat it from . . .**
69. Up and about, say

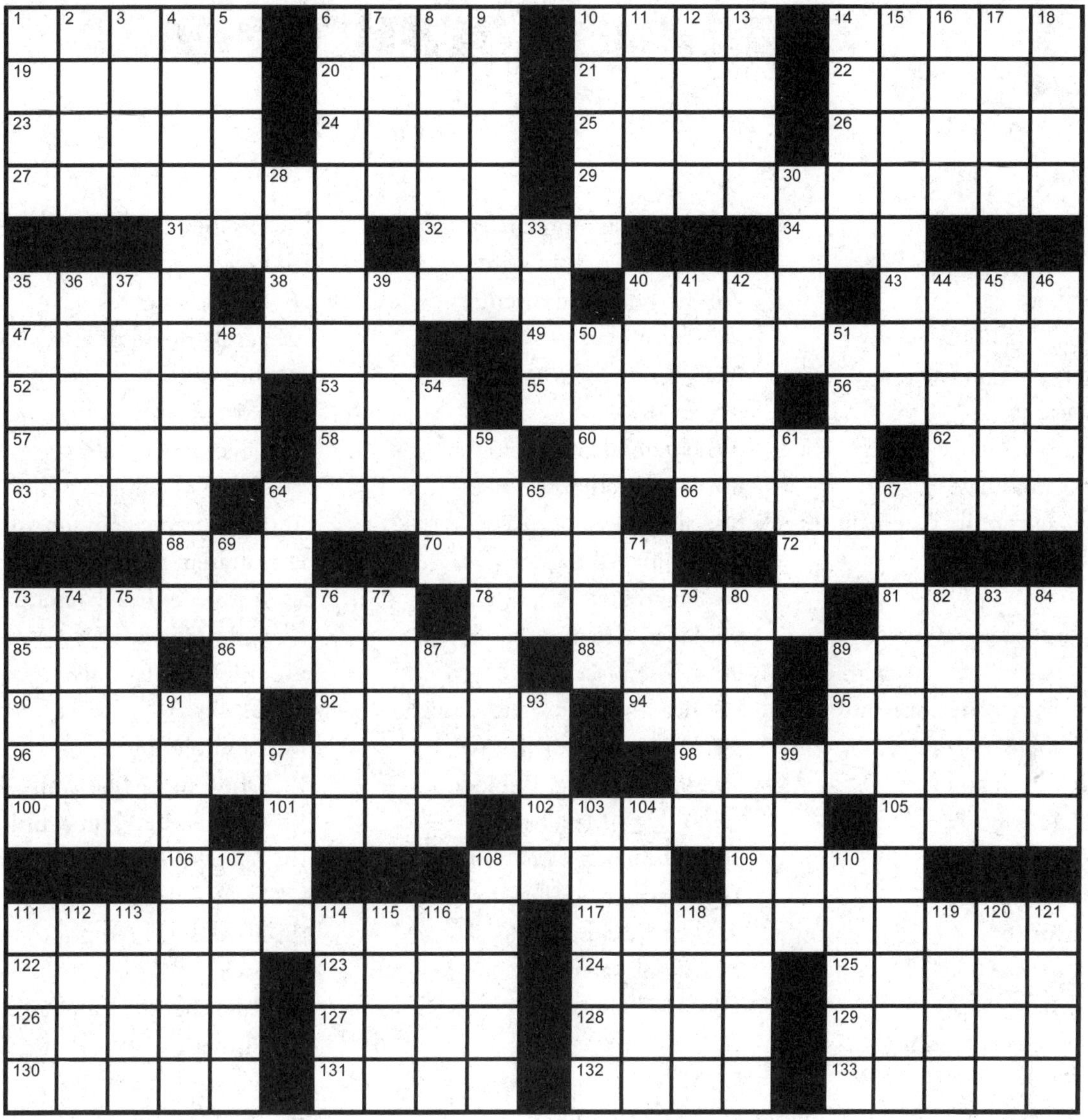

(Crossword grid)

71. Tide type
73. Frankfurt "fox"
74. Type of Inuit dwelling
75. Hamilton-born *SCTV* actor Martin
76. Glenn Close thriller: _____ *Attraction*
77. Weaken a levee
79. Armed forces blockade
80. Daunt
82. Nigerian buck
83. Old European coin
84. Type of infection
87. Shouts, in Shawinigan

89. Gone _____ not forgotten
91. Margaret Atwood book: *The Blind _____*
93. Cobbler's "Get lost!"?
97. An engine might make this sound
99. 2007 Rush song: "Bravest _____"
103. Prepare for burial
104. Luv
107. Prepare bread dough
108. The 23rd is one
110. INVISTA Centre, in Kingston
111. 117-A, for example

112. Russian river
113. *Project Runway* judge Garcia
114. Some tubers
115. Aching
116. White Rock-born actor Nicholas
118. NDP and Liberals, say
119. Wile E. Coyote's product supplier
120. She envisions the future
121. Former cabinet ministers Gray or Dhaliwal

ACROSS

1. Emeril's interjection
4. Seafood entree
10. "Black" missions
13. Letters seen on wedding invitations
17. Canadian Yanofsky who was a chess grandmaster
18. Language family that includes Turkish
19. Droll
20. List shortening abbr.
21. Molson stubby, for example
23. Neuville negative response
24. Type of pastry (var.)
25. Switch back and forth
26. Worked at 86-A
28. Bloodsucker
29. Wall decorator
30. Fibre for rope
33. Stick for shish kebab
35. Golden
39. Enlightened Buddhist
41. Heats
43. Participated in a National Ballet of Canada production
44. Sweet, dark wine
47. Malign, to Marlowe
49. Property document
50. Famed Nova Scotia schooner
52. Land of leprechauns
53. Late
54. Magistrate or minister, say
57. Like an airhead (var.)
61. Juliet's query: "_____ thou love me?"
62. Makes lots of money
67. Move like molasses
68. Carbohydrate-binding protein
70. Sign for some born in October
71. Canada tried to keep the peace here in the '90s
73. Saints' shining circlets
75. With _____ in sight
76. Astronomical distances
78. Cut molars
81. US singer Suzanne
82. Erodes
84. No-good entomologist?
86. Slaughterhouses
89. Blue jeans
93. Major AB highway
94. Furtive
95. Chad Kroeger's band
96. Loosen laces
97. Beaufort, in Canada's Arctic
98. Find oneself in Tokyo?
99. 2010 Michael Bublé song: "_____ Me a River"
100. Dean anagram
101. Former NHLers Jovanovski and Belfour
102. Looks at steps?
103. Peach or plum

DOWN

1. _____ ghanouj
2. Jennifer who won synchro springboard Olympic bronze in 2012
3. Robert DeNiro movie: _____ the Parents
4. Tim Horton was one in the '70s
5. Genetic copies
6. Besiege
7. Anne of Green Gables Cuthbert
8. Stack of stuff
9. It's been filmed in Manitoba: _____ Road Truckers
10. Admit to
11. African shrub
12. Major Canadian oil company
13. Newfoundland held two of these in 1948 (var.)
14. Hubbub
15. Low-lying area
16. Slog through
22. Parole Board of Canada does this
26. Skirt-wearing pub staffer
27. Olympian goddess
29. Statistics computations
30. Door frame component
31. Eurasian mountain range
32. It features heavy rescue on the Coq: Highway _____ Hell
34. 1989 Richler book: Solomon Gursky _____ Here
36. Laptop brand
37. Drove like Mike Weir?
38. Uninhabited Nunavut island
40. Yellow-flowered perennial
42. Slice of bacon
45. He was advised not to look back
46. Parenthetical comment
48. Listens to a Who?
51. Geologic period
53. "Four Strong Winds" singer Ian
55. Expansive properties
56. Rest Of Canada (abbr.)
57. South African hamlet
58. Sioux City state
59. Old Russian ruler (var.)
60. Dazzling doyen
63. Memorable saying
64. Duel tool
65. _____ Around the Rosy
66. Coke or Pepsi
68. Canada's official summer game
69. Derbyshire river
72. Canadian reality show: Til _____ Do Us Part
74. Caribbean island
77. Set out on a 97-A
79. Canada goose, say

80. *SCTV* star Levy
83. _____ a bone
85. Bath or smelling follower
86. Greenish-blue colour

87. Southern Ontario community: Grand _____
88. Politician's helper
89. Grime or grit

90. 1951 Hugh MacLennan novel: _____ *Man's Son*
91. Almond shade
92. Kind of terrier
95. Our, in Chibougamau

53 French-Canadian Fellows

Men of Québec

ACROSS

1. Partly detached house?
5. Build on _____
9. Pairs
14. Verve
17. **NHLer Cournoyer or actor Ducharme**
18. ZZ Top, for example
19. Description of some non-Hollywood films
20. Groom's declaration
21. Geek
22. Victoria historic site: Fort _____ Hill
23. Moved like a pendulum
24. I, to Caesar
25. Rare mineral once found in Greenland
27. Single hydrocarbon?
28. Estate owner description
30. Exercises too much
33. Lira anagram
34. **Politician Parizeau or goalie Plante**
38. Surgical probe
39. **Premier Lévesque or singer Simard**
40. Portion out
41. 1987 Paul Carrack hit: "Don't Shed a _____"
43. Laundry room appliance
45. Spill over the top
46. How you shift in a standard
48. Places, to Tiberius
51. Thumbtacks
53. Order of Canada science journalist Ingram
54. Grandfather clock part
56. Central Netherlands city
57. Preceding month (abbr.)
58. **NHLer Lafleur or Cirque du Soleil founder Laliberté**
59. BC place: Pacific _____ National Park Reserve
60. Advanced math degree?
61. What a raconteur does
63. 1984 Bruce Cockburn single: "If I _____ a Rocket Launcher"
64. Sign up at U of A
66. Sleep wherever, in Wales
67. Choppers' landing places
69. Osprey's cousin
70. Canadian singer Vickers, for example
72. Yield
73. Poke fun at
74. **Writer Carrier or singer Voisine**
77. Sightlessness
79. **Speed skater Hamelin or businessman Bronfman**
81. _____-bodied
82. Riot police wear this
84. Moves toward
86. _____ Up the Rim to Win
87. Gardens where trees are grown and shown (var.)
92. French vineyard
93. Greek poetry Muse
95. She perjures
96. River in southwestern Ontario
97. Coal scuttle
98. Show you've seen before on CTV
99. _____-inflammatory drug
100. **NHLer Beliveau or prime minister Chrétien**
101. Low digit
102. Bottomless pit
103. Average grades
104. AM's "A"

DOWN

1. 1990s boy band: 'N _____
2. Eternally
3. *CODCO* star Walsh
4. _____-European
5. Endeavour to achieve a goal
6. Christian church member
7. Source of pillow feathers
8. Fish type
9. This movie mogul's father was Canadian
10. Naive
11. Theme of *The Scarlet Letter*
12. Cacophony
13. Japanese video game company
14. **Prime minister Trudeau or CFLer Lavertu**
15. Park carefully
16. Curly-haired dog breed
26. Oaf
27. Not authorized by a court
29. Munchie for Bugs
31. Twin in Genesis
32. Possible home for Wilbur
34. Alberta landmark: _____ National Park
35. Made reference to
36. In the vicinity
37. It comes between sadhe and resh
42. Rank for some sailors (abbr.)
44. Incense ingredient
46. Domtar has one in Kamloops
47. 1979 Triumph tune: "_____ It on the Line"
49. Manitoba standard time zone
50. Strong
52. Blender setting
54. Preps a bed for planting
55. Ritter/Somers sitcom: _____ *Company*
58. Eight pints (abbr.)
59. Apply a new paint colour

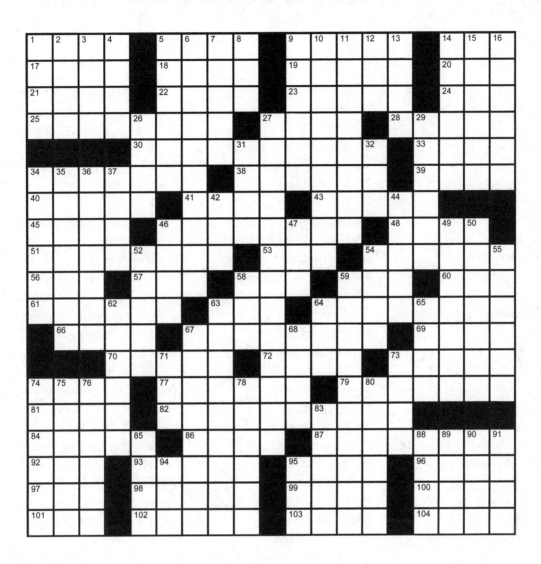

62. Rolle who played housekeeper Florida on *Maude*
63. Ancient Greek historian
64. X-ray unit
65. Sibyl
67. The Order of Canada appoints five of these members annually
68. Type of tree a partridge sat in
71. Collar a criminal

73. It's also known as eddo
74. California city: _____ Mirage
75. 1930s actress Merle
76. **Politician Ryan or Habs coach Julien**
78. Road safety cones
80. Presumptuous pride
83. State bordered by two Canadian provinces

85. Word repeated in a Doris Day song
88. Royal male, in India
89. Equally balanced
90. Suit _____
91. Famed L.M. Montgomery character: _____ Shirley
94. Yank's Civil War rival
95. Mistassini, to a Quebecer

ACROSS

1. Hover over, menacingly
5. Walkway in 13-D
9. Mace anagram
13. Niels of physics fame
17. Early Peruvian
18. Narcissus' mythological admirer
19. Pond hopper
20. Small case for Cherie
21. Security for a debt
22. Newlyweds' entranceway?
24. Archers' goals?
25. South American palm berry
26. Three vowels for Old MacDonald
27. Celebrity news magazine: _____! Canada
28. Manage a situation
29. Square metre
31. Shortened name for Canadian tennis pro Bouchard
32. Prices
33. 19th-C. Canadian poet Goldsmith
35. Canadian Bar Association member
37. Okra-based dish
40. Banish
42. "A Boy Named _____"
43. Chinese and Thais
45. Deplete one's resources
47. Update kitchen cabinets
52. 1984 Bryan Adams single: "_____ to You"
53. "Canada's magazine for successful retirement"
56. Golden Olympic Canadian triathlete Whitfield
57. Cousin of Camembert
59. Gift for mom: _____ day
60. Like unanalyzed data
62. Hatchlings' home
63. Logic proposition
65. Scythe sharpening tools
70. 2004 hit from Canada's Terri Clark: "Girls _____ Too"
71. Chalkboard cleaner
73. Cash for a trip to Calais
74. More frenetic
76. Break in time
78. Abs exercise
80. Honey-based beverages
81. Early settler in Québec
85. Heroic, in literature
87. Asian perennial with showy flowers
88. Stirs up sediment
90. Vancouver hotel: Pan _____
94. Makes like Mike Myers
95. Note taking clerk
96. _____ capita
97. Anna Neagle movie: _____, Nanette
98. Royal Canadian Air Farce offering
99. Put a part into the whole
101. U of T alum
102. Like a desert
103. Easter hymn: "_____ Risen!"
104. Profit-sharing percentages
105. Lab burner
106. Court announcement
107. Electrical discharges
108. Alexander Keith's brews
109. Deli loaves

DOWN

1. Scented shrub
2. Annual Canadian tour: Stars _____
3. 2007 Arcade Fire track: "_____ of Noise"
4. Brandon's province
5. Tsar Ivan V's co-ruler
6. Attain a goal
7. "Comin' _____ the Rye"
8. Garden groundbreaker
9. Reading room
10. "Calm down!"
11. Croquet clubs
12. Tuber type
13. Victoria park: _____ Hill
14. Idle
15. Half a nursery rhyme character's name
16. Moves up the corporate ladder
23. Pronoun for her
30. Bob Dylan composition: "All _____ the Watchtower"
31. It's for the mill?
32. Some residents of 4-D
34. Bodily secretion
36. "_____ home and native land"
37. Mangle a message
38. Shylock, say
39. Smallest amounts possible (var.)
41. Flower necklace
44. CQD follower
46. Enlivens
48. Shark part
49. Earhart who disappeared
50. Nestled up to (var.)
51. Goes in
54. Roman goddess
55. Actor Mineo
58. Typography measures
61. WWW component
64. Protection
66. Oxidation
67. Industrial Research Institute (abbr.)
68. Shacks for sheep
69. Shrub with red drupes
72. 1960s ABC series: The _____ Patrol
75. 21st premier of 4-D
77. Virtue to Moir, at the rink
79. Lab tube
81. Canada's official winter sport

82. Clothing
83. Shoe company mascot: _____ Brown
84. Mindful?
86. Pet a Persian?

87. Cowboy's rope
89. Keep a written record
91. Geographical landmark: _____-ninth parallel
92. Just plain stupid

93. Composition endings
95. Bantu language
96. Canadian country singer Brandt
100. Canadian arts institution since 1880 (abbr.)

As you play this game

ACROSS

1. Cross for King Tut
5. Estimate
10. Canadian new wave group: Men Without _____
14. Book for a Greek Titan?
19. Not common
20. Winged, like Pegasus
21. Tinker with text
22. Deciduous tree
23. **Actor Russell's raven?**
25. **Dalai's camelid?**
27. Aging process
28. Provide funds in advance
29. Minute bit?
30. Old-style tailor
31. Canadian-born NHLer Letang
33. Limb
34. Secretary or rolltop
35. City in Italy: _____ Remo
36. Little lady
37. Seed on a bun or bagel
39. Carpentry or cobbling tool
42. Beginners, in Bath
44. Treads the boards
46. Call to court?
50. 2012 hit from Canada's Carly Rae Jepsen: "Call Me _____"
52. Decides on
54. It precedes Minor or Major
56. Shampoo for a sophisticated chap?
57. Narcissistic people
59. Container weight for a shipment
61. Prosecuted again after a hung jury
63. Ontario-born NHLers Hutton and Harpur
64. Dined at Swiss Chalet
67. Semester at Dalhousie
69. Goof up
70. Yellowknife landmark: Ragged _____ Road
71. **1932 Olympian Buster's crustacean?**
73. Possessive in Port-Cartier
75. City of the NFL's Browns, for short
77. _____ is not to wonder why
78. Strawberry seed
79. Peking nursemaid
80. Early East Indian religion
82. State from which you can't wake
84. Transform subtly, like colours
86. **Vera's plants?**
87. Five-card poker game
89. Drink to excess
92. Read over in detail
93. Literature categories
95. Neck of the woods, perhaps
97. Former Montréal Expos pitcher Martinez
99. RNs might work here
100. Radiator cover
102. Cried
104. Reno and Ashcroft, in previous US administrations (abbr.)
106. See espionage in action?
109. Goose egg
110. 1979 Neil Young & Crazy Horse hit: "Hey Hey, My My (_____ the Black)"
111. Some Michelangelo works
114. Hot anagram
115. TSN hockey "insider" Craig
117. Like a no-bid item on eBay
120. **Actor Ethan's bird?**
122. **Machine man John's mammal?**
123. Crunchy cookies
124. Famed general Robert
125. Step inside
126. Thing of interest, perhaps?
127. Spar
128. Shred
129. They're honoured on Canada's Walk of Fame
130. Pooch in *The Thin Man* movies

DOWN

1. Circle parts
2. Nostrils
3. Stockholm spending money
4. Loggers, say
5. Old region in France
6. Stomach discomfort cause
7. Provide a paycheque
8. British goods purveyor
9. Waste pipes
10. Aids
11. Sixth Jewish month
12. Like a watch that never goes out of style?
13. Ear bone
14. With competence
15. _____ Aviv
16. You might have one on your car
17. High points
18. Former Toronto Maple Leafs star Eddie
24. Lairds' lands
26. Drawn-out dramas
32. 1991 Tom Cochrane tune: "Life _____ Highway"
34. Reserved
36. Clean floors
37. Pre-exercise exercise
38. Has to
39. Tiny organism (var.)
40. Weight Watchers manager's concern?
41. **Novelist Annabel's big cat?**
43. Public speaking platforms (var.)
45. **Jeff's mutt?**
47. **Commentator Rafe's roan?**

48. Glutton
49. 19th-C. Aussie outlaw Kelly
51. Grafton mystery offering: _____ for Burglar
53. Hurt your "piggy"
55. Planned in advance
58. Tex-Mex servings
60. 2011 Ed Sheeran hit: "The _____"
62. Remnant of a blaze
65. You'll find a canal here
66. Unclear
68. Environmental Research and Education (abbr.)
72. Ella's "Shoo!"?
74. Outdoor storage buildings

76. Atomic _____ of Canada Limited
79. Benedick's kerfuffle?
80. Bout of bawling
81. European river that might rise?
83. Provincial anthem: "_____ to Newfoundland"
85. See 17-D
88. Stilt walker's fanciful story?
90. Foe
91. He lived at 24 Sussex in the '70s (abbr.)
94. Kind of cold?
96. Bristle on a barley stem
98. VIA critics?
101. More agile
103. Practice pieces

105. Rose Bowl and Cotton Bowl (var.)
106. Spirit of a people
107. Four Seasons Hotels and Resorts founder Isadore
108. _____ Corporation of Canada
110. Signed with a BIC?
111. Sous-chef's tool
112. See 10-D
113. It creates dangerous driving conditions
115. 1980 album: The _____ of Burton Cummings
116. Ontario place: _____ Sound
118. Bristle
119. US humorist Bombeck
121. Ornamental carp

ACROSS

1. FDR's mother, et al.
6. Nunavut Quest vehicle
10. Canadian agricultural lender (abbr.)
13. Irritate
17. Suffix meaning "science"
18. *Beverly Hills 90210* star Spelling
19. American's retirement savings account (abbr.)
20. Raw silk hue
21. Abandoned infants
23. White Spot founder Bailey
24. Several grand?
25. Creating harmony?
26. Treble and bass
28. Emollient found in lotion
29. Hide-and-_____
30. *The Dean Martin Celebrity* _____
31. Crosses over
32. New Brunswick attraction: _____ Trail Parkway
35. Flu symptom
37. BC premier Horgan as of July 2017
38. 7-D is on the northwest shore of this lake
39. Stick in one's _____
40. Roundworms
44. Commonwealth Stadium CFLer
46. British sky gazing org. founded in 1820
48. *Fatso* star DeLuise
49. *Decree* _____
50. Light bulb inventor's initials
51. Province of 37-D
54. Things
56. Showy
58. Allegation maker
61. Earls staffers
62. Hot spring
65. Underhill who competed with Duguay on *Battle of the Blades*
66. Diamond or ruby
68. *Golden Girls* actress Arthur
69. Carved glass, say
71. Hooked on yarn?
74. Cutting-_____
76. Daughter of Cronus
77. Word of woe
78. Perilous job at an old royal court?
80. Canadian sandwich shop since 1968
81. New Zealand parrots
83. Bob Seger hit: "Night _____"
84. Double reed woodwind
86. Pals, in Papineau
87. Uganda neighbour
88. Canada's Kyle Shewfelt won Commonwealth Games gold doing this
92. Beethoven contemporary Ferdinand
93. 1995 Shania Twain hit: "_____ Man of Mine"
94. He doesn't regain the weight he lost
96. Lees anagram
97. Philosopher's area of study, for short
98. Nave neighbour
99. Scouting mission, for short
100. Earns income from fishing?
101. "No" vote
102. Rip up paper, say
103. Serpentine

DOWN

1. Chesterfield
2. "Thanks _____!"
3. Trounce, competitively
4. Liturgical "Lamb of God" prayer
5. Cape Breton city
6. Smelly reprobate?
7. Ontario provincial park: _____ Point
8. Unit of energy
9. Bee Gees' nightclubs?
10. Used subtlety to avoid an issue
11. Trump-appointed US ambassador to Canada Kelly
12. Turkish Angora, et al.
13. Big communication devices?
14. Like Kópavogur residents
15. Banned refrigerant
16. They sometimes blow
22. Falsehood
27. Nail anagram
30. Air Miles offers these
31. Heavy drinker
32. Tender tootsies?
33. "Little Bear" constellation: _____ Minor
34. World's largest supplier of athletic shoes and apparel
36. 2017 best country solo performance Grammy winner Morris
37. Annual music event: Big Valley _____
39. Humber and Seneca, in Toronto
41. Giller Prize nominee Lisa
42. Kingston clock setting (abbr.)
43. _____-boom-bah
45. Atlas pages
47. 1980s Blue Jays pitcher Dave
52. Chibougamau chapeau?
53. Demons, in Middle Eastern mythology
55. 1981 April Wine hit: "_____ Between You and Me"
56. Taxonomic categories
57. Elude
58. Initial alphabet letters
59. Volvo or Volkswagen
60. Most hoarse

62. Beatles song: "_____ Leaving Home"
63. See 89-D
64. _____ hand
67. Figure of speech type
70. Former prime minister Jean
72. "Morning _____ Broken"
73. American folk hero Crockett
75. *Pun*ishing phrase?

79. Ocean floor rug?
80. Back teeth
81. National Ballet of Canada artistic director (with 87-D)
82. 1970 Elvis live show song: "Walk _____ In My Shoes"
83. High-IQ grp. in Canada since 1967
85. Silent _____ deadly

87. See 81-D
88. You might use this card at West Edmonton Mall
89. They lived in 63-D
90. A flamingo has a long one
91. Annual CFL game: _____ Cup
95. Animal that's bananas for bananas?

57 Who Am I? 2

Name this artist

ACROSS

1. Theatrical curtain fabric
6. Fingerprints, to a bobby
10. Canada's Ken Taylor, from 1977–80 (abbr.)
13. Kirkland Lake's favourite son Thicke
17. **This indigenous group's art inspired her**
18. Once more, to a Scot
19. Canada's Nickelback, for example
21. Restaurant patron's request
22. Cancellation at Cape Canaveral
23. Heavily treed
24. Share scripture
26. **Her autobiography completed in 1945**
28. Federal program for seniors (abbr.)
30. Top of a pyramid, say
31. Run like a well-oiled machine?
32. Give and take?
36. Averted: _____ off
38. Winnipeg NHLer
39. Chair part
42. Girl or man Friday
43. Woodbine competitor
44. Happy-go-lucky
46. Fury
48. Baked beans can
49. Reserved
50. Aerie hatchling
51. Like Canada's prairies, for example
53. Utah tribe
54. Barn compartments
56. **Her painting that sold for $3.39 million in 2013**
59. Tape deck button
62. *Love Story* star MacGraw
63. Varnishes
67. Former Chevy subcompact

68. Puppy's bite
69. Where Springsteen was born?
70. Citrus fruit
71. China's third-largest city
74. Smell
76. *Stars Wars* general: Han _____
77. Rocky Mountain _____
78. Sigh sound
79. Boxer's confusion?
80. Angle, awkwardly
81. Ready–fire link
82. Arequipa country
83. He designed Canada's first postage stamp: _____ Sandford Fleming
85. **Canadian artists who said, "You are one of us"**
90. These parrot other birds?
95. Eastern European principality of old
96. "Nasty" Nastase
98. Purity of gold measurement
99. On balance
100. Canada's acting Cariou, et al.
101. **She is (with 2-D)**
102. Opposite of messy
103. Stage of sleep, for short
104. Abbreviated arrivals?
105. Said, old style

DOWN

1. Browse at The Brick
2. **See 101-A**
3. RCMP spectacular: Musical _____
4. Anagram for 42-A
5. Québec playwright Micone
6. Ottawa-born NHL player Boyle
7. Like a pop-eyed sailor man?
8. **1931 oil on canvas**
9. Busybody
10. Attach

11. Five-time Eskimos Grey Cup quarterback Warren
12. Old European's fast food meal?
13. Indian tea type
14. Money spent in Lesotho
15. End of a minister's message
16. Canadian rower Hanlan, et al.
20. Good standing
25. Padlock part
27. Tie the knot
29. _____ cling
32. Loggers' adages?
33. Cable
34. Montréal-born singer-songwriter Cohen
35. Protest document
37. Eastern Canada pollution problem
38. Blue bird seen in Toronto?
39. Benzene compound
40. True-to-life
41. Facility for hungry officers
44. It contains kings and queens
45. Not scared of anything
47. Jessica who posed for *Playboy* after the 1987 PTL Club scandal
49. Hogs' dwelling
52. Canadian flag colour
53. Six-Day War weapon
54. Standard American English (abbr.)
55. Cashier's drawer
57. Peak in Europe
58. Scottish lords
59. Evaluate
60. Diabolical
61. Calendar span
64. Crazily
65. Jazz singer Holly from Nova Scotia
66. Canadian winter white stuff
68. US fed. health org.

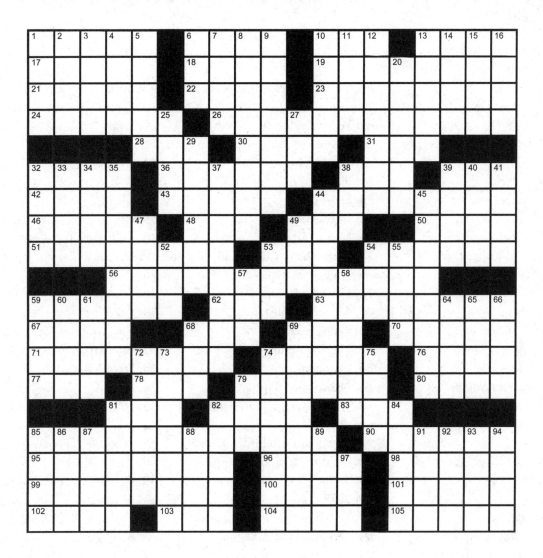

69. This BC village made "a lasting impression" on her

72. Deadly Australasian snake

73. Tea urn, in Tarko-Sale

74. Like a meek maid?

75. Well-groomed

79. Teensy

81. Examine accounting procedures

82. Sacred song

84. Clears a casino table

85. Fellow FBI worker?

86. Anne Shirley, for Canada's Megan Follows

87. Paella pot

88. Place to put papers

89. *Degrassi: The Next Generation* actress Dobrev

91. RV owner's destination

92. Song for Jessye Norman

93. 1907 Post-Impressionist painting: Totem _____ at Sitka

94. Eye irritant

97. Hairpin turn, say

58 Canada Cornucopia 29

ACROSS

1. _____ for knowledge
7. Trounces
12. Canada's 1996 Olympics hero Donovan
18. Chemical salt
19. Classical architecture style
20. Attached, in biology
21. Diefenbaker government minister of justice Davie
22. Former Governor General Jules
23. Cossack military commander
24. Make bacon
25. Stamkos' aspiration?
27. _____ Mountains
29. Christmas songs
30. Two make a sawbuck
31. Irish Rovers stalwart Jimmy
33. Canadian sprinting star De Grasse
36. 19th PEI premier Campbell
38. Nikons and Kodaks
42. Cad
43. Colourful leaf
44. Horror film actor Lugosi
45. Adam's partner
46. Upper court description
48. Retina receptor
49. Parasite on a pooch
50. Antwerp country (abbr.)
51. Moray
52. Toothpaste brand
54. Damp
55. "Zounds!"
57. Magnetic field density unit
58. NL coastline sight
59. Order of Canada jazz musician Dutch
61. Causes snoozing?
62. Chili _____ carne
63. 1968 Bee Gees hit: "_____ Gotta Get a Message to You"

66. Concordia research lab, for short
67. Fix, at the farm?
68. Chinese cooking ingredient
71. Japanese carp
72. Pleased
73. Ship's officer
74. Interjection of disgust
75. Makes certain
77. Retail chain with Canadian origins?
78. Church sections
79. City of 99-A
81. Fluish feeling
83. Locking devices
86. Cuts cordwood
87. Narrow opening
88. 1970s "Lucky Man" band, for short
91. Like a wise old bird?
93. Fertilizer component
95. Twain who released *Now* in 2017
97. One who dons duds
98. Melancholy, on the moors?
99. Percival _____ Memorial Stadium
100. Landscapers' trimming tools
101. Long-time Hab Savard
102. Christie classic: *Murder on the _____ Express*

DOWN

1. Annual Toronto cinematic celebration (abbr.)
2. Long-running CBC comedy: *This _____ Has 22 Minutes*
3. In a lazy manner
4. Squealer
5. Cheap smoke
6. Carpenter's joint
7. Bandmate of 31-A Millar
8. Gardening tool

9. Salve
10. Berton who wrote *The Last Spike*
11. Animal's neck
12. Sis boom _____
13. Benign tumour type
14. Chant
15. Crippled
16. Abbr. for "Them as well"
17. Desires to shop in Japan?
26. _____ projection
28. Radiant
30. Priceless?
31. King or queen, in a deck
32. Bay Days, say
33. Steed for a Saudi?
34. "Uh-uh"
35. 16th premier of Québec Maurice
37. Trilby or toque
39. Pious
40. Greetings in old Rome
41. MP's place in Parliament
43. Drained, like a radiator
44. Manager
47. Low in fat
48. Cistern
49. Bestseller from Canada's Sara Gruen: *Water _____ Elephants*
53. Street in 79-A: _____ Sainte-Catherine
54. Waiter's handout
56. 2013 Michael Bublé track: "I _____ It Easy"
57. Colour of medal for 12-A
58. Birthplace of Beethoven
59. Former premiers Harcourt or Harris
60. Unknown, briefly?
61. Ogres and orangutans
62. Giving rise to
64. Bad habit for Pence?
65. Some lodge fellows

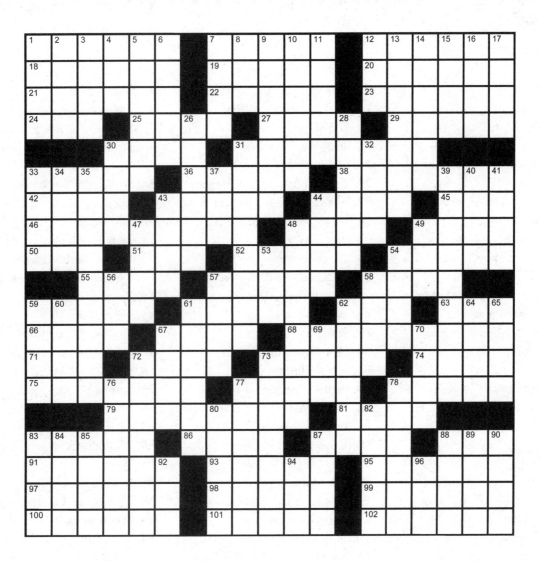

67. The Canadian Golf Hall of Fame and Museum is at this course: _____ Abbey
69. Timmins time (abbr.)
70. Class or category
72. More icky
73. Braggart
76. Official at a Blue Jays game

77. Replace the electrical
78. Munro or Atwood
80. South African banknotes
82. Gadget (var.)
83. Miss Universe Canada 2017 Lauren
84. Impressed
85. Dross from Dofasco

87. Erse anagram
88. Massachusetts motto starter
89. Roughrider competitor
90. Breathe heavily
92. They're posted on store doors (abbr.)
94. Harass a maid?
96. He floated like a butterfly

(59) Pathologically Speaking

Adjectives for medicos

ACROSS

1. Stubble remover
6. Discriminator against granddad, say (var.)
11. Scotiabank foyer machine (abbr.)
14. Bargain basement priced
19. "Be-Bop-_____"
20. Bullring procession
21. Signal for a pool shark?
22. Hunting season gun
23. **Strange, to the psychologist?**
25. Pregnancy timeframe
27. Decorative drapery items
28. "Sh," for example
29. Settle your debts
30. Scottish lord
32. Satchel for a cleaner?
37. Blubber
40. Phone service company: Sask_____
41. Throat clearer's interjection
42. Piece for a classical pianist
44. You might listen like this
46. More opulent
48. Dubai VIP (var.)
49. Like notebook paper
50. Earlier
52. BC arena: Richmond Olympic _____
54. Salve
55. Kelly Clarkson hit: "All I _____ Wanted"
56. Fashionista's blade?
58. Understatement, to an English major
60. Willing to listen
62. Native of Novi Sad
64. Reggae singer Peter
65. Greyish blonde?
66. Mammal on a Vancouver Canuck's jersey
67. YUL posting
68. Acronym for "immediately"
70. Stomach, colloquially
73. Not active
75. Star's car
77. Make sense of French?
79. Turned outward, like fingers
82. In an extremely excellent way
84. Religious image in a Russian church (var.)
85. *The Incredible _____*
86. You used to pay this on BC's Coquihalla Highway
88. It follows ecto
89. Perks?
90. He pursued the Pleiades
92. In a sordid way
94. Pacific islands group
96. Entered
98. Tropical cuckoos
99. Title, in Témiscaming
100. *Has Anybody Seen My _____?*
101. Overturn
102. Little sticks
104. Managerial monk
106. Track meet races
108. Without equal, in England?
111. Ontario Iroquoian language
115. **Scary, to the dermatologist?**
118. 1970s Canadian music group: _____ in Coldwater
119. Software Development Tool (abbr.)
120. Traditional Irish song: "Robin _____"
121. Glacier groove
122. Vehicle brand since 1900
123. Time zone for Trenton (abbr.)
124. Amble
125. Too quick to judge

DOWN

1. Truck sold by 122-A
2. Landed (on)
3. Western New Mexico Native
4. Further on, in years
5. Made a joint, like a carpenter
6. Like a doomsday prediction
7. Ungainly
8. Hieroglyphs female figure
9. Ottawa NHLer
10. Got anagram
11. Be part of a film
12. Russian author Ivan
13. Former Israeli prime minister
14. Prepare for inurnment
15. That fellow's
16. Newt
17. Labatt 50, for example
18. Each
24. Suit jacket component
26. Quebecer Favreau who portrayed Sol the clown
28. "Frankly, my dear, I don't give a _____"
30. Paroxysm
31. **Creepy, to the cardiologist?**
33. Cajun soups
34. **Uncanny, to the pulmonologist?**
35. Anoint, archaically
36. Microbes
37. Optic membrane
38. Martini fruits
39. **Odd, to the orthopaedist?**
41. Lithe
43. _____ hygiene
45. Xeric
47. Sliding glass _____
51. Flame to an Oiler, say
53. Long list of complaints
56. 1980s CBC show: *The Kids of Degrassi _____*
57. It's sometimes for two?
59. Music group: The Four _____
61. Suspect's test, for short
63. Brier trimmer's zingers?

67. Bird that doesn't fly
69. Rose family bramble
71. Perfect place to live?
72. Monthly, old style
74. South or North state
76. California's Catalina
77. You carry these in cafeterias
78. Former currency in Italy
79. Exhibited
80. Baby's food consistency
81. Question from Juliet: "_____ thou love me?"

83. 16-season Toronto Maple Leaf Ron
87. National Ballet of Canada dancers' leggings
89. Destroy
91. Fertilizer chemical
93. Royal platform
95. Snake with a hood
97. It comes before "-do-well"
103. 19th.-C. Canadian painter Eaton
104. Secluded nest on a cliff
105. Seed shell, in science

107. Get rid of the weight
108. Actress Zadora, et al.
109. Laurier and Macdonald, for example
110. State of pique
111. Slight degree of difference
112. ETs fly in this
113. Put down grass
114. Part of a gear
115. Deli counter purchase
116. Hubbub
117. Canadian children's author–illustrator Marie-Louise

60 Canada Cornucopia 30

ACROSS

1. Gossipy newspapers
5. 701, in Roman numerals
9. Québec town
13. Erudite Clue character?
17. Canada to the US, politically
18. Edmonton Homebuilt Aircraft Association (abbr.)
19. Ragged Ass, in Yellowknife
20. Yorkshire river
21. Former Québec premier (with 46-D)
22. Leon's sell this
24. Like some Tim Hortons coffee servings
25. US oil giant
26. MPs, say
27. Derived sustenance from
28. One of Columbus' ships
29. Canadian humorist Leacock
31. Former Governor General of Canada LeBlanc
32. Hamilton's Dofasco produces this
33. Bullring worker
35. Babes in the woods, say
37. Middle Eastern important personage
40. Order of Canada military man MacKenzie
42. Fish type
43. Welcome break from the federal government
45. Goal-orientated
47. Military units
51. Loaf type
52. Long Yiddish stories?
55. One of Canada's territories
56. Zing
58. We breathe it
59. "Caught you!"
61. Tropical tuber
62. Prepare for an event
64. They bid on contract work
69. Tu, en anglais
70. Organized method
72. Expansive accommodations at the Royal York
73. Most ashy, in appearance
75. Mound
77. Be environmentally conscientious
79. Feet, in zoology
80. Trade blockades
84. Firenze nation
86. Shoppers Drug stores
87. They contain irises
89. What a Batman character did?
93. Gator's relation
94. Mixes batter
95. Rachel Carson wrote about this pesticide
96. Dry sherry
97. JavaScript inventor Brendan
98. Go-go dancer's attire
100. Glowing critique
101. 1960s Hollywood starlet Sommer
102. Fairy tale first word
103. Teens' hero
104. Greek love god
105. Ferret out the details
106. Turns a horse to the right
107. Sulk
108. Revise a script

DOWN

1. Some Indian royalty
2. Watchful Nunavut community?
3. It precedes Bay in Cape Breton
4. Like a comprehensive overview
5. Rule breaker
6. Railway link between England and France
7. Hyundais and Hondas
8. "Painted Ladies" singer Thomas
9. Shrub with greyish foliage
10. Amp up the volume
11. Abandons on an island
12. Red Sea port for a Dane to visit?
13. Indicated
14. Bloc Québécois founder Bouchard
15. News readers' online forum
16. Canada won 22 of these at the Rio Olympics
23. Income From Operations (abbr.)
30. Inanity
31. Wheel on a spur
32. Terrifying
34. Begins receiving CPP
36. Mo. of Canada's 2008 federal election
37. This can cause high blood pressure
38. Wickenheiser of women's hockey fame
39. Priests' approved absences
41. Unwell
44. Sri Lankan export
46. See 21-A
48. Authorized
49. Full of holes (var.)
50. Pigs' noses
53. "Scram!"
54. Pronoun for an ocean liner
57. Short-tailed songbirds
60. German–French sculptor Jean
63. Looks at lords?
65. Bedrooms for babies
66. It's sometimes cast?
67. Petite French cases
68. Full of flavour
71. Cosmo or GQ

126

74. Like Petro-Canada gas
76. Quintessentially Canadian grub
78. Remedy for otitis externa
80. *Canada's Walk of Fame Tribute Show* hosts
81. *Taxi* actress Henner

82. Ontario-born NHLer McGinn, et al.
83. Show emotion
85. Canadian Rich who made a big impression?
88. Nincompoop

90. River that flows south through 55-A
91. Coda, in an old poem
92. Second-person verb, old style
94. Big Smoke miasma
95. English "Thank You" songstress
99. 1993 prime minister Campbell

61 Canadian Christmas Singalong

Match the song with the person

ACROSS

1. Painful contraction
6. Seal a crack (var.)
10. Virgo's brightest star
15. Deeply engrossed
19. 1972 War hit: "The _____ Kid"
20. Curvy architectural moulding
21. Canadian decor retailer: _____ Barn
22. Arabic ruler
23. Canadian pianist Peterson
24. Like permed hair
25. CBC show from 2009–11: _____ *Erica*
26. Burrard Inlet span: Lions _____ Bridge
27. **Favourite of labour leader Bob?**
30. Parasites
32. James Clavell novel: _____-*Pan*
33. Unexpressive
34. Sustenance
35. Trade (var.)
39. US prescription drug overseer (abbr.)
41. In trouble at a Leafs game?
43. **Classic for Charmion, Clancy and William Lyon Mackenzie?**
46. "Put a _____ in it!"
47. Like actress Tina?
50. Play by the rules
51. Anger, in Athlone?
52. She often gets flowers in May
53. Omit an "a," say
55. *Dateline* network
56. Dirty trick
59. Two-masted vessels
62. Often
63. Rolled oats cereal
64. Loblaws generic brand: No _____
65. **Holiday song for swimmer Cindy?**
71. Fiery or milky gemstone
72. Sounding catty?
73. Important historical times
74. Cause
76. Gusset
78. Dog food brand: _____ Kan
81. "_____ You Glad You're You"
82. Pen name?
83. South American blackbird
84. Hot dish for a cold day?
86. "It _____ to Be You"
87. Influenza symptom
89. **Ditty for goalie Glenn and emcee Monty?**
93. So that
95. Gender
96. Bean rich in protein (var.)
97. Shark's stick?
100. Blood collection containers
102. Help out
104. Dental clinic instrument
105. **Carol for Nova Scotia singer Cole (with "The")**
111. African ethnic group
112. Gut bit
114. Groom a goatee
115. Sleep _____
116. Some Labatt brews
117. Student in *une école*
118. Lighten a burden
119. Metric volume measurement (var.)
120. Sagacious
121. Did some bathroom DIY
122. Tibia locale
123. Disrespect

DOWN

1. Barge for garbage
2. "Poppycock!"
3. Sacs for spores
4. "Get lost!"
5. *Inside Edition* correspondent Jim
6. A rancher's boots might be made of this?
7. Lab gel
8. Popular blue jeans
9. Pipeline that runs from Alberta to the Gulf Coast
10. Yields
11. Speak from the pulpit
12. Everglades avian
13. Container for Molson's Old Style Pilsner
14. Like a cherubic cherub?
15. Junta, for example
16. Flabbergast
17. Spike used by rock climbers
18. Trick-or-_____
28. Long-time CBC Radio show: *The Vinyl* _____
29. Chinese secret society
31. Striker who's on the fence?
34. Deviations
35. Alberta place: _____ Hills
36. *Dragnet* actor Jack
37. Of hearing
38. U of M degree option
40. Like
42. Weather map line
44. Answer
45. Be bothersome
47. Last exam of the semester?
48. Cause of swelling
49. Okay answers?
52. Girl Guides of Canada cookie flavour
54. They cover some floors
57. Kitchens and dens
58. Euphemism for "unemployed"
59. Salty liquid
60. Dinged a doorbell
61. Shell's interior
62. 1950s *Maclean's* editor Ralph
63. Dressage ring pace

65. "Jack Was Every Inch a Sailor" is loosely based on him
66. *Place des Arts* company: _____ de Montréal
67. Helped a lady into her corset
68. Like some polkas?
69. Tremble in the wind
70. Submarine's "door"
75. Important position for a golfer?
76. Squid squirt this
77. Parasite eggs
78. Drug bust amount, often
79. US to Canada, for example

80. NL-born Giller nominee Moore
83. Ministers' helpers
85. Owns
88. Classic Canadian cooking show: *The Galloping* _____
89. Looked for oil
90. And others, to Augustus
91. Male managers?
92. QEW off-ramp, say
93. Treat badly
94. Come about over time
97. See 2-D
98. Circular windows

99. Pop duo: Hall & _____
101. HGTV Canada design star Richardson
103. Lentils, peas and beans (var.)
105. Cad
106. Like conditional court decrees
107. Vast
108. Burst _____ tears
109. Turn off course
110. Knitter's story?
113. Roman-style 151

ACROSS

1. Impale
5. Chicken _____ king
8. 1998 Paul Brandt single
12. Roots or RONA
17. 2010 Grammy-winning Beyoncé song
18. Brandon-born ex-NHLer Hextall
19. In 1851, this charitable org. launched in Canada
20. Marvelled out loud
21. Yoked pair
22. South American birds
24. Rope
25. As dull as _____
27. Subtracted by
29. Sinclair Ross short story: "The Lamp at _____"
30. Granola bar bit
31. Canadian Triple Crown event
33. Actresses Thompson and Michele
35. Hindu mystic
38. Travelled by Red Arrow
39. 1989 Rush single: "Show Don't _____"
40. _____ Hortons
43. Sit at Rogers Centre?
46. Like Marilyn's dress in *The Seven Year Itch*
48. Came anagram
49. Lengthy letters
51. Gravitational path
52. Plaything
53. Bathtime powder
54. Plumber's Windsor Castle fix?
56. Spanakopita ingredient
57. Spanish hero: El _____
58. Metallic fabric
59. Québec is our largest producer of this
63. Hoodwink

64. Electrical current unit
67. Like 22-A
68. Corrects before a press run
70. Sorrowful interjection
71. Airbnb offering
73. Rudolph Valentino, et al.
75. 2004 Nelly Furtado hit
76. Pant
78. Hebrew prophet
79. Refine
80. Rope fibre
81. European range
82. International Literary Institute (abbr.)
83. Vancouver or Victoria
86. Saskatchewan's 14th premier Wall
88. The Church of Jesus Christ of _____ Saints
93. Bassoons' kin
95. Canadian golf greats Gary Cowan and Marlene Streit
97. Sere anagram
98. Anne Shirley's bosom friend
99. Approaching, old style
100. "Yo ho ho" libation
101. Wading bird
102. Northern African antelope
103. Reform Party's first MP Deb
104. Cut of beef, in Scotland
105. _____ meet

DOWN

1. Clad in footwear
2. *Cash Cab* vehicle
3. Hemsky who's played for the Habs, Sens and Oilers
4. Québec Winter Carnival mascot
5. Buddhist who attains nirvana
6. Purloined goods
7. Exercise type
8. Pearson International Airport code

9. Former archbishop of Montréal: Paul-_____ Léger
10. A dermatologist might treat this
11. Bother
12. Support Our Troops (abbr.)
13. 2015 MacLean book: *Hockey _____*
14. Indiana neighbour
15. Activity on HGTV Canada's *Worst to First*
16. Garden of _____
23. Does business on the TSX
26. Hurry up and _____
28. _____-discipline
32. Moving towards the middle
34. 2009 Anne Murray autobiography
35. Bat at a fly
36. Texas city
37. Soldiers' employer
38. Sports broadcast second looks
39. *The Harder _____ Fall*
40. *Life of Pi* actress
41. "How Sweet _____"
42. Legendary tale
44. Preliminary track and field races
45. Dolt's divot?
47. Heraldic border on a shield
50. Proposes a toast
53. _____ Mutant Ninja Turtles
55. Expire, like a membership
56. Clef symbol
57. About one-third of annual visitors to this country are Canadian
59. BC and AB retailer: Value Drug _____
60. State with conviction
61. Like the scent of a Christmas tree lot (var.)
62. Keister or can
63. Their bones are displayed at Alberta's Royal Tyrrell Museum

64. Sunburn gel
65. West Edmonton _____
66. Hardly audible attention-getter
69. Golf ball depression
70. They might be secret
72. Souvlaki meat
74. Somerset river
77. "I _____ from the bed to see what was the matter"

80. Serengeti scavenger
81. "Time is money," for example
82. Lesley Gore hit: "_____ Party"
83. Ending of a musical piece
84. Essay writer's footnote abbr.
85. Natterjack
87. Arab world dignitary
89. "The _____ North strong and free"

90. No-win situation for the artist?
91. 1982 "Heat of the Moment" supergroup
92. Kennel cry
94. Instrument for Cdn. jazz musician Kelly Jefferson
96. Your, of yore

Either/Or

Movies or songs

ACROSS

1. Scientists' dogs?
5. Play divisions
9. Security deposits
14. Had the nerve to
19. Came to rest
20. Food for the sty
21. Medical clinic employee
22. Edmonton's Rogers Place
23. Australasian palm
24. Small marsh bird
25. **Roy Orbison hit or Julia Roberts movie**
27. **Song by The Seekers or Lynn Redgrave film**
30. Astonishment
31. At the scene
32. Earned anagram
33. Smoked delicacy
35. Big egg layer
37. Margaret and Pierre, say
38. Take a whiff
41. High water indicator
45. Catch red-handed
48. Monetary unit in Nigeria
50. Copperhead or rattlesnake
51. On the Adriatic?
56. Tool for a logger
57. Arranged for a train trip?
59. Unruffled
60. Went to dreamland
62. Some eye drops do this
63. Clark Gable spouse Carole
64. Mister, in Munich
65. Canadian Navy rank: Able _____
67. Adorns with leaves
68. **Céline Dion duet or Disney animated offering**
72. Pauses, in poetry
74. Front-end _____
75. "Arrivederci"
78. Provides a favour
79. Inured
81. Old-style verses
82. Metal worker
83. Money moguls
86. Third-person pronoun
87. More crafty
88. Like some gloves
89. 1960s Canadian sprinting star Jerome
90. Norse god of strife
91. Screenwriter's initial output
94. Architectural blueprint details
96. Make a purchase at Mark's
100. Tailor a pair of pants
101. Flock female
103. Sandbanks
107. Puffy clouds
109. Boater's blade
112. **Joan Jett staple or Michael J. Fox movie**
115. **Don McLean hit or 1999 teen comedy**
118. Senator's score?
119. Undecided
120. Moons, in Montréal
121. Nettle
122. Press ballyhoo
123. Consequently
124. RBC Global _____ Management
125. Newfoundlander Michael who won the Cup with the Bruins
126. Soviet-era news agency
127. Require

DOWN

1. *The Ghost & Mrs. Muir* star Hope
2. Extraterrestrial being
3. Two-legged stand
4. Takes a good, hard look
5. Language in old Mesopotamia
6. Sink blockage
7. Author/actress Spelling
8. Extra tire
9. National economic measurement (abbr.)
10. Angel's glow
11. Sprouted up
12. Well-respected
13. Game, _____, match
14. Early morning moment
15. ". . . the roof there _____ such a clatter"
16. Music producers do this in a studio
17. Related through one's mother
18. Aalborg residents
26. 2007 Tegan and Sara track: "Burn _____ Life Down"
28. Coastal islands bird
29. *Frozen* song: "_____ It Go"
34. **Paul McCartney theme song or Bond franchise film**
36. Disfigure
39. Dried or fresh fruit type
40. Restaurant chain in Canada: TGI _____
42. Gossip or grime
43. Tool for a duel
44. Evergreen shrub
45. Mansbridge's predecessor
46. Automobile shaft
47. Molson muscle
49. True inner self
52. Spicy sauce
53. Most absent-minded
54. Ireland's alternate name
55. Tallies up
58. Panache
59. Gondolier, for one
61. Rule the roost, say
63. Brain segment
65. Less unreliable
66. YVR postings, for short
67. Indiana Jones' haberdashery items

69. Plumbing snakes
70. _____ list
71. Come out of one's shell?
72. Holsteins and Herefords
73. *Maclean's* contributor Allen
76. Pasty in the face
77. Criminal court: _____ and terminer
79. Bone in the arm
80. Legal petitioner
81. Classic Hitchcock film
83. Seamstresses' pocket change?
84. Dadaist sculptor Jean
85. Bridge supports

88. Canadian *Bubblegum Delicious* poet Dennis
92. Forward, in fashion
93. Archibald Belaney's fraudulent First Nations name: Grey _____
95. Cushion a blow
96. Milan performance place: La _____
97. Organic soil component
98. Signs of things to come
99. Blender button word
102. Canada won gold in this 2008 Olympics event: Men's _____
104. Love

105. Like Great Bear Lake?
106. Meeting of ecclesiastical minds
108. W Network offering: *Love It or _____ It Vancouver*
110. Acted like an orangutan?
111. Bank of the Gatineau
113. Most represented artist at the Prado
114. Hockey Hall of Fame inductee Day, et al.
116. Important mo. on the CRA calendar
117. Always, in olden verse

ACROSS

1. Five-pin bowling frame score
6. Canadian who won cycling gold at the Athens Olympics: _____-Ann Muenzer
10. Ball belles
14. Hermey, in *Rudolph the Red-nosed Reindeer*
17. Fire extinguishing gas
18. 2001 Cowboy Junkies album
19. Canadian ex-NHLer Mike Bossy was one for 10 years
21. Monastery head
22. "_____ said"
23. Window cleaning gizmo
24. Goopy substance
25. Joyfulness
26. Billiards stick
27. Canada _____ Foundation
28. Stereo system receivers
30. Slip up
31. Vision
33. Libidinous love
36. Unhealthy atmospheres
40. Female relative
41. It's sung in church
43. Princeton-to-Kelowna direction (abbr.)
44. Cleopatra's snakes
48. Golfer's wear?
49. Rapidly alternate notes, in music
50. Canadian children's author Mélanie
51. Swindled
53. Musculoskeletal disorders network: Bone and _____ Canada
54. Suggest
55. Complained about the fish?
56. Fathoms measurement
57. Torrential rain storm
58. Town west of Edmonton
59. Adorable one
60. Release from Stony Mountain Institution
61. Christian _____
62. Former Canadian senate speaker Kinsella, et al.
63. Adriatic Sea country (abbr.)
64. Marshes
65. Dusk, in poetry of old
66. He's been visiting a Bracebridge village since 1955
67. Take in information
69. Severe
71. Ontario body of water
77. Orange road safety device
79. Deg. from 59-D
80. Curly, Larry or Moe
81. It accompanies ready and willing
84. To and _____
85. Wagers, at Woodbine
87. Soft palate part
88. Agree with
90. Salve from a plant
91. Uses a sieve
92. Stringed instrument
93. To laugh, in Lévis
94. Razzle-dazzle
95. Point on a Québec compass
96. Alberta place: _____ Man's Flats AB
97. Character from *The Legend of Zelda: Breath of the Wild*
98. Judges

DOWN

1. California volcano
2. Toronto Hospital For Sick Children invention in 1930
3. Pigment deficient
4. Tenant who has lots of space?
5. Barge in
6. It's on the shore of Lake Erie: _____ Point Biosphere Reserve
7. Sumptuousness
8. Flames game official
9. Uses deductive reasoning
10. Vertebrae parts
11. Canada's Pacific coast naval base
12. Warm-water fish in Ontario
13. Society of Automotive Engineers (abbr.)
14. Somerset Maugham novel: *The Razor's* _____
15. Canadian singer Aaron, et al.
16. Worry
20. Colourful salamanders
29. Put on haz-mat gear: _____ up
32. Black Forest _____
34. Ovum
35. Playful pixie
37. Use a ruler
38. Immunity-building enzyme
39. Parlour pieces
42. Trig abbr.
44. Consented
45. More protected from the sun
46. _____ *non grata*
47. Quality of taste
49. African grasslands antelopes
50. *The Fault in Our Stars* star Nat
52. Nine–eleven connector
53. Issue after some Air Canada flights
54. _____ Food Association of Canada
56. Bryan Adams sang one with Barbra Streisand in 1996
57. Detritus
59. Montréal post-secondary institution
60. Insult, in Ipswich
62. Manicurist's tool
63. Lawn maintenance machines
66. Piglets' place

67. Garden bloomer
68. Ill-_____
70. Use Canadian Tire money?
72. Leave on a journey
73. Neophyte
74. Knobby fabric

75. Shining, to Robert W. Service
76. Bakery leavening agents
78. Interminably
81. Pinnacle
82. Feathery scarves

83. Canadian fantasy fiction novelist: Charles de _____
86. Catches a glimpse
89. Canada placed a moratorium on fishing for this in 1992

Canadian in the City

Demonyms

ACROSS

1. This might sit on a parlour trolley
7. ET transports
11. Audio Visual Aids Department (abbr.)
15. A beard covers this
19. Cranky or contrary
20. Wander without a destination
21. Marquis de _____
22. Aesop fable contestant
23. **Gateway to the West resident**
25. Social slighter
26. Russian figure skaters Kulik or Klimkin
27. Paleo- opposite
28. Brain hemispheres
29. Shade of light silk
30. Nub
31. Yours, in Rimouski
33. Defensive ditch
34. Treating unjustly
36. Red Serge garment
38. Doctored drink for Mickey in Helsinki?
39. _____ *Andronicus*
40. Entrances for Jim Morrison?
43. **Nation's capital inhabitant**
45. Jewish calendar month
47. Female donkey
48. _____ Beta Kappa
49. Hole-in-one
50. Inner circle
51. With no difficulty at all
52. Cancels privileges, say
54. Had on
55. Exterminator's expletive?
57. Have the flu
58. Rugged mountain ridges
59. Lorgnette component
60. Briton
61. Story starter
62. TSX employees

64. Band's gig tunes
66. Chauffeur-driven vehicle
69. Cast your ballot
70. Saturday night outing
71. Faucet
75. Altar declaration
76. _____ and kin
77. Louise Penny's first mystery: *Still _____*
78. "Absolutely!"
79. 2009 Giller Prize-winning author MacIntyre
81. It precedes Trail or Peninsula in Ontario
83. Singer DiFranco
84. Diamonds?
85. Carrying
86. Go-karts
88. **Queen City citizen**
90. Go off the beaten path
91. Canadian funny guys Mercer and Moranis
92. Pasture posse
94. Capone's foe
95. How winners might celebrate
97. Inst. that seeks 7-A
98. Québécois-style _____ soup
99. Crate board
101. Frenzy
102. Panacea plant?
104. Canada's Eugenie Bouchard, for example
107. Angel's topper
108. Fail to mention
109. **Citizen in half of Kay-Doubleyah**
111. It follows Dutch or microwave
112. Fertilizer from a fen
113. Not bumpy
114. An American in Paris, perhaps?
115. Weedy vetch
116. Marine flier

117. As dry as a bone, say
118. Intuits

DOWN

1. Burg
2. One of the Great Lakes
3. Like explanatory text notes
4. State rep in DC
5. Long-time NHLers Lindros and Staal
6. Click on the keyboard
7. Prod
8. You might see one off Newfoundland's coast
9. Obvious
10. An evening in Italy?
11. Claimant
12. **Gastown urban dweller**
13. Decorates
14. Clean up computer code
15. Hélène's hairstyles?
16. **City of Trees inhabitant**
17. Anglo–Irish novelist Murdoch
18. Like a drink lacking ice
24. They're white in winter
32. Time for tea at the airport?
34. Untamed author Oscar?
35. Aides' concepts?
36. Dried coconut meat
37. 1990 Céline song: "(If There Was) Any _____ Way"
38. Act that preserves your image
39. Former Russian rulers
41. Archaeologist's find
42. Canadian magazine: _____ *at Home*
44. Rouser
46. Hansen and Fox, to many Canadians
47. Kicked off the airplane?
53. 20-year House of Commons Conservative Jelinek

54. Sandra Bullock movie: *While You _____ Sleeping*
56. Knee ligament (abbr.)
59. **Windy City resident**
60. 1970s NHL star Mahovlich
61. It manufactures escalators and elevators
63. _____-com
64. Canadian-born *60 Minutes* correspondent Morley
65. Oak offshoot?
66. Airs
67. Dolt
68. **City of Saints local**

70. Cuts into cubes
72. Residential rodents
73. Pacific coast predators
74. They're younger than adults
76. Nairobi nation
77. Blessed by good fortune
78. He's great at horseshoes?
80. Sound heard through a handset
82. Swiss dish
87. Structure at a bus stop
89. Tchaikovsky composition: *Symphony No. 5 _____ minor*
91. Fruit squeezing device
93. Flammable gas

96. Metaphor, i.e.
97. Great _____ Lake
98. Puff of smoke
99. Canada's Schwartz wrote this Benatar cover: "Hit Me With Your Best _____"
100. Volcanic flow
102. Bedazzles
103. Some Molson products
105. Highly unusual
106. Singles
110. Chardonnay, in Chicoutimi

ACROSS

1. Fettuccine or fusilli
6. Tree trunk
10. Tactical Response Team (abbr.)
13. The government ceased sales of these in Nov. 2017 (abbr.)
17. Garnish for a burger
18. Alternative to DOS
19. Strike down with an axe
20. Geisha's obi purse
21. Most wicked
23. Bob Ballard, when he found *Titanic*
25. Hair wisps
26. Troops' training
28. Temporarily gave to
29. Welland-born NHLer Clutterbuck
30. *Star Trek: Deep Space Nine* character
31. See 3-D
32. *The Taming of the _____*
35. Muslim rulers' decrees
38. Underwater craft, for short
40. Genoa goodbye
41. En masse
43. Growls
47. NL skater Kaetlyn who won 2018 World Championship gold
49. Long-time Winnipeg NDP MP Martin
50. Victoria Day month, in Val-d'Or
52. Canadian Cory Monteith starred on this Fox series
53. Liquid medicine dose (abbr.)
54. Gives in
57. Remove a hairpiece?
59. Rhododendron kin
60. Like a crude gardener?
62. Home of BC's Harbour Publishing: _____ Park

65. Nickel Belt city
67. Friend
70. *Lawrence of Arabia* actor Sharif
71. Garnier hair product
73. Essence of a matter
74. Fossilize
76. Former Canadian corporation: Sun _____
78. Ancient nomadic Arabs
81. Fictional protagonist
82. Gnome's kin
84. Night flight from Vancouver to Montréal, say
85. Wears
86. RBC foyer machine
89. Little green veggie
91. _____'easter
92. Baby's early syllables
94. Alberta Royal Tyrrell Museum town
97. 2017 biography: *Reckless _____: A Portrait of Joni Mitchell*
101. Like a Match.com user
102. Eliminate a threat
104. Sitcom starring Canada's Michael J. Fox: *Family _____*
105. Federation of _____ Societies of Canada
106. 2014 Nickelback single: "_____ of a Revolution"
107. Saltpetre
108. Cutlass or Delta 88, for short
109. Den anagram
110. Sleep in cheap lodgings
111. Chewing tobacco brand since 1934

DOWN

1. Be huffy
2. *Interview with the Vampire* writer Rice
3. Cancer, for example
4. "Bye-bye!"

5. Host of 29-D Younghusband
6. Like some cabinetry
7. Loonies, say
8. Road in Cape Breton: Fleur-de-_____ Trail
9. Return an accused to another country
10. Ten Commandments pronoun
11. Odd-numbered page
12. Fabrics for some jackets
13. Canadian Indigenous Nurses Association (abbr.)
14. Tangle
15. Ontario hikers' route (with 87-D)
16. Bantu speaker
22. Vietnam Veterans Memorial designer Maya
24. Love, in Lachine
27. Chiapas cheers
29. Discovery show: _____ *Worst Driver*
32. William Wallace, for one
33. Snake's warning sound
34. Turnpike turnoff
36. New Delhi money
37. Kyrgyzstan currency
39. One over par, for Ontario's Brooke Henderson
41. Driver's licence, for example
42. Island in Micronesia
44. American Lung Association (abbr.)
45. Press on the gas pedal
46. Get a look at
48. German character on 85-D
51. Short beginnings?
55. Muhammad Ali's pottery materials?
56. Lothario
58. _____ and wherefores
59. Eagles' roost

61. Mission BC monks' community: Westminster _____

62. 1990s CBC show: _____ *PI*

63. Soul, in Saguenay

64. Pierre, to Justin and Sacha

66. Plain

67. Pizzeria products

68. Bushy hairstyle

69. William _____ Mackenzie King

72. Corn cob

75. Lamb kebab

77. _____ male

79. Former Québec premier Lévesque

80. Nullifies

83. Weak

85. Bob Crane sitcom: _____ *Heroes*

86. Increase

87. See 15-D

88. Silenced sound

90. Long-time *Maclean's* columnist Fotheringham

93. 1981 Peter Gzowski book: *The Game of _____ Lives*

95. Shoddy situation

96. Ribald

97. Udders

98. Long-time leader of Yugoslavia

99. Old Testament book

100. Old cinematic spool

103. Nigerian state

67 Beware the Ides of March

Find the letter pattern

ACROSS

1. Like a pixie
7. Long-time CBC entertainer Messer
10. Laundry appliances
17. 1984–90 Stornoway resident John
18. Pre-holiday nights
20. Like bile, say
21. **Actors' parenthetical comments**
22. Indigenous Brazilians
23. Sort and list
24. Preceded
25. _____ power
26. Secured with links?
27. States of rage
28. Twofold
29. Cut off, like locks
30. Objective of the Borg
33. Provincial capital named for a queen
37. Make fizzy
38. Oared
40. Greek letters
41. Landscapers lay this
44. 2014 Tom Cruise film: _____ of Tomorrow
45. Fatigued
46. Village, in Afrikaans
47. Nimoy or Shatner fan, say
49. Burrito bean
50. Rocky Mountains landmark: Kicking _____ Pass
51. Vilify
52. **Mopeds and motorcycles**
53. More doting
54. Terrible torment
55. Canadian media entrepreneur Znaimer
56. Tops
57. Fortune
58. Amazing stunts
59. Shakespeare was this of Avon
60. *The Catcher in the* _____
61. Toronto-to-Peterborough dir.
62. Urban dwelling, for short
63. Long-time London school for boys
65. Someone who sleeps around?
67. Incapable of reforming
72. Military academy frosh
74. Nocturnal primate
75. Tor
76. Brimming
79. Artists' unclad subjects
80. Cellphone message sound
81. Wall tapestries
82. Jannings who won the first acting Oscar
83. **Girl _____ of Canada**
84. Lethbridge Viaduct, for example
85. Fencer's weapon
86. Certify to be true
87. Paving substance
88. Suffield AB airport code
89. They carry burdens?

DOWN

1. Bologna homeland
2. They think things over
3. **Groups of lions**
4. Spore membranes
5. Leak
6. A day has 24 of these (abbr.)
7. Blow up
8. Release eggs
9. Language spoken in Kathmandu
10. Hit from BC's Poppy Family: "_____ Way You Goin' Billy?"
11. Wrote a book
12. Blackened someone's name
13. _____ pigeon
14. Julia Roberts role: _____ Brockovich
15. Completely destroy
16. Children's winter toy
19. _____ Robert Borden
25. Fodder source on the farm
28. One under par at Glen Abbey
29. Nasal noises
31. Without much gumption
32. Expresses one's thoughts
34. "Set thine house _____"
35. Place to purchase plants
36. Malign
39. Ontario-born Hockey Hall of Famer Boivin
41. Attacked from the air
42. Spice rack spice
43. Dedicates oneself, say
45. **The Bay of Fundy has the highest of these in the world**
46. 2005 Shania Twain song
48. Cattle, in days of yore
49. Engine component
50. Frank's spicy frank?
52. Band's rigger
53. 1986 comedy: _____ *Bueller's Day Off*
55. Cape Breton singers: _____ of the Deeps
56. Early *Front Page Challenge* personality Alex
58. Predict
59. Raced quickly, at a Rhode Island rodeo?
62. Keyboard created in 1886
63. Thugs' sweatshirts?
64. Largest city in Kansas
66. Soak the people at poolside
68. Like divots
69. **They walk down aisles**
70. Most hobbled
71. Discharges
73. Plagued by
76. It precedes "tat-tat"
77. Screws up

78. Get ready, for short
79. Born as (Fr.)

80. Precious
83. Chat

ACROSS

1. Hadfield who wrote *An Astronaut's Guide to Life on Earth*
6. US political campaign grps.
10. Capricorn animal
14. "Disgusting!" interjection
17. _____ of Commons
18. American civil rights org. since 1920
19. Canadian ergonomic products company: _____Forme
20. On the _____
21. Jubilee, in Edmonton or Calgary
23. Slow running pace
24. Have a brief meal?
25. Foreshadowed
26. Where keynoters speak from (var.)
28. Al rival, in the CFL
29. Pioneering Canadian physician: _____ Johnson Macleod
31. Quit your job
33. Pasta type
38. Unveil a new product, say
42. Arm bones
43. 56-A is part of this: National Highway _____
45. "Parting is such sweet _____ . . ."
46. Some mood disorders
48. 2003 Martina McBride hit: "This _____ for the Girls"
50. 2012 Neil Young autobiography: *Waging Heavy* _____
51. Type of fatty acid
53. Petro-Canada pumps tell you this number
55. Banned orchard spray
56. Road that spans the nation
59. Feels nauseous
63. Relating to Virginia or Vermont
64. Fudge family confection
69. Meet and _____
71. Turkey roasting rod
72. Your sister's son, to you
73. Like a good-looking Victorian cab driver?
75. Rogue card sharps?
79. Longest river in France
80. Southern Spain autonomous region
82. Pressing needs (var.)
84. Contraction for "should not"
85. Estate entranceway
86. Newfoundland place: _____ Bonavista
89. South African semi-desert region
91. Hamilton university
97. G8 ally of Canada
98. Sopranos' moments in the spotlight
99. Juxtaposed, in grammar
101. Adverb in a vintage verse
102. Analogous, like your aunt?
103. National _____ Board of Canada
104. *Cybill* co-star Pfeiffer
105. US terr. that split into two states
106. Old CBC Radio show: *The Happy* _____
107. Gets the gist
108. Go on a shopping spree

DOWN

1. Crack like skin in winter
2. Time increment
3. Impolite
4. Osiris' consort
5. _____ record
6. Mila and Brian, to Ben
7. This might cause you to take a TUMS
8. *The Virginian* actor Gulager
9. Waste water receptacle
10. Aristotelian precept
11. Woodwind section performer
12. Two nannies?
13. Former Canadian trading floor (abbr.)
14. CDA hockey rival
15. Guzzling sound
16. Syringe, for short
22. Arch style
27. Monopoly game avenue
28. *The Goods* host Bain
30. Badmouth
32. Slime
33. Totals
34. _____ du jour
35. Québec resort: Mont-Sainte-_____
36. Greek goddess
37. Céline Dion #1: "My _____ Will Go On"
39. Range or river in Russia
40. _____-Cola
41. Decorative jug
44. Baroque keyboard composition
47. Canadian doctors Macphail and Banting
49. Coat closer
52. CFL squad: Hamilton Tiger-_____
53. Repeated motif, in music
54. Canadian writer Robinson
57. Serviette holder
58. Anoint, old style
59. Ottoman Empire rank (var.)
60. Armenia neighbour
61. Extend credit
62. Ernie and Bert's street
65. 2010 Sarah McLachlan track: "Don't Give _____ Us"
66. Like fashion show models
67. "Is there an echo in _____?"

68. Meadow birthers
70. Perfume resin
74. Ontario cottage country area
76. Cuke or spud
77. Specimen
78. *Mr. D* and *Kim's Convenience*, on CBC
81. A Russian city was named for him in 1925

83. Aquamarines and emeralds
86. Signalled an actor
87. Out on the ocean?
88. Iconic Vancouver place: Stanley _____
90. Buffoons
92. Pitches in to help out
93. Aerobics movement
94. Laundry detergent brand

95. 1986 Luba song: "_____ in the Darkest Moments"
96. Mouthpiece for 11-D
98. Settle down?
100. 1974 Dennis Lee poetry collection: *Alligator* _____

69 Destination: Fredericton

Take a local tour

ACROSS

1. Canada's Coco Rocha, for one
6. Supports
10. Popular '70s hairdo
14. Singer Jordan's backtalk?
18. Unescorted
19. Rung kin
21. Young salmon
22. Sous-chef's undertaking
23. Actors Guinness and Baldwin
24. Water park feature
25. Bit of plankton
26. Slick
27. **19th-C. textile factory that's now a National Historic Site**
31. Dates
32. Chat (var.)
33. Père _____
34. Most insensible
37. See 26-A
40. Ropes in?
44. Coming or going
45. Large tree
46. Ceremonial bodyguard for the Queen
48. Prompt for a pool player?
49. Reward, old style
50. She, in Sherbrooke
52. US Plains Natives
53. Malice
55. Uneven?
56. Some central Europeans
58. Tirana nation (abbr.)
60. Conduct the orchestra
61. Sir Adam Beck, in Ontario
63. Most minute
66. Push over the edge of reason
68. Place of refuge
71. Collection for Canada's Milos Raonic?
72. Resistance unit, in physics
74. Only horse to win the Kentucky Derby and the Queen's Plate: Northern _____
75. Retailers' reimbursements
77. Beef or pork
80. Hudson River crossing: Tappen _____ Bridge
81. State firmly
82. You might get Molson on this
84. State of bliss
86. Large-leafed plant: Elephant _____
89. Juices
91. Beach treat: Salt water _____
94. Long-running game show: *What's My _____?*
95. Neck part
96. Car anagram
97. Breakfast cereal
99. Pot for Peter?
100. Stick used in Canada's official summer game
102. Iranian city
104. Metro Vancouver regional district city
106. Intimidated
107. Fluid for an etcher
109. Former Middle Eastern royal
110. Part of MIT
111. **19th-C. building that once housed a market and the judiciary**
119. Handout, in Hampshire
120. Folklore fiend
121. Grieve for
122. Kick out of school
123. Sword fight
124. Northern European capital
125. Lessened tension, say
126. Bar mitzvah and bat mitzvah
127. Calgary-born Murray who played for the Jets and Sens
128. Homophone of 114-D
129. Canvasback's colourful cousin
130. Emulate Oiler Connor McDavid

DOWN

1. Palindrome for her?
2. Cantina cooker
3. Canada's former US ambassador Gary
4. Closed in a sac, biologically
5. Tenants
6. Helping hand, from Howe?
7. "_____ all come out in the wash"
8. **You might read this while you're there**
9. Pistol or revolver
10. Spouses' set-to
11. Suspend
12. Inert gas
13. See 97-A
14. Ruins
15. Seed sheath for a liar?
16. Divest stocks
17. Something to do with your little eye?
20. Short survey?
28. Ship
29. Sanctions
30. Intends
34. Short audition tape?
35. Matured
36. **Long-time city nickname**
38. Arabian or Aegean
39. Exercise for artist Francisco?
41. **Technology museum housed in a former jail**
42. Temporary loss of electricity
43. Farming machine
45. Stars on Ice star Stojko
47. Go down, in canasta
51. Auction grouping
52. Sugary suffix
54. Dash 8 or Twin Otter

Solution on page 224

56. Plant fungus
57. Breezy day toy
59. King or queen
62. Cause concern
64. *Brave New World* drug
65. **Performance venue**
67. Bulldoze a building
68. Turkey's highest peak
69. Extreme
70. Bumped into
73. Morning, in Châteauguay
76. Appease hunger
78. Xeric
79. Large barrel

83. BC/AB National Historic Site: Athabasca _____
85. Renounce one's beliefs
87. Church section
88. 1960s TV actress Donna
90. Coastal cutter
92. Seasonal illness
93. National organization: Assembly of _____ Nations
95. Safe, as opposed to poisonous
98. 1968 Irish Rovers hit: "The _____"
99. Sailor's garment
101. Tardy CFLers?
103. Hardly ever

105. Write like Canada's Dennis Lee
106. Frock for a fräulein
108. Calf without a mama
111. *Global National* photo segment: _____ Canada
112. Parkay product
113. Suggest strongly
114. Close to
115. Formaldehyde insulation type banned in Canada
116. "What have you been _____?"
117. Crystal ball gazer
118. Something _____ again
119. Old pesticide

ACROSS

1. Early Irish alphabet
6. Yellowknife Highway locale: _____ Lake Territorial Park
10. Juno and Grammy winner k.d.
14. U of T prof's deg.
17. New Zealand tree type
18. Cosmetic surgery procedure, for short
19. Instrument for Mitch Miller
20. US education grp. founded in 1857
21. Illicit activity instigator
23. Bearded
25. Word with an opposite meaning
26. Committee note takers
28. Facile La-Z-Boy furniture purchase?
30. Cost an _____ and a leg
31. Highlanders' headgear
35. Android viewing app
36. Shakespeare festival town in Ontario
40. Not fully round
42. Seer anagram
44. Let go the reins
45. Scandinavian country (abbr.)
46. Prominent Toronto neighbourhood
48. Newfoundland city: St. _____
50. Former *Le Devoir* editor-in-chief Bissonnette
51. Quill user's pot
52. Catlike African animal
53. Inclined to fix computers?
54. Pump up the volume
55. Two-_____
56. SK-born Shore wore this number as a 1930s Boston Bruin
57. Pelvic bones
60. Itemizes
61. Mechanical keyboard

65. Margaret Atwood creation
66. Pile of rock rubble
67. Heavy weights?
68. Motoring org. in AB
69. Thomas who opposed Henry VIII
70. Canadian Country Music Association award winner: Carolyn _____ Johnson
72. "The _____ Gretzky"
73. Toast topper
76. Georgian and James
78. Canadian *Jalna* author: Mazo _____ Roche
79. Set the dogs on
80. Bad bard?
83. In working order
86. Sea that connects to the Persian Gulf
91. Space Shuttle robotic equipment
92. Adaptable
94. 2014 Chris Hadfield book: *You _____ Here*
95. Skin cream additive
96. Lone anagram
97. Pens for swine
98. Groovy digs
99. Make repairs
100. Snugs
101. T-bill or bond

DOWN

1. Gumbo cook's ingredient
2. Bear market success
3. Tom Clancy's debut novel: *The _____ for Red October*
4. Redblack rival
5. A.A. who created Piglet and Pooh
6. Hydraulic bucket type
7. Secreted
8. Brief references, in Repentigny?

9. Jazzy songstress Jones
10. Like tenor and bass singers
11. Despicable
12. Black, in Bécancour
13. Develop in the womb
14. Relating to a lung illness
15. Frau's mate
16. Freddy Fender hit: "Wasted _____ and Wasted Nights"
22. Young hawk
24. Saw cut
27. Dads
29. Bygone times
31. Donut shapes
32. River in 36-A
33. 1994 Jim Carrey film: *The _____*
34. Long-time Canadian publisher: McClelland & _____
37. Canadian Tire promos
38. _____ Hashanah
39. Squirrel's home
41. Tissue swelling condition
43. Removed a cassette tape
47. Peak near Zermatt
49. Bills printed in the US, but not Canada
50. Montréal-born singer Cohen
52. Saguenay station
53. 1989 album by 10-A: *Absolute Torch and _____*
55. Destined for disaster
56. Cookie can
57. Unwanted email
58. American soprano Gluck
59. Roughed up?
60. Recyclable metal
61. Equestriennes' hairstyles?
62. Moulding with a double curve
63. *Dreamgirls* actress Sharon
64. Nick and Nora's dog, in the movies
66. Costa del _____

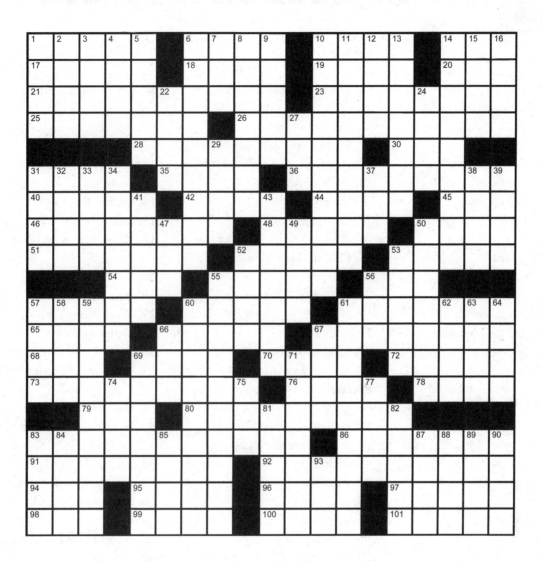

67. "_____ the night before
    Christmas . . . "
69. Road building material
71. Marine gastropod
74. Oscar winner Sorvino
75. Ending for eight

77. Medieval worker
81. Made a wild dog docile
82. Mrs. Gorbachev
83. Ontario Coalition of Aboriginal
    People (abbr.)
84. Yugoslavian monetary unit

85. Yarn
87. They sleep upside-down
88. Bird venerated in ancient Egypt
89. Out of the wind, nautically
90. 39-D, for example
93. Canadian humorist Harron

The Gods Must Be Crazy

Some mythology merriment

ACROSS

1. Repressive Soviet prison
6. Paint layer
10. CCCP, in English
14. 1970s show: *The _____ Squad*
17. Without any company
18. Rounded entryway
19. Reluctant (var.)
20. *Aladdin* song: "Prince _____"
21. **Government for an underworld god?**
23. Agile
24. Canadians Oleksiak and Wiebe won 2016 gold here
25. _____, drink and be merry
26. Waistline ruffle
27. River in Kamloops
29. Canada Post designation: Postal _____
30. Royal Electrical and Mechanical Engineers (abbr.)
32. South American country
33. Stonehenge, et al.
37. Arachnid or crustacean
41. Ticks
42. Edible Asian leaf
44. Breathe easily again
45. White-rumped songbird
47. Bulldozes, in Bath
49. NASCAR event
50. What you're doing now
51. Works hard
52. Threadlike
53. Card that can be low or high
54. Québec-born *Rookie Blue* actress Peregrym
55. "Runaround _____"
56. Sports stars Mikita and Musial
59. She discovered radium
60. Canadian C&W singer Wilf, et al.
64. Quaker product
65. 1980 Rush hit: "The Spirit of _____"
66. Birth city of 54-A
67. Globes
69. _____ a sour note
71. Phrixus' twin, in Greek mythology
72. Gilbert and Sullivan productions
74. Like an infected tooth
76. Henpecks
77. 2016 Kiefer Sutherland single: "Can't _____ Away"
79. Rocky crags
80. Like an ordinary prairie?
83. Smeltery scum
85. Austin Powers, for one
88. Untruth
89. Indigo dye source
90. **Wild party for an agriculture god?**
92. Australian bird
93. California region: _____ Valley
94. Large lake partially in Ontario
95. Metallic sound
96. Coquitlam River structure
97. Pre-revolutionary Russian monarch
98. _____ *of the D'Urbervilles*
99. Santa's assistants

DOWN

1. Stare in amazement
2. Yellow-fleshed potato type
3. Galoot
4. Minute insect
5. Study of international relations
6. Mary Poppins' tote
7. ____ rehydration therapy
8. From *The Two Gentlemen of Verona*: "O time most _____!"
9. Stew seasoning
10. Northern Ireland outdoor attire?
11. Second-year high-schooler, for short
12. Lyric poem sections
13. Poets, say
14. **Pet for a war god?**
15. Stewed meat dish
16. Edmonton-born NHLer Phaneuf
22. Ghanaian money
28. Business woman?
29. Silk Road-era inn
31. Listlessness
33. Supersized mouths
34. 1980 Juno-winning single: "_____ Beach"
35. Highlander, for example
36. Lazenby's only Bond film: *On _____ Majesty's Secret Service*
38. Very, in Ville-Marie
39. West Coast waters mammal
40. Burnaby landmark: _____ Lake Park
43. **Weight loss for a love god?**
46. Toronto-to-Oshawa dir.
48. Sneaky
51. Most bog-like
52. Advancement
54. Wet earth
55. _____ Diego
56. Garden variety, say
57. Long-time Canadian entertainer Gordie
58. **Reading room for a wise goddess?**
59. *CODCO* comic ensemble
60. Interprets
61. Long fish
62. Unhealthy breath
63. Canadian Challenge _____ Dog Race
65. Greek wines

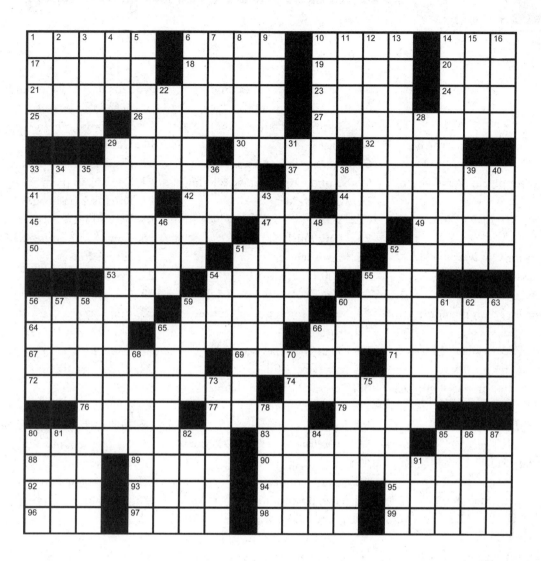

66. Mafia members running amok?
68. On the throne
70. Parent's morning drop-off location
73. Building facing stone
75. Coconut fibre

78. BMO GIC, for example
80. Implored
81. City in 32-A
82. Traditional Philippines game
84. "(Sittin' On) The Dock of the Bay" singer Redding

85. Czech, for example
86. Pass and river name in BC
87. Tibetan bovines
91. 2013 Michael Bublé song with Bryan Adams: "After _____"

ACROSS

1. It airs on HGTV Canada: _____ *Town*
5. Canada has one on its northern coast
10. Plumbing pipe material (abbr.)
13. Cookbook abbr.
17. Sudbury's Trebek of *Jeopardy!*
18. *Objets d'art*
19. Letters for Old MacDonald
20. Utah ski area
21. Highway 417 exit
22. It preceded flash memory
23. Garden trellis
25. Former Calgary Flame Fleury
26. Shape with four sides
27. 31st Québec premier (with 34-D)
28. Dining linens
31. _____ tide
32. First-lap leader at the Molson Indy
35. Early spring bloomer
37. Office of Labor-Management Standards (abbr.)
41. Cash in electronic form
42. "My Cherie _____"
43. Bend down
44. Borders on
45. Ocean Spray flavour: _____-Apple
46. American actor and TV presenter Michael
49. Country of 37-A
50. Ethnic group in India
51. Saskatchewan city: _____ Jaw
52. Jane's disaster?
54. Jesus raised him from the dead
56. Beach and Carlton, in Toronto
57. Detritus at BC's Highland Valley Copper mine
59. Herbs that yield dyes
60. Chicken _____

63. Org. for a US prosecutor
64. Offspring of Chaos
65. Colony insects
66. Hoist
67. *Growing Pains* actress Joanna
69. Second Cup beverage offering
71. Woodworker
72. 1930s Hollywood star Nelson
73. Daffy Duck, for one
75. Raisin type
76. 1960 Billboard #1: "_____ Angel"
78. Stony Mountain Institution "guest"
80. Quality of a permanent hairstyle?
84. Toronto _____ Exchange
85. *The Seven Year _____*
89. Related, chemically
90. Therefore
91. _____ Cup
92. Ceramic square
93. YHZ posting
94. First Nations leader
95. Group on a ranch
96. Berets and bowlers
97. Give a nickname
98. Canadian historian Gwynne, et al.
99. Noggin, in Nicolet

DOWN

1. Order of Canada ballerina Evelyn
2. 1994 Nobel Prize-winning chemist George
3. The same, in 48-D
4. Like some mathematical notations
5. Get gouged, perhaps
6. Coded communication
7. Computer message you don't want to see
8. Explosive measurement?

9. Shania's "Any Man of Mine" reached this chart spot
10. Nest noise
11. Hindu deity
12. Duplicates
13. Sri Lankan palm
14. Radar screen image
15. Baby's first one is big news
16. *Company's Coming* cookbooks author Jean
24. Hank Aaron's home state (abbr.)
29. Canada's Billy Bishop, et al.
30. Pittance
32. BC's Mount Robson, for example
33. Old-style pulpit
34. See 27-A
36. _____ ligament
38. This included Alberta and Saskatchewan land: _____ Purchase
39. Lion's share
40. Fix a feline
42. Libidinous awakenings?
43. Clothesline?
45. Welsh dog breed
47. South African currency units
48. Québec locale: Sept-_____
51. Supernatural life force
53. Mike Holmes catchphrase and book title
55. Swerves sharply
56. In a rueful way
57. Seize profits?
58. Book from SK author Braithwaite: *Never Sleep Three in _____*
59. Hudson Bay drainage basin, for example
61. k.d. lang soundtrack album: _____ *Cowgirls Get the Blues*
62. Wartime singer Lynn
66. _____-in-one

68. Big Apple paper
70. Snapchat, for example
71. Beat-up cars
73. Looked in a lecherous way
74. Undisturbed, to an archaeologist
75. Canada's Christine Sinclair excels at this
77. Expected Negative Exposure (abbr.)
79. Environmental probe
80. Autobiography by 25-A: *Playing _____ Fire*
81. Nepal's continent
82. Battery unit
83. Unpopular employee during a strike
86. Maple or magnolia
87. First Dick Francis novel: *Dead _____*
88. Jekyll's dark side

Solution on page 225

73 Island Life

... in British Columbia

ACROSS

1. Lamb serving
5. Brian Mulroney's spouse
9. Hydroelectric facility location
12. Food and Drug Administration (abbr.)
15. Rogers Arena game official, for short
18. Money you can spend in Sofia
19. Top-notch server?
20. In 2016, Canada won four Olympic golds here
21. Baleen whale type
23. Televangelist Roberts
24. Abominable snowman
25. Much bother about nothing?
26. Where a river meets the sea
27. **Dionisio Point Provincial Park island**
29. Driver, for example
32. L.M. Montgomery heroine
33. It doesn't hold water?
35. Like Oslo residents
36. Move unsteadily
38. Trap for speeders
41. Equitably meted
43. Ears anagram
45. Alums
46. Old interjection?
47. Conducive to peace
49. **Longest Strait of Georgia island**
51. Scribe, in Shawinigan
53. Carbon compound
55. Upper part of a glacier
56. University student's advanced deg.
59. Petite green veggie
60. Gritty fruit
63. Moan or groan
65. Involve, as a consequence
67. Robert who played the young Vito Corleone
69. Nastier
71. Belleville-born ex-NHLer Brett
72. Like far north regions
75. **Provincial capital island**
77. Hefty
78. "Praise the Lord!"
79. Mythological king of Pylos
80. Some written works
82. Caribbean music style
84. Old-style elixirs
86. Splinter group
87. Motion in the gym
90. Brian of Roxy Music fame
91. Not present or future
93. Cold-shoulder
95. Blacken someone's name
97. **Fraser River island at New Westminster**
99. Medium's mystical state
102. Distant
103. Common BC tree
106. Sorrels
108. Lady of the house, in Hamburg
109. Bloodhound's trail
110. Brownies might earn these?
112. 2007 Tegan and Sara track: "_____ Going In"
114. Like a small, precious gem?
116. *The _____ of the Rings*
117. Men who rub you the right way?
120. **Island with the East Point lighthouse**
124. Similar to a Cyclops
126. Sphere-shaped object
127. Toronto-born Corey of *The Lost Boys* fame
129. Faddy 1970s ring name
130. Incorrectly interpret text?
131. Title for 5-A
132. Bird that soars by the seashore
133. Sicilian volcano
134. Casino wager
135. Attempt
136. 1992 Bryan Adams song: "Do I Have to _____ the Words?"
137. Grasps your point of view
138. Judge

DOWN

1. Wooden shoe
2. Spouse of Zeus
3. University of Calgary ice sports facility: Olympic _____
4. Fortifying fence
5. **It separates 27-A from 120-A**
6. Freeze up?
7. Call from a tennis umpire
8. Ovule enclosure
9. He judged harshly, in ancient Greece
10. Helpers
11. Lunar descent
12. ". . . land glorious and _____"
13. Administered medication
14. The National Gallery of Canada highlights this
15. It became two African countries in 1962: _____-Urundi
16. Made a wage
17. Ads to attract WestJet pilots?
22. **Largest of the Discovery Islands**
28. It sometimes lacks quality?
30. Blue Jays game segment
31. Calm
34. *All About _____*
37. *M*A*S*H* actor: David _____ Stiers
38. Bring in crops
39. Tropical fever
40. *Star Trek: The Next Generation* android
42. It's opposite WSW
44. Lumberjack's tool

47. Curling _____
48. **Queen Charlotte Strait island**
50. State strongly
52. Computerphile
54. "In _____ of flowers"
56. See 44-D
57. Fleece
58. McBeal's confederate?
61. Seine bank
62. Upholsterers might get down to these?
64. Smooth over a road
66. Ergo
67. "Shoot!" synonym
68. "I'm _____ your tricks!"
70. Irish or Scottish language
72. Trim down

73. Indicator of potential future events
74. Danish building toy maker
76. Internet startups: Dot-_____
77. Digital info unit
79. Ebb's opposite number
81. Large vegetable patch, say
83. To the left, nautically
85. Wave rider
87. Widespread
88. Sparkle
89. Sassy
92. It precedes -pitch or -mo
94. Clef segment
96. Used the Hoover
97. **Gulf of Georgia island**
98. Kidnappers demand these
100. Catch a bad guy

101. Fine French food?
103. Poise
104. Canadian currency coin
105. Most desperate
107. African country: _____ Leone
109. Alky
111. See 95-A
113. Plump, in Poole
115. **Haro Strait island**
118. *The Full Monty* actor Mark
119. Cyndi Lauper album: _____ *So Unusual*
121. Memorization by repetition
122. Nil
123. Canadian C&W singer Gregory
125. Still
128. Often used verb

ACROSS

1. Wise guys
6. Crime boss
10. Eponymous physics resistance unit
13. Celebrated hockey star Messier
17. Robert Munsch book: *Andrew's* _____ *Tooth*
18. Cosmetics company founded in 1886
19. Nottawasaga, in Ontario
20. Fencing blade
21. Spousal family member
22. Eyesore at a CFB?
23. "_____! The Witch Is Dead!"
25. Jellyfish
27. Material world people?
29. Roman magistrates
31. 1998 Nickelback track: "Hold _____ Your Hand"
32. Mattress frameworks
37. Right-of-birth inheritance
41. Humpty Dumptyish
42. Get the _____ out of
44. *Scooby-Doo*, for short
45. Farm field
46. Spinal cord membranes
48. Make text corrections
50. Canadian comedian Mercer
51. Manitoba city newspaper: _____ *Sun*
52. Fence steps
53. Kisses from Gregory?
54. Harrison who painted Yukon scenes
55. Vancouver-born ex-NHLer Beck
56. Loo
57. Less polite
60. Caterpillar hairs
61. Pudding type
65. Old-style oath
66. Eminent
67. Port city on Lake Ontario
68. US furniture retailer with stores in three Canadian cities: West _____
69. Run away from lightning?
70. Crusty skin bit
72. Determined to do something
73. Federal government department: _____ and Oceans
76. Physical form of an element
78. Play by _____
79. Walked all over
81. Canadian Olivia Poole invented this baby bouncer
84. Kim Mitchell's group: Max _____
90. Connected series of rooms
91. Not yet final, in legalese
93. Pig in _____
94. Lose vitality
95. CTV *Your Morning* host Mulroney
96. Medical procedure
97. Microwaved, colloquially speaking
98. Cause of a red eye
99. Supersonic flyer, for short
100. Blood pigment
101. Bridesmaid offering from Canadian designer Alfred Sung

DOWN

1. Slight in build
2. Top-rated
3. Hayley Wickenheiser has four Olympic medals of this colour
4. Biblical grandson of Sarah
5. Works on a Singer
6. Some CBC employees
7. Road atlas abbr.
8. Hold title to
9. Get-go, say
10. In a stubborn manner
11. Potentially destructive pellet
12. Chatty bird
13. So-so spiritualist?
14. Like Peter or Paul, say
15. Tenant's expense
16. Beer barrels
24. Lower abdomen
26. Copy a primatologist?
28. Calgary venue for February 1988 competitions (abbr.)
30. Benedick's brouhahas?
32. Do poorly at the box office
33. *Camelot* song: "If _____ I Would Leave You"
34. *China Beach* star Delany
35. Cut corners
36. Like a sore spot?
38. Gemini-nominated sports announcer Black
39. Adam's apple locale
40. Talks to some animals?
43. Groups of four
47. 1966 Margaret Laurence novel: *A Jest of* _____
49. Mud
50. Harsh critic
52. Satisfy
53. Olden days Church of England foe
55. Progressive development
56. Canadian *Bloodletting and Miraculous Cures* writer Vincent
57. Place to find coral
58. Unattractive fruit?
59. Insect that bothers a lady in distress?
60. 1945 Governor General's Award fiction winner: *Two* _____
61. Chardonnay, for example
62. School bus driver on *The Simpsons*

63. Western Canada grocery store chain

64. Chrétien and Martin cabinet minister McLellan

66. Fin. neighbour

67. Winnipeg-born game show emcee Monty

69. Gemstone mined in some parts of Canada

71. Whimsical impulse

74. Rock salt

75. Source of maple syrup

77. Doe anagram

80. Good guy, in Yiddish (var.)

81. They attend Kiever Synagogue in Toronto

82. Attentive

83. Elbows

85. 84-A, for example

86. Bone _____

87. Puff on a reefer

88. Gets the most from

89. Some of 61-D are this

92. Long-time Toronto retailer: _____ the Record Man

Making a Splash

Jump into these movies

ACROSS

1. Some snakes
5. One-liner, for example
9. Yellowhammer State
16. Copy a tape
19. Central Alberta lake
20. Somewhat
21. Popular Dodge
22. YXE abbr.
23. **2009 Joseph Fiennes drama**
26. Nutritional std. info
27. Judicial writ type
28. Showed again, on TV
29. Nonsense
31. Apollo's twin sister
32. NBC morning program
33. Newfoundland fishing village: _____ River
35. Outlaws
37. "Roaring" era
40. Make certain
43. Saguenay streets
44. Disney dog
45. Change hair colour
46. Canadian charity founded in 1922: Easter _____
47. Buddhist temples
48. Canada is virtually free of this disease
49. She might read tea leaves
50. Secure, like a Blue Jay?
51. Talk wildly
52. Frilly ornamentation
54. Levin or Glass
55. Tree native to India
57. Hamilton island
61. Wrote a film
63. Three Musketeers' motto word, x2
64. Heart contractions
65. Disappear into _____
66. Highway markers

68. Eastern New Brunswick village founded in 1780: _____-Pelé
69. In a sleepy manner
71. Stuns
72. Dried out
73. 2007 Diana Krall "very best" track: "You _____ My Head"
76. Actor Coward, et al.
77. _____ *iacta est*
78. _____ Goldfinger
79. "Obviously!"
80. Rowed the boat ashore?
81. Canada signed this international agreement in 1947
82. Group within a group
83. Markets a product before it's released
85. The universe as a whole
87. Helped
88. Afro or shrub description
89. Inuit soapstone carver, for example
93. Synagogue theologian
95. *Royal Canadian Air* _____
96. Annoy
97. Like a slick Whitehorse street
98. **1972 "disaster" movie (with "*The*")**
102. Manitoba place: The _____
103. Like food left on one's plate
104. Fruit rind
105. English children's literature author Blyton
106. Canadian singer Anna, to Kate
107. Zealous nonconformist
108. Smidgens
109. Bobs the bait

DOWN

1. Old World lizard
2. Guess Who tune segment: "No _____ Tonight"

3. Manufacturing facility
4. It came before the calculator
5. Fragrant shrub
6. Dense, mentally
7. Young foxes
8. African country (abbr.)
9. Yields
10. Historical figure Secord, et al.
11. Set out neatly
12. Farm structure
13. Old Roman greeting
14. Expo 67 legacy until 1984: _____ and His World
15. Long-time Alouettes quarterback Calvillo
16. **2012 Halle Berry adventure movie**
17. Language of Pakistan
18. Canadian children's entertainers: Sharon & _____
24. They christen
25. Wears away
30. Not at home
32. Tighten up
33. **1996 Sandra Bullock romcom**
34. Plants a new crop of trees
36. Pregnant
37. Cough medicine ingredient
38. Needle part
39. Msg. on Sunday morning
40. Be of service to Stamkos?
41. Seek out
42. Southern Ontario tourists' destination: African Lion _____
44. Canadian country group: The _____ Brothers
47. **1995 Kevin Costner action film**
48. Common man
49. Type of wrestling in Tokyo
51. Logic
52. Silly structure?
53. Bits of food

55. Tussle
56. Keens
58. Stomach troubles
59. Sweetie
60. Facet
62. It can precede -European or -Chinese
64. Johannesburg area
66. Fairly warm
67. Scant
70. Understands
72. Sent in an entry

73. National economic indicator (abbr.)
74. *Days of _____ Lives*
75. **1989 sci-fi film from James Cameron**
77. German spa city
78. Texas capital city
80. He had a complex?
81. Former region in France
82. Reddish-brown horses
84. See 106-A
85. _____ *on the Orient Express*

86. Did woodwork
88. Hut in the Alps
90. Health club feature
91. Take _____ down memory lane
92. Requires
93. Pulls paper apart
94. Berry variety
95. Act of derring-do
96. It might be big?
99. _____-trick pony
100. US trading overseer (abbr.)
101. Suitable

76

Canada Cornucopia 38

ACROSS

1. Chess match ploy
7. Cause consternation
13. Binge at Hudson's Bay?
18. Ontario First Nation
19. Millhaven Institution "guest"
20. Abuser, on the Internet
21. 49th parallel, for example
22. Old Greek city state
23. Twin of Romulus
24. Ready to roll?
25. West Indian fruit
27. Sparkling wine
28. 1939 Lombard/Stewart movie: *Made for Each _____*
29. American actor Torn
30. Alberta's 11th premier Getty
32. 2014 Michael Bublé bonus track: "_____ of May"
34. The Vancouver Canucks retired this Pavel Bure jersey number
35. Michael Ondaatje novel: *The English _____*
39. Approximation words
41. Was compatible (var.)
43. 1975 Neil Young and Crazy Horse track: "Don't _____ No Tears"
44. 1998 Drew Barrymore movie: *_____ After*
45. Breaks down in tears
47. Dispirited
48. US rapper: Dr. _____
49. Eater anagram
50. Ontario city
52. Tenant
54. Sound of a snake
55. Jellyfish type
58. Gun an engine
61. Deserved
62. Horse-drawn carriage
66. 2014 Arcade Fire single: "We _____"

68. Suffix with pamphlet
69. 1963 Chiffons song: "_____ So Fine"
70. Game fish
71. Build to particular requirements
72. Track wager
73. Tumults
75. Bangladesh bread
76. Long-tailed finches
78. Keyboard key, briefly
79. Tragically Hip song: "_____ Orleans is Sinking"
81. Robinson or Miniver, in the movies
82. Horatian work
83. Discharges a weapon
85. Moist
87. Like unfair boxing allegations?
91. Language family that includes Hungarian
94. Tarzan's transport
95. Greek Muse of astronomy
96. Noisy insect
97. European abalone
98. Surgery tool
99. In a creepy manner
100. Uncle Sam facial feature
101. Birch kin
102. Queen bee's fellows

DOWN

1. Desert that abuts China
2. Before long, in poetry
3. Water bird
4. Sits tight
5. Conceive
6. It preceded feathering
7. Genre for the Bee Gees
8. Filled a spreadsheet
9. Alberta historical site: Head _____-In Buffalo Jump
10. Native species: Newfoundland pine _____

11. Rose-scented liquid
12. 2009 Margaret Atwood novel: *The _____ of the Flood*
13. Haro or Hecate, in BC
14. More like an Ivy League student?
15. Play around?
16. Hebrew month name
17. 2014 Blake Shelton song: "Anyone _____"
26. Sturdy cart
30. Classic by Canada's Elizabeth Smart: *By Grand Central Station I Sat _____ and Wept*
31. Nabisco cookie: Golden _____
33. Rejects another's opinion
35. Early time for the Leafs?
36. Actress Arden, et al.
37. Tennis court crossers
38. Very, in Val-d'Or
40. Makes a choice
42. Knife affixed to a rifle
43. Found fault with the seafood?
46. Conductor's need: _____ music
48. 1976 Elton John duet partner Kiki
49. Man-made BC reservoir: Upper _____ Lake
51. Cote bleat
52. Hippies dropped this in the '60s
53. Go off the rails
56. "_____ the ramparts we watched . . ."
57. Beijing money
58. Take a time out
59. Vancouver world's fair: _____ 86
60. Watch Whoopi Goldberg's show?
63. Bridge name in Ottawa and Montréal
64. Window covering in winter

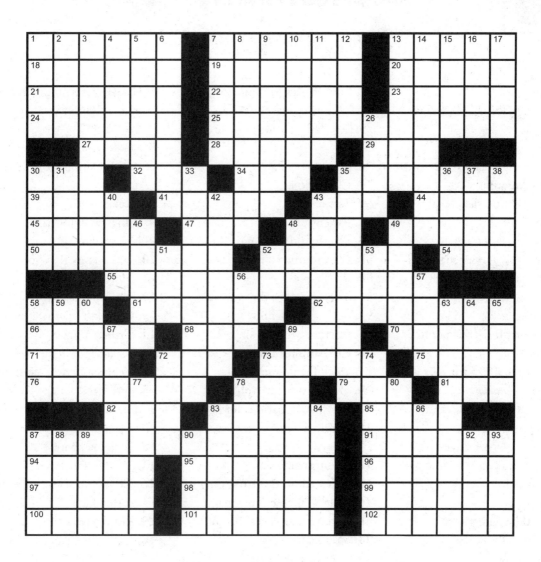

65. Very long periods of time
67. Canada's *Bluenose*, for example
69. Toronto's Isadore Sharp, for example
72. Red vegetable
73. Canadian documentary filmmaker McKenna
74. Lured into lust

77. Prince _____ Island
78. Ships' Atlantic crossing accolade: Blue _____
80. More cautious
83. Untamed
84. Blue Jays ERAs, for example
86. Large-scale
87. Shapeless form

88. Literary name for the Emerald Isle
89. Eastern priest
90. Hawaiian Islands dance
92. Bone _____
93. Little islands

Solution on page 226

Broadway Lights

Tony-winning Canadian thespians

ACROSS

1. Vojvodina capital: _____ Sad
5. Not nigh
9. Nikola Tesla, for one
13. 19th-C. Canadian settler and author Susanna
19. Men Without Hats vocalist Doroschuk
20. National arm of a global aid agency: _____ Canada
21. Canadian calling necessity: _____ code
22. Horrifies (var.)
23. **Winnipeg-born winner in 1979**
25. **He won in 1993 for *Kiss of the Spider Woman***
27. Big moment for a Blue Jay at bat
28. Boys, in Bonnybridge
29. Plant pores (var.)
31. Manatee, for example
33. Poses a question
37. Rushed headlong
38. Latin phrase: Pro _____
39. Unshorn sheep
40. **Play that earned the award for 43-D**
42. Hither and _____
43. Semi or scow, say
45. Alkaloid that helps control high blood pressure
47. Curly-tailed Asiatic dogs
48. Religious offshoot group
51. Place for sentimentality?
52. Stainless steel component
56. Muddy the waters?
58. Utmost degree
59. Gradually creating more noise
61. Garlands for Hawaii visitors
63. Army provisions provider
68. _____ nerve
69. Divers' milieu
72. Local leader in some provinces
73. Take away weapons
75. 2012 Alice Munro book: *Dear _____*
76. Scented stale air
78. Clumsy one
80. Teapot bit
82. Pretension
83. Like Byron's writing?
88. Great burden
90. _____-poly
91. They dive into the data lake?
93. _____ fibrillation
95. Cosmetics brand since 2004
98. **Christopher Plummer won in 1974 for this musical**
99. Orange or white tuber
101. Flying formations for geese
102. Former West Coast line: BC _____
103. Trump has two
104. Fit well, to the ornithologist?
106. Mel C's "spicy" nickname
108. You're often near this in PEI
110. Standard gear?
112. **Musical for which 23-A won**
116. **Christopher Plummer won in 1997 for this play**
119. _____ balloon
120. Word in a New Year's song
121. Cookie first produced in 1912
122. Jet black, in old poems
123. Like rising dough
124. Three on a domino
125. Strike sharply, old style
126. Property owner's document

DOWN

1. Zero
2. Lowe's Canada line: _____ Decors
3. Texas town
4. Federal government document with 3,000+ pages: _____ Tax Act
5. Oodles of land
6. Pacific National Exhibition, for one
7. Awakening
8. Brings back together
9. Nova Scotia place: _____ Island
10. Like a stray slapshot
11. More high-pitched
12. Wraps for sprains
13. Pumpkin pie spice
14. Greek cheers
15. Switchboard employee (abbr.)
16. *Captain Underpants* kidlit author Pilkey
17. St. Lawrence River landmark: _____ d'Orléans
18. Extreme Speed Racing (abbr.)
24. US doctors' grp.
26. China is the leading exporter of this metal
29. Pen for swine
30. 1994 Tragically Hip hit: "Grace, _____"
32. Less common
33. National charitable organization: The War _____
34. Freudian fall?
35. Casino game
36. Editor's word
38. Countrified
40. Lifts
41. **1963 winner for *Who's Afraid of Virginia Woolf?***
43. **He won in 1964 for a Shakespearean role**
44. Opposed to, in Dogpatch
46. Marty Howe, to Gordie
47. Lecterns (var.)
49. **Actress Dewhurst who won twice (1961 and 1974)**

50. Stadium ticket stub information
52. Divot
53. Western US Native
54. Bumps in the dirt road?
55. Ether form
57. Willingly, old style
60. You're working on one . . .
62. Rase anagram
64. Wee
65. American singer Lovich
66. Ontario premier Ernie (2002–03)
67. Chianti and Cabernet
70. US newspaper: *Baltimore _____-American*
71. _____ wheel
74. Passover foodstuff
77. Walkway with colonnades in old Greece
79. Line from *King Lear*: "_____, foh and fum . . ."
81. Tropical fruit
83. Honda Indy Toronto, for one
84. Black gemstone
85. Paddock parent
86. "'Tis a pity"
87. Device that maintains low temperatures
89. African antelope
92. Rescuer
94. Brush up on knowledge
95. Place for a piercing
96. Ignited
97. Michael Bublé live album: *Come _____ With Me*
100. Intrude on another's affairs
102. Drifted aimlessly
104. Victoria _____
105. Canadian Taxpayers Federation government waste "award" name
106. Sharpen shaving equipment
107. Use a crowbar
108. Tizzy
109. Frightening (var.)
111. Compound in ammonia
112. Reticent, socially
113. Mental distress
114. Greek letter
115. _____ in "elephant"
117. Salty seafood
118. It precedes plate or point

Solution on page 227

ACROSS

1. Gaiter
5. Wheat or canola, in Western Canada
9. Black birds
13. Avril Lavigne fragrance: Black _____
17. With the bow, to the violin section
18. Pueblo person
19. ICU word
20. Stage of insect development
21. Lesotho money
22. First name of Toronto-born singer The Weeknd
23. Canada has six of these
25. Canadian–American Pulitzer Prize-winning writer Bellow
26. He came after Claudius
27. Winnipeg pedestrian bridge: _____ Riel
28. 16:9, vis-à-vis HDTV
31. Track runners' circuits
32. Breach of duty, in law
33. Indian currency
35. Had arrears
39. Torontonians' transit option
42. _____ in the pan
44. Play genre
45. Kilt crease
46. Song for a pair
47. 1847 Herman Melville novel
50. Energy
51. Circular accommodations
52. Canada's Larry Cain won 1984 Olympic gold in this craft
53. Obsession for Felix Unger
55. Feudal fellows
57. _____ Original—Canada's Favourite Caramel™
58. Part of a province name
59. Bitty bugs
60. Line with stucco, old style
62. Suffix with Vancouver
63. Northwest Territories employer: Diavik Diamond _____
64. Automated Fingerprint Identification System (abbr.)
65. Gumption
66. The _____ Wives of Windsor
68. It came before sonar
70. They need to be cleaned up
71. 1997 Sarah McLachlan hit
72. Mea _____
74. Comes in _____ and starts
75. Synagogue
77. Idealistic or unrealistic
83. BC's Joseph Coyle invented this in 1911
87. Indian currency unit
88. "Nonsense!" in Newcastle
89. US film director Quentin
90. Bright thought for an aide?
91. "Diana" singer Paul
92. Uzbekistan sea
93. Large Aussie birds
94. Canadian Critical _____ Society
95. Golf bag pegs
96. 2006 Neil Young song: "_____ Impeach the President"
97. Valentine's Day gift
98. Lyra anagram
99. Scandinavian mythology source

DOWN

1. Taco chip topper
2. Indonesian outriggers (var.)
3. Behave badly
4. Cologne kin
5. Endowed church chapel
6. Prolific Canadian children's author Munsch
7. Canadian _____ Company
8. Air Canada crew member
9. Obedient, poetically
10. See 9-A
11. Nun's wear
12. Ancient tombstone markers
13. Provide seed money
14. Fish for a sandwich
15. Emulated a gorilla?
16. Tear down, in Tottenham
24. Microwave, colloquially
29. Winter wear
30. Very mad
34. Speech sounds related
36. Indecisive people
37. Giving off light, say
38. Revelstoke and Keenleyside, in BC
39. Intrepid agent?
40. Emitted sorrowful cries
41. Thiamine deficiency disease
42. Sombre
43. Former NHL centre Rochefort
44. Shakespearean verb
46. Saskatchewan-born NHLer Severson
48. Témiscaming moms
49. Sow one's wild _____
52. Accra cash
54. Entail
56. Pungent meat description
57. Plug-free Internet access
58. Bean variety
59. Ethel Merman film: Call Me _____
61. 1982 Canadian film: _____ Plouffe
65. After deductions (var.)
67. Little imps
69. Like 97-A
70. Burnaby-born singer Bublé
72. More brusque
73. Preceding month, to Tiberius
74. Forger's skill
76. Star Wars Solo
78. Skin fold

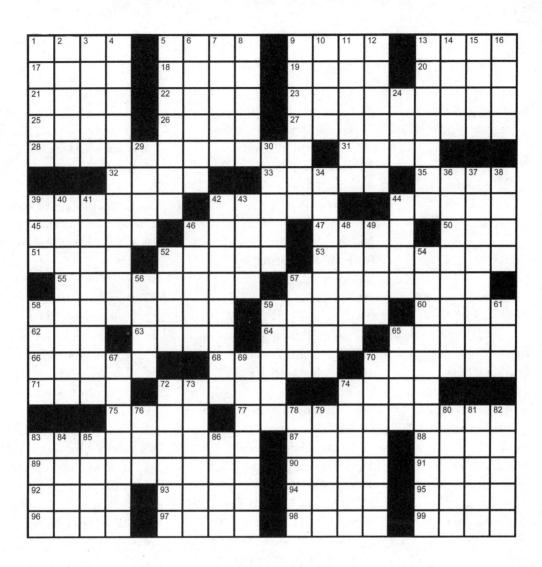

79. Gary Burghoff *M*A*S*H* role
80. Funnel-shaped
81. Queried
82. Tibetan capital

83. Common Latin abbreviation
84. Montréal commuter hub:
_____ *Centrale*

85. Nova Scotia island: Petit-
de-_____
86. Weighty burden

79 On the Move

Punny passages

ACROSS

1. Stuffing for a scarecrow
6. Has a mortgage held by BMO, say
10. Stage set item
14. Canada's Peace Tower is here (abbr.)
17. Canadian boreal forest, for example
18. Basic instinct?
19. Start over
20. Toronto Raptor, for example
21. **Excursion in a Ford SUV?**
23. Organic chemical radical
24. Dusk, to a bard
25. Errs, like Monty or Howie?
26. Carps' kin
28. Like the squirt of a squid
29. Hit hard, in olden days
31. Equilibrium
33. Ayn's coin?
37. Canadian telecommunications firm
38. Like a stubborn tanner?
42. Entangle
44. Disproves
46. _____ ki-yay
47. **Fantastic junket for a 1966 movie cast?**
49. Madagascar mammal
51. Loves too much
52. Old hobbies?
54. Teenaged Canadian Forces program participant
56. Nerdy one
57. Reserve in Ontario: _____ Nations of the Grand River
58. Early Rush album: _____ *By Night*
59. Dracula, in another form
61. Big pig
65. Tropical Asian perennial
67. Official estimator

72. Oohed
74. Morning, in Madrid
76. **Ocean trip for actor Tom?**
77. 1984 Leon Uris novel
79. Taxonomic groups
81. Toll of a bad news bell
82. Automatons
84. Droop
86. 2004 Brad Pitt movie
87. Finnish hot spots?
88. Spicy ballroom dance?
90. See 18-A
93. Breathing rasps
95. Early Christian paid to pray
100. Dairy farm sound
101. Singing Murray from Springhill
102. **Crusade for director John Ford?**
104. Civic Holiday mo.
105. Hammer part
106. Not in the wind, at sea
107. Extreme, in Saint-Eustache
108. Canadian non-profit: Cancer Research Society (abbr.)
109. Conflagration for cremation
110. Tree trunk growth
111. Place

DOWN

1. Originate (from)
2. Joni Mitchell hit: "Big Yellow _____"
3. Tears up
4. Ripened over time
5. Walks in water
6. Deviant one
7. Some prom corsages
8. It's sometimes ideal?
9. "_____ in the Clowns"
10. Played an étude, say
11. Enjoy a book once more
12. **Homer's long holiday?**

13. Grit or Tory
14. Lisa Moore Giller Prize nominee
15. **Actor Shatner's excursion to space?**
16. 1970s CFL stalwart Gabriel
22. Foot, in poetry structure
27. Cigar smoker's receptacle
28. Crustacean with seven pairs of legs
30. Czech river
32. Footnote abbr.
33. Invitee's answer
34. Midget mammal
35. Negative votes
36. "Darn!"
39. _____ the minute
40. Poet's contraction
41. Workstation
43. Breastplate (var.)
45. Dirty
48. Kuwaiti VIP
50. Canadian Electric Bicycle Association (abbr.)
53. Checkup
55. Silky powder
58. Smooth move, say
60. Nestlé Canada confection: Big _____
61. City in England
62. Hawaiian island
63. Throat clearer's noise
64. Make leftovers?
66. Mary _____
67. X and Y, in algebra
68. Jemima or Mame
69. Tire anagram
70. Capital city on a fjord
71. Lean (on)
73. Actors Andrews or Carvey
75. *CTV National* _____
78. **Adventure for a famous band?**
80. Makes an accusation

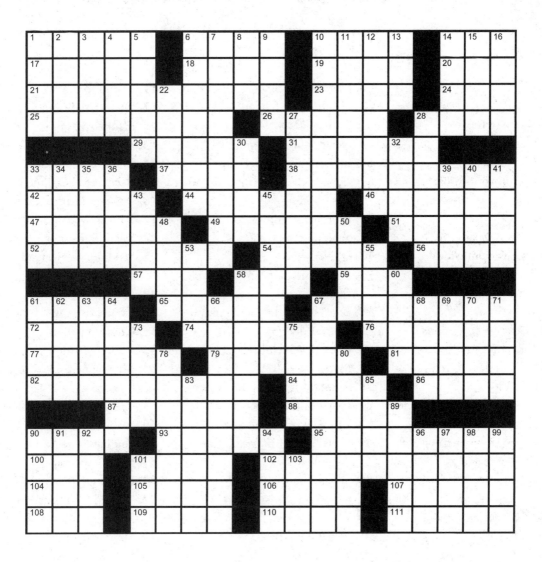

83. More ridiculous

85. Alexander II, for one

89. Goodbye, in Guadalajara

90. Apple computer type

91. Beatles magical mystery passage?

92. Machine gear wheels

94. Tinned meat brand

96. Dirty reading

97. Partner

98. India tourist's stop

99. Fiscal distress

101. Electronic device software, for short

103. International Labour Office (abbr.)

Solution on page 227

ACROSS

1. Fun times for explosives experts?
7. Wild West search party
12. Tosses a pigskin
18. Dress for success?
19. It dangles in your throat
20. Like some Margaret Atwood works
21. Sherries from Spain
23. BC whale-watching locale
24. Pet owner's funny poem?
25. Like some *Globe and Mail* pieces
27. Plant with two cotyledons
28. Compass point in Québec
29. Canada won three medals in this at Torino
31. Chart-topping Canadian singer Bryan
35. Bell and Shaw competitor
37. Sister city of Calgary
41. It's a highway, to Canadian singer Cochrane
42. Plant fibres for sack making
43. Sorrowful word
44. You might have one to the ground
45. Bicuspid bane
47. Religious work of art
48. Arizona indigenous group
49. Parry Sound-born NHL legend Bobby
50. Saskatoon-to-Prince Albert direction (abbr.)
51. Golden Canadian Olympic swimmer Oleksiak
53. Canada participates in this sport's Pacific Nations Cup
54. Bird at the seashore
56. He created Tigger and Piglet
57. You might get some from Scotiabank
58. Arabic bigwigs

60. Dessert that jiggles
61. Swindle
62. Rotten
65. Neighbour of Cambodia
66. In a proper manner
67. Canada's Curt Harnett shone in this building
70. A human thing to do . . .
71. Schooner pole
72. USNA word
73. Feeling no pain, in the dental chair
74. Blue Mountain people mover
76. Pigeons' lodgings
77. Deck that includes The Hanged Man
78. Autobody shop figure
80. Catch onto a concept
82. Essential oil from roses
85. Canadian-born *Scream* star Campbell
86. Where the Jets play
91. See 37-A
93. Having consequences
95. Genetic variation
96. Mark a test
97. It curdles milk
98. Thatched
99. Opposite of broadside
100. Glycerides, for example

DOWN

1. Canada's 2017 world champion curler Gushue
2. Short vehicle that's long?
3. Enthralled
4. Lyrics + music = this
5. Learners
6. Uproars
7. Yank on
8. Gametes
9. Alternative to crosswords
10. Hills at Whistler

11. Tripod for an artist
12. Driver's tight quarters manoeuvre (abbr.)
13. Alberta land formation
14. Remove impurities
15. Related to hearing
16. Big Beaujolais drinker?
17. John A. Macdonald, originally
22. Salad ingredient
26. Send out the Canadian Armed Forces
29. In a drowsy way
30. Comparison word
31. Choir member
32. Famous fashion surname
33. More conclusively, to Julius Caesar
34. Greeted at a New York opera?
36. It abuts Djibouti (abbr.)
38. You have one next door
39. Foot, in poetry
40. Like Superman's vision
42. "Could I Be Your Girl" singer Arden
43. Skin breakout
46. Half of a towel set?
47. Bring a new concept to the table
48. Cyst contents
52. Pipe's bend
53. South African currency
55. Speech hesitations
56. Thaw in the spring?
57. Poise
58. Products from Labatt and Molson
59. Former CFL commissioner Cohon
60. Prime minister Trudeau
61. "American Woman," for example
63. Soldier's stock, for short
64. Monies owed

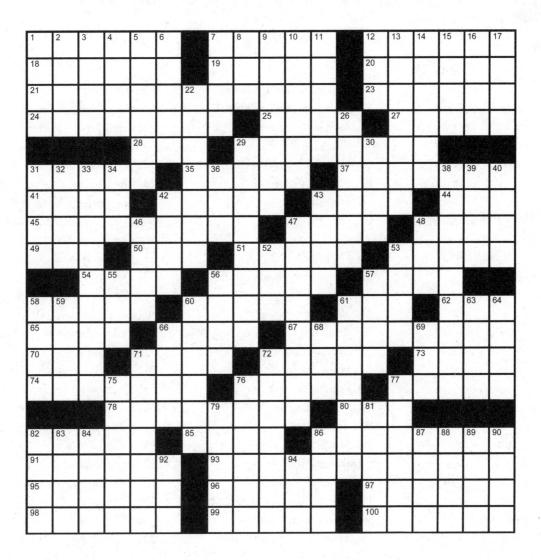

66. Goofy

68. A Bette Davis movie was all about her

69. Health care worker (abbr.)

71. Bad government

72. Stenographer's tablet

75. Jumped

76. Bats' digs

77. Clenches

79. Unite

81. Habituate to (var.)

82. A little bit open

83. Story

84. Scrabble square

86. Architect Christopher

87. Ain't correct?

88. You might decorate one at Christmas

89. Always

90. Comes down with an illness

92. River in 86-A

94. Old name for a city in Japan

81 A Penny Saved

Investments for Canadians

ACROSS

1. Tangy pastries?
6. 1950s CBC cooking program: _____ in the Kitchen
10. Comedic trio: The Three _____
17. Up in the air?
18. Assist
19. Populous Chinese city
20. Hiatus
21. Johnny Cash movie: Five Minutes to _____
22. Food prep pros
23. Meringue ingredient
26. Sew up hawks' eyes
27. English actor Alastair
28. Samuel Pepys, et al.
30. "Pronto!"
34. Nearby
36. He has an apartment to let
40. Traditional teachings
41. Dogwood
42. Gene Vincent hit: "Be-_____-Alula"
43. Serving of corn
44. French region on the English Channel
46. Non-elastic
48. Some investment funds (abbr.)
49. Hit from Canada's Terry Jacks: "_____ in the Sun"
50. Rankin Family song: "Rise _____"
52. Bracelet fastener
53. W.O. Mitchell novel: Who _____ Seen the Wind?
54. Low-risk government investment offering (abbr.)
55. Air Canada acquired this flyer in 2001 (abbr.)
56. Provide fresh soil for a fern
59. Chop finely
60. Fish native to Japan

64. Matched savings for those with disabilities (abbr.)
65. It separates Greenland and Ellesmere Island: _____ Basin
66. He led his army over the Alps
67. SINs, for example
68. Doberman's doc
69. Urchins
72. 1984 Nobel Peace Prize winner Desmond
73. Cause chubbiness
75. Attempt
76. Like a lone male?
77. Bone inflammation condition
79. Molson Stock _____
81. Hot tuna sandwich
83. Pirate's booty bin
89. Serif, perhaps
91. Apprentice (var.)
92. Jungle vine
93. Bantu tribal spears
94. Mixed bag, say
95. Up and about in the morning
96. Ocean birds
97. Some Canadian crops
98. There's no accounting for this?

DOWN

1. Magnesium silicate mineral
2. Old orchard spray
3. Lariat
4. Non-taxable investment account (abbr.)
5. These may have thorns
6. Celestial crescents
7. Not so much?
8. Reno resident
9. Barren
10. Ventriloquist Lewis
11. Tit for _____
12. Early ballroom dance
13. Shrek's spouse, for example
14. Asian cooking ingredient

15. Saskatchewan village: _____ Grey
16. Tegan, to Sara, in Canadian music
19. Terror inducing
24. Grease monkeys' containers
25. Statuesque scribe's story?
29. Pop machine opening
30. Clerical garments
31. Painful skin ulcer?
32. "Mi chiamano Mimi," for one
33. "West End Girls" group: _____ Boys
35. Farley Mowat book: Never _____ Wolf
37. _____ precedent
38. Klutzes
39. Long-term savings option (abbr.)
42. Hot dog holder
45. Perfectly suited?
47. Be under the weather
48. Draws a response
50. Renounce
51. It offers a guaranteed rate of return (abbr.)
52. 1984 Olympics golden Canadian canoeist Larry
54. Soup container
55. Car's instrument panel
56. Retirement money payout plan (abbr.)
57. Icelandic poetry
58. Barely audible summons
59. Yoga class pad
60. Aussie hoppers
61. Lie adjacent to
62. Pro follower, in a Latin phrase
63. Plumber's pitch?
65. Ontario area: Chatham-_____
66. AB health info regulations
68. Trace

70. Canada's Max Ward, for example
71. In a slipshod manner
74. 1970s Canadian figure skater Cranston
75. Root beer brand
78. Cases for mesdames
80. Public glory
81. Thalia or Urania
82. Ago, in the past
84. *Ugly Betty* actor Michael
85. **Account that offers higher interest (abbr.)**
86. Stomachs?
87. Pother
88. Rate anagram
89. Headgear for a Blue Jay
90. Baseballer Ripken

ACROSS

1. TD or BMO
5. Calgary _____ of Education
10. Bill and Hillary's grp.
13. 99-A, for example
17. Stir up sediment
18. Tripoli nation
19. Coffee dispenser
20. 1971 Poppy Family hit: "Where _____ Grows"
21. Even less attractive
23. Deodorant brand
24. Land of llamas
25. Like the littlest adolescent?
26. Forest plant?
29. Numbskull
30. Dakota dwellings (var.)
31. Plasterer's box
32. Thrash wildly
35. ERA word
37. 1973 April Wine hit: "Weeping _____"
39. SCTV hoser portrayer Moranis
40. Canada _____ ginger ale
41. University with campuses in 54-D
44. Temper glass
47. Basketball plays: Give-and-_____
49. Strong alkali
50. Nucleus container
51. Type of intersection
52. Fix a photo
55. Ebbed
57. Transfers Canadian government authority to the provinces
59. Takes into custody
62. Consoled
63. Enjoy a Blue Mountain run
66. Iacocca, et al.
67. Global superpower (abbr.)
69. Chips and _____

70. Canadian Olympic rowing medallist Laumann
72. Priests' poems?
75. Charge at 1-A
77. Diana Krall song: "When I Look in Your _____"
78. Canadian Olympic Hall of Fame swimming inductee Bob
79. Pubs, in Paddington
81. Resided
82. Horse colouring
83. Take it easy
84. Queen of hearts, for example
86. Racing vehicle at the Calgary Stampede
89. Devouring
93. Warmth
94. Earned Day Off (abbr.)
95. New Brunswick island frequented by Franklin Roosevelt
97. Northern European city
98. Regional flyer: _____ Inuit
99. Hélène Joy's Murdoch Mysteries character: Dr. Julia _____
100. 1972 Edward Bear hit: "Last _____"
101. See 67-A
102. 1930s leading lady Myrna
103. Like 97-A residents
104. Influence

DOWN

1. Champagne descriptive
2. Blue ribbon
3. Agatha Christie mystery: Death on the _____
4. West central Yukon region
5. TV censor's sound
6. Castor bean, for example
7. 1992 Dixie Chicks track: "Just _____ Like Me"
8. Crop grown in Western Canada

9. English scientist Charles
10. Die shaped
11. Alumni of 41-A
12. B&Bs
13. Procreates
14. Took too many drugs
15. Old Italian currency units
16. It comes before Tishrei
22. 15th-C. stringed instrument
27. Newspaper column, for short
28. Toledo state
30. Edmonton Eskimo pre-season sessions
32. Male undergrads' grp.
33. 1979 Triumph hit: "Lay It on the _____"
34. Cane anagram
36. Atmospheric inert gas
37. Breathes with difficulty
38. Singular stratagem?
42. Words of 20-A
43. Antiquity
45. Offspring of Zeus
46. University of Calgary class
48. Fish type
53. Three-time world champion ice dancer from Canada: _____ Virtue
54. Nova Scotia city
56. Dice anagram
57. One who razes
58. Place for a pin
59. Yodeller's milieu
60. Gather the crops
61. Payments for Canadian musicians
63. _____ terrier
64. Boat bottom
65. Workplace for a research grp.
68. Moral story, in literature
71. Obscene behaviour
73. Sty sound

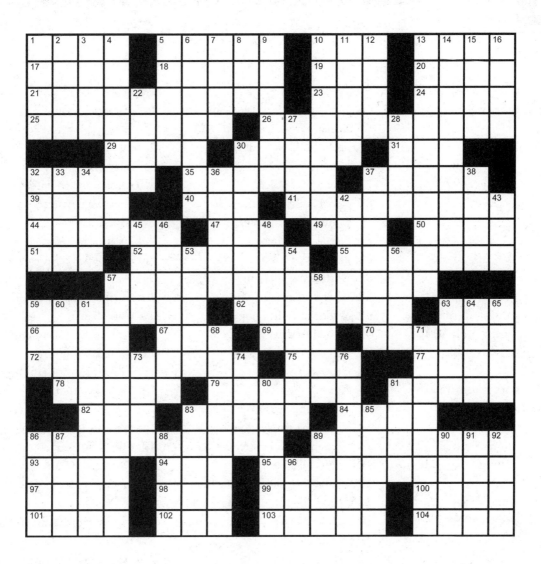

74. Unaccompanied U.N.C.L.E. agent?
76. Bath Institution breakouts
80. CRTC material requirement
81. Small amount
83. CBC _____ One
85. Repent

86. Cabbage, in Chicoutimi
87. Canadian-born actress Elizabeth
88. Raised skin mark
89. Therapy technique: Eye Movement Desensitization and Reprocessing (abbr.)
90. Aura

91. Radius neighbour
92. Unemployed person's GC payment (var.)
96. Provincial gallery in ON

Double-barrelled animals

ACROSS

1. Thomas Paine's religious belief
6. Greek letter
10. Little sausage?
14. Cotton-tipped sticks
19. Slip away to Vegas for a wedding?
20. Wicked
21. Baseball star Babe
22. Book, in Boisbriand
23. Buzzing
24. Places a wager
25. Succulent tropical plant
26. Carousel tune: "This Was _____ Nice Clambake"
27. Better prepared
29. **Equestrian's favourite fish?**
32. Italian mountain
33. Sore anagram
34. 1974 Bachman-Turner Overdrive song: "_____ It Ride"
35. Maple genus
38. 24 hours when you're not on your game?
40. Noon, in Châteauguay
43. Where Laos is
47. Scientific classification of 4-D and 67-D
49. Using connections to impress
52. Viola player's stroke
53. *The Voice* network
55. Female vampire
56. September bloomer
57. Heavy lifter
58. Ontario's Black Donnellys, for one
60. Right winger, for short
62. Levin who wrote *Deathtrap*
63. Role for Canada's Shatner
64. That being the case, in legalese
66. Rapidly alternating notes, in music

68. Tea anagram
70. Montréal sister city in South Korea
72. She who likes Fridays?
73. Lambaste
77. Like a sexy voice?
80. Rebel Alliance base in *The Empire Strikes Back*
84. Signal at Sotheby's
85. Pager
87. Kosher shopper's mart
88. Chef's covering
89. Wine valley in France
91. It used to drive engines?
93. KFC bucket piece
94. Gnaws on
95. Among the stars
98. Tree that grows from eastern Manitoba to Newfoundland
100. Barely audible interjection
101. Bankrolls
102. Largest of the Toronto Islands
104. See 124-A
105. Desert attire (var.)
107. Spicy swami?
108. Thin wooden strip
110. **Bird within a bird?**
116. Reflexive pronoun
120. Broadcasting now
121. Small sewing case
122. Scandinavian mythology anthology
124. Mountaintop roost
125. Call the Canucks don't like to hear
126. Indian bread
127. Epithet
128. Upcoming marriage announcements
129. Yearns for
130. Hoodlum
131. Search out
132. Icy rain

DOWN

1. 2007 track from Canada's Sum 41: "_____ Father"
2. If all _____ fails
3. Scarce amount, in Sparta?
4. **Tropical insect eater?**
5. Deserve a pay raise
6. **Striped bird?**
7. Christmas _____
8. Gave 10 per cent
9. Loser
10. Music group since 1970: Canadian _____
11. True crime author Ann
12. Molecular bit
13. "Take _____ Train"
14. Satisfy a thirst
15. Surreptitiously listens in
16. Declare
17. Highlands slope
18. Hawk, like Hudson's Bay
28. Chemical compound
30. RCMP word
31. Mythological history Muse
35. Run _____ (var.)
36. Bay of Naples island
37. Imprison, old style
39. Aesop offering
40. The same, in Shawinigan
41. Local jargon
42. Harry Potter's foil Malfoy
44. 1960s protest type
45. Like certain gases
46. Raga might be played here?
48. Amazement
50. Roof style
51. Toronto Zoo exhibit animal until spring 2018
54. Mechanic's energy source?
59. Not on one side or the other
61. Bacchanalia
64. Diminish
65. Tree type

67. Huge sea creature?
69. River in Italy
71. Oasis brother Gallagher
73. BC CFL pros
74. Miners travel through these
75. Seed shell
76. Preferred one over the other
78. Make aware of danger
79. Catfish kin?
81. Suzette's serving?
82. Coyotes' cries
83. Commencement
84. Small abnormality
86. They wriggle underwater

88. Academy of Country Music (abbr.)
90. Getting back territory, say
92. Neighbour of Hong Kong
96. Move back and forth
97. Fall back into old habits
99. Tottenham Hotspur midfielder Alli
103. Stick for a seamstress
106. You can see these in an alley off Newfoundland's coast
107. One-named British singer
109. Cairo citizens
110. Hard labour

111. Odd, to a Scotsman
112. Ucluelet set the Canadian daily record for this
113. Air one's grievances
114. Canada's Marc Gagnon won three medals at this state's Olympics
115. Kauai social gathering
117. Irish river
118. Stanza segment
119. Former Regina winter event: Kona-_____
123. Old CTV series: _____ South

Solution on page 228

ACROSS

1. Bachelor's final destination?
6. Covers one's emotions?
11. Interior wall panels
16. Prepares a WestJet flight in winter
18. Cereal meal
19. Very portly
20. Daytimer
21. Old Roman magistrate's aide
22. Material for a veil
23. David Bowie hit: "_____ Love"
24. Occupancy
26. SPCA visitors, hopefully?
28. _____ candy
29. South-central BC lake
33. Burden bearer, in the Bible
34. Numbers next to plus signs
38. Fringe benefit
39. Permissible
41. It airs *60 Minutes*
42. Canadian mining industry founding father Timmins
43. Many-eyed giant of myth
45. Sally Field show: *The Flying _____*
46. Former Ontario premier Rae
47. Jane Urquhart Giller nominee: *The _____ Carvers*
48. Academic's paper
50. Micro-organism
52. Birth province of 70-A: _____ Brunswick
53. Monarchs' dominions
56. Gender-neutral pronoun
59. Young student's text
60. Remote
64. Naomi Klein book: *The _____ Doctrine*
66. Sun god
67. Canadian Tire Centre official, for short
68. Slippery incline?

69. American actress Suvari
70. Secretariat jockey Turcotte
71. Long-legged bird
73. Former dictator Idi
74. House of Commons sitting
76. _____ a plea
77. Vote in an MP again
79. Recipe abbr.
80. Canadian magazine (1887–2005): _____ *Night*
82. US magazine since 1932
86. Women's group since 1998: _____ Society
91. Old Greek plaza
92. Sense of misgiving
93. Cocktail created in Calgary: _____ Caesar
94. Québec-born novelist Louis
95. Played for pay
96. Agreeable fellows?
97. Thing in *Vogue*?
98. Curvy letters
99. 2012 track from Canada's Melanie Fiona: "Break Down _____ Walls"

DOWN

1. Oates whose final NHL team was the Oilers
2. Children's building blocks toy
3. Fit to be _____
4. Pimple problem
5. Change boundaries, say
6. Keep up appearances?
7. Most playful, to William Tell?
8. Indian instruments
9. Door handles
10. Goa girl's garb
11. Feeble man
12. Bridge support
13. Sobeys section
14. City to visit solo?

15. Children should be this, but not heard
17. Summertime shoe
18. Switch sides, say
25. Small fry
27. Hunters' favourite time of year?
29. Lovers' tiff
30. München mister
31. Exhort
32. Some seabirds
34. BC city
35. Time for lunch
36. Copenhagen resident
37. Ed Sullivan's program?
40. Old-style reward
41. More hokey
44. See 71-A
46. Entreat
47. Blinds a hawk
49. 1987 Canadian film: _____ *Heard the Mermaids Singing*
50. It precedes Canada or Transat
51. Al Strachan's *99: Gretzky: His Game, His Story*
54. Lee anagram
55. Berry shrub
56. Doctrines, for short
57. Rankin Family song: "Fare _____ Well Love"
58. Justin and Sacha, to Margaret
61. Encyclopedia volume
62. "Beowulf," for one
63. Bump on a bumper
65. Like some stomachs
67. Disgusts
70. Shoddily made
71. It's fresh off the griddle
72. Close
75. Vancouver or Salt Spring
76. Affectionate touch
78. Slot on a shoe
80. Hole in the head
81. Film critic Rex

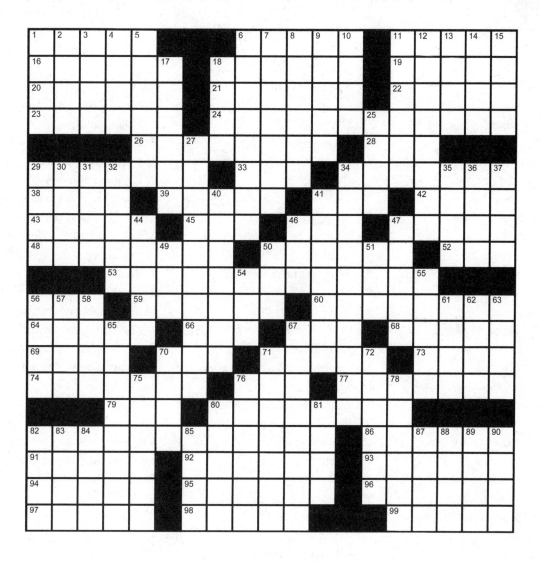

82. StatCan data bit

83. Toronto NEWSTALK 1010 program: *The Jerry _____ Show*

84. Unsated person's request

85. Rubik's preferred shape?

87. Money, in Manchester

88. Canadian retailer since 1964: _____ Hardware

89. Sweet drinks, for short

90. Northeast England river

Saskatchewan

ACROSS

1. Arachnid's feeler
5. House of Commons sceptre
9. Hawaiian dance
13. Like a pale complexion
19. Crowd's din
20. Greeting from one matey to another
21. Son of Zeus
22. **Provincial capital**
23. It secretes hormones
26. More cockamamie
27. City in France
28. Official language of India
29. Harangue
30. Droning insects
33. Prefix with care
34. Members of 93-A
36. Ancient Greek temple sanctums
37. *The Voice* contestant, for example
40. Summer astrological sign
41. Engine speed (abbr.)
44. They were banished to colonies in olden days
46. Menopause treatment (abbr.)
47. Layer above the Earth
50. Never seen spouse on *The Mary Tyler Moore Show*
51. City in Poland
54. Closed
55. New Brunswick provides dulse to this US company: _____ Foods
56. Supped
57. Old phone discs
58. "Don't get _____ of yourself"
60. Bores with gemstones?
61. Sees Mata Hari?
63. 1980s Edmonton Oilers winger Anderson
64. Calgary's Saddledome, for example

65. Symbolic bird
70. In one ear and out the _____
72. Sharpened a blade
73. Crotchety
75. Northwestern Ontario town: _____ River
76. Lively
77. Apple or orange
79. Toronto cultural attraction (abbr.)
81. With adroit skill
82. Sexy skirt feature
83. Solvent solution
85. 2007 Nickelback single: "_____ of a Bullet"
86. _____ damage
89. Cobra
90. Set of door slats, in Savannah
92. Retail outlet sign info
93. Unruly group of Mafia members?
94. NDPer
97. Compete in a bee
98. Mike's seven-season show: *Holmes on* _____
100. Waste piece of wool
101. Dip into?
103. Arid expanse in Africa
106. Japanese musical instruments
108. Small step for man?
109. Right-leaning type style
110. Math mavens
115. **Official provincial mineral**
116. Opposite of short
117. Mane anagram
118. This-and-that miscellany
119. Refines ore, say
120. Ultimatum component
121. Retailer since 1922: Canadian _____
122. Completely absorbed

DOWN

1. Nova Scotia National Historic Site: Grand-_____
2. British-based insurer
3. Young chappie
4. Divides equitably
5. Louis Hémon CanLit classic: _____ *Chapdelaine*
6. Doctrine of non-violence in Buddhism
7. They sit across from Libs in the House of Commons
8. Non-profit organization: _____ Foundation of Canada
9. Silvery chemical compound
10. **Much-mined mineral**
11. Give credit to?
12. Sonar predecessor
13. Like the most fresh lettuce
14. Birds' building on the farm
15. Petri dish culture mediums
16. Hard hit at Rogers Centre: _____ drive
17. Leg part
18. Outdoor space behind your house
24. BC tree: Western red _____
25. Tenement district
30. Lily type
31. Imagine
32. **Highest point in the province**
33. Canadian apparel retailer
35. Spoken
38. Serving at The Keg
39. Forward a message again
41. **South Saskatchewan tributary**
42. Groom oneself with care
43. "High IQ Society" group in Canada
45. Nancy Greene, for one
48. Bronze Age Chinese dynasty
49. Funeral procession vehicle
52. Sound of a hoarse voice

53. Official provincial fish
57. Journal
59. Take advice
60. Pleasure trip
62. Chemical group derived from benzene
63. Foolish person, colloquially
66. Possessive pronoun
67. Related to a heart part
68. Decisive defeat
69. Window seat bay
70. Spinachy plant (var.)
71. Small drum
74. "Sings" in the Alps

76. Annapolis newcomer
77. Flintlock musket
78. Knocks
80. Cosmetics queen Norman
82. Tolerates unpalatable food?
84. Not quite on time
85. Largest Great Lake
87. Casanova, for one
88. Pulse crop
91. Containing element #76
95. Talk nonsense, in Norwich
96. Laugh nervously
98. Proper, in Islamic diets

99. National sports body: _____ Canada
102. US neighbour of Québec
103. Takes a taste of a liquid
104. Bit of matter
105. Joan Jett classic: "I _____ Myself for Loving You"
107. See 35-D
108. Truck for a trucker
111. Front porch square
112. Tuscaloosa state (abbr.)
113. Bit of tang
114. Habitual drinker

ACROSS

1. Tomato _____
6. 1960s dance
10. Sleep stage acronym
13. Hay is the most common this in Ontario
17. Steppe in South America
18. Greek liqueur
19. Sapporo sash
20. 1978 Trooper hit: "Raise a Little _____"
21. Northern hemisphere swallow
23. Brett Hull, to Bobby
24. Out on the Pacific
25. Most favourable conditions (var.)
26. Editor's revision
29. Lomé country
30. Spacious
31. *Waking _____ Devine*
32. Eat enthusiastically, in the garden?
35. Earthy pigment
37. Pester, in a hostile manner
40. Club for Canada's Mike Weir
41. Astronauts' drink
42. Civic statute
44. Cialis competitor
46. Fred Penner children's song: "The _____ Came Back"
48. Permissive answer
49. Societal hero
50. Hamilton clock setting (abbr.)
51. Modernizes
54. Canada's 11th prime minister
56. Seasonal sapling
58. Nova Scotia-born folksinger: John Allan _____
61. Congenital absence of organ development
62. This Canadian channel aired *The Guest Book* in 2017
65. Frigg's spouse
66. Paddle for 59-D
68. Parliament Hill's home (abbr.)
69. Artist who works with acid
71. Ultimate provocation at the soda fountain?
74. Averages, at Cabot Cliffs
76. Canada–US _____ Pact
77. Areas of operation
78. Beach shelter
80. Pismire
81. Large bird
82. Four-door car
83. Garbage heap place
85. Gossiper
88. Incendiary weapon
92. Intensive care _____
93. A Tudor Henry
94. 6/8 time piece
96. Person on the move?
97. I, to Octavia
98. Warming or convection appliance
99. Tale of Troy (with *"The"*)
100. Educational organization: Child _____ Canada
101. American trumpeter Adderley
102. NBA squad: Brooklyn _____
103. 2013 Michael Bublé single: "_____ Your Eyes"

DOWN

1. As well, in Laos?
2. Blow from a palm
3. Struggle for air
4. Composing, old style
5. 2014 Justin Trudeau book: _____ *Ground*
6. Taiwan's old name
7. Boring routines
8. Submachine gun type
9. Crazy about
10. *The National* co-anchor (with 79-D)
11. Tropical tree
12. Intellect
13. Canadian women's magazine
14. 1 Sussex Drive, for example
15. Margarine
16. Canada Pension _____
22. It precedes Sept.
27. "Sleeping sickness," for short
28. "Auth. unknown" citation
30. Ships' meet
32. Go underwater
33. Mythological rainbow goddess
34. Animal with a beard
36. Early Andeans
37. Trials and tribulations
38. Tommy Douglas, by birth
39. Bivouac shelter
41. Plant parts that grow down from the stem
43. Monies you owe
45. Industrial area in Germany
47. Musical piece speed
52. Middle Eastern currency unit
53. Desert basin
55. Organized
56. Metric measurement
57. Beelzebub
58. Fizzy drink
59. Canadian kayaker van Koeverden who's won four Olympic medals
60. Erroneous tenet
62. Long-time Toronto radio station
63. Teem anagram
64. Woodbine racetrack pace
67. Brouhaha based on bigotry
70. Canadian women's hockey icon Cassie
72. Bump your toe
73. Redden who played for the Sens for 11 seasons
75. Angles

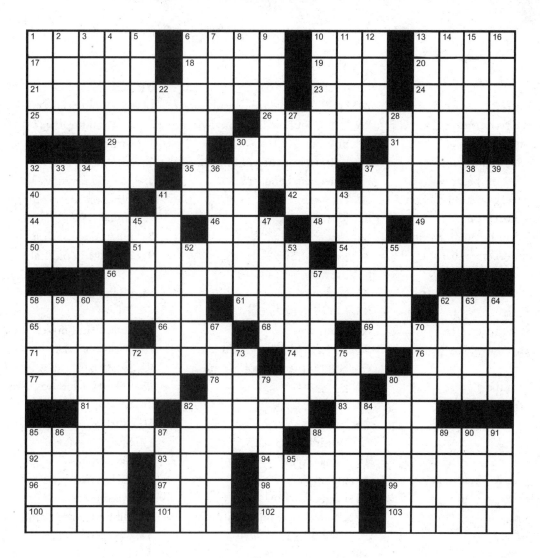

79. See 10-D
80. It induces vomiting
82. Eurasian antelope
84. Coffee-making appliance

85. Halifax Harbour boats
86. Asian animal
87. Like a tied score
88. Banjo component

89. Eclectic mixture
90. Some provincial riding reps
91. Ordered
95. Blvd.

ACROSS

1. Flower feature
6. Sourness or sweetness
11. Places monies in trust
18. Oozes confidence, say
20. Pitted fruit, in Frontenac
21. Early Hollywood star Charlie
22. **African antelope**
23. Woolly South American animal
24. *Laverne & Shirley* character Ragusa
25. Direction in Dorval
26. Font flourish
28. Short-lived rage?
29. Squeeze resources to the limit
30. By way of
31. Ticket remnant
33. *Canada's _____ Driver*
35. Cheese-topped chip
37. Smell awful
38. You do a McTwist on this
41. Athlete who plays for pay
42. Western Canada pie type: Saskatoon _____
43. Dull driller?
44. Segment of 34-D
45. **Small drum**
47. They elect MPs
50. Sorrow
52. Shortly
53. US DOJ org.
56. Food recall bacteria
57. *Buffy the Vampire Slayer* villains: _____ of the First Evil
59. Get
61. CIBC _____ for the Cure
62. Battle of Britain flying grp.
63. Visionaries?
65. Hops kilns
66. Extremely cold
69. *Ben-Hur*, for example
71. Filth in a flue
72. Tally mark

73. Micronesian island
74. HGTV Canada show subject
76. Canadian Norris Trophy winner Bourque
77. Palindromic interjection
78. Ethereally handsome?
80. Hate crime
82. Rattan worker
84. Aesop offering: *The _____ in the Lion's Skin*
85. Busy former premier?
87. Kraków residents
88. Most white, facially
89. **Luau attire**
91. Sir John A. Macdonald Day falls on the 11th of this mo.
92. _____ harrow (var.)
93. Twinkle
96. Waste can
97. South Pole locale
101. Roast type
102. Complete
104. Street urchin
105. Nanaimo is on this side of Vancouver Island
107. Fast tennis serve
108. Belonging to that fellow
109. Frequent forecast word for the West Coast
111. Historical wall hanging
113. To the _____ degree
114. Shreddies and Cheerios
116. Aphrodite loved him
118. **Ballroom dance**
120. Phrase heard on a piste
121. Calgary Stampede competitions
122. Deli purchase
123. Kept in a manuscript
124. Lancashire village: Knott-_____-Sea
125. Actresses Lollobrigida and Gershon

DOWN

1. Feet, zoologically speaking
2. Lives and breathes
3. **Motorized rickshaw**
4. Build on
5. Accoutrements with 89-A
6. Falling on the sword, say
7. Annual Rate of Payment (abbr.)
8. French singer Edith
9. Language in old Italy
10. Make adjustments again
11. "Behold the man," said Pontius Pilate
12. Cylindrical military hat
13. Show concern
14. Dashboard gauge info (abbr.)
15. 19th-C. Ontario premier Mowat
16. With a stronger bouquet, say
17. Sly
19. Satay sticks
20. Egyptian capital
27. Choir member's garment
32. Biblical tower name
34. *Rocky Mountaineer*, for example
36. Popular Calgary market
37. "Losing My Religion" US band
39. Eight-time Grammy nominee Amos
40. Lees
42. **Filled candy**
46. Unduly
47. Partially enclosed porch
48. Microscope lenses
49. Giraffes have purple ones
50. Citrus crop
51. Students' charges
53. Sprinter's ploy?
54. Female dogs
55. Briefly, to actor Martin?
57. Engendered
58. Navigator's change of focus?
60. Eastern philosophy principle

64. Eye irritant
67. Famed lyricist Gershwin
68. Hollow-nosed bullet
70. Provide a free pass, say
75. Spanish wine
79. Gordon Lightfoot classic: "If _____ Could Read My Mind"
81. Metallic sound
82. *SCTV* ensemble
83. Heavy imbiber (var.)
86. Like some wedding invitations

88. Summertime meals
89. Get the lay of the land?
90. Out of the loop
92. IVs do this
93. Adds charm to
94. Agleam
95. Come out of a cocoon
98. Gather a lot of stuff?
99. Cabaret dance
100. Respiratory illness
102. Portuguese language symbol

103. Induced
106. Bangkok citizens
108. Canadian "Sunglasses at Night" singer Corey
110. Former Flame and Canuck Bertuzzi
112. Nova Scotia community: _____ Harbour
115. Dine at Swiss Chalet
117. Prefix with Gothic
119. _____ Baba

Solution on page 229

O Canada Crosswords Book 19 ■ *181*

ACROSS

1. Anti-aircraft fire
5. Remote Access Service (abbr.)
8. Bachelor's final party
12. Centre of things
17. 1969 Barbra Streisand role: Dolly _____
18. Feeling of elation
20. Ammonia derivative
21. Kiln
22. Evoking emotions
23. Canada's oldest university
24. Sweaters
26. Dog with a curly tail
27. Gawping
28. CTV aired this sitcom: *Two _____ Half Men*
29. Eyelid problem
31. Run easily
33. Cote compartment?
36. *King _____*
37. Weird Al Yankovic parody: "_____ It"
40. Commits a puck error at Rogers Place
41. Thug's threat
43. Search like swine
45. Latin dance
47. Vivid coloured oxide
49. Temporary cessation
50. 1998 novel by Canada's Lawrence Hill: _____ *Known Blood*
51. 1970 Margaret Laurence literary offering: *A _____ in the House*
53. Hostile House of Commons group?
55. Italian dish: _____ bucco
56. Terr. of 30-D
57. *Entertainment Tonight* staffer John (1986–96)
58. Elvis chart-topper: "_____ Hotel"
62. Skin irritation salve
63. Small amt. of sugar
66. Concur
67. Über economizer
69. 2017 CBC TV show: *The _____ of Life*
71. Puget Sound city
73. Far _____
74. She shares her name with a flower
75. North Carolina river
76. Classifications
78. This cost hurdler Felicien her place on Canada's 2012 Olympic team
81. Popular 18th-C. metalware
82. Eagle's home (var.)
83. A Norse goddess of destiny
84. Catty sound in Chicoutimi?
87. Bark like 26-A
89. _____ taffy
93. Peruvian peaks
94. *SNL* role for Canada's Lorne Michaels
96. Long-time attire for Karen Kain
97. Frown
98. Neurological communication disorder
99. Israeli airline
100. Pert, like Canadian singer Jordan?
101. Rotted, like wood
102. Clairvoyant's extra sense
103. Ex-NHLer Hawerchuk who played for the Jets

DOWN

1. Particle mass
2. Bulgarian currency
3. Reasonably on par?
4. 2004 novel by 81-D: *A Complicated _____*
5. Mulroney's US contemporary
6. Ambiance
7. Supported the Tim Hortons Brier
8. Hillary Clinton's former role (abbr.)
9. Hard to stomach entree?
10. Kuril Islands ethnic group
11. Group of Canada geese
12. Magician's incantation errors?
13. Upon reflection, you'll see this?
14. Former Canadian specialty channel: Showcase _____
15. Click your fingers
16. Prefix with graph or scope
19. Danced in a disco?
25. Bride's words to her groom
30. Ragged Ass Road city
32. Paddle
33. Leaning tower town
34. Mag Ruffmann W Network show: *Anything _____ Do*
35. Awful expression?
36. This emerged during Canada's 2015 federal election: _____ Manifesto
37. Camille's small case
38. Too
39. Nirvana hit: "Smells Like _____ Spirit"
42. Birth mo. for some Virgos
44. Presidential swear words?
46. Sparingly, when it comes to alcohol
48. Anile oldsters
52. Investors Service Bureau (abbr.)
54. Table condiment, in Saguenay
55. "Sandwich" cookie
56. Inexperienced person
58. Dislike a lot

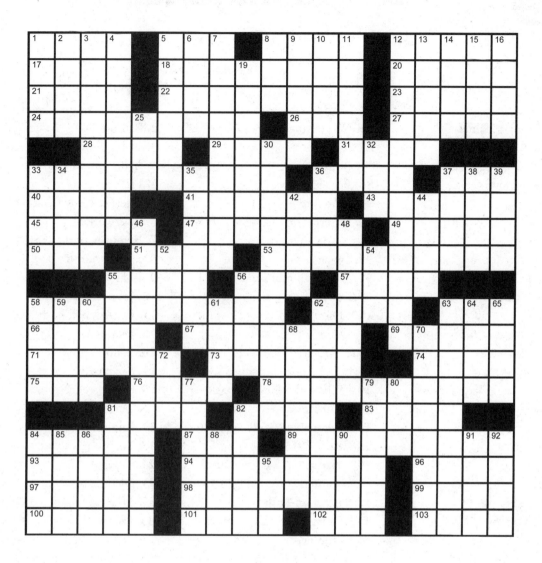

59. Former Blue Rodeo member Bob
60. With the bow, to Isaac Stern
61. YSJ postings, for short
62. Carp about tummy trouble?
63. Big hairy spider
64. Awaken
65. Beckoning whisper
68. Becomes weepy

70. Tested a chemical's strength
72. Justin Bieber hit: "_____ Around the World"
77. Safe opening device
79. Sting
80. Plant
81. Two-time Giller Prize finalist Miriam
82. Towards the left, at sea

84. Church service for many?
85. Indigenous people of 93-A
86. Bothers
88. Toronto BMO Field athlete
90. Floral garlands
91. Abbr. for others who are late?
92. Principle to be obeyed
95. Annual July celebration: Canada _____

89 Money Men

Canadian government finance gurus

ACROSS

1. Commoner
5. Frosting for a Flame?
10. Sound of a hoof
14. Frowned on, in society
19. Mystical glow
20. CB _____
21. LP player
22. How you read to a child
23. Puzzle type for magician Angel?
25. Bell MTS Place officials, for short
26. Loop on the gallows
27. Past, present or future, in grammar
28. Run out of time?
30. Decorative display shelves
32. The _____ Society of Upper Canada
34. Juicy fruit
36. Cutlet (var.)
41. Den
42. **Marc (1982–84)**
47. Stretch across
48. Orderly brothers?
50. Birds' beaks
52. _____ than thou
53. Smart
54. Run up debts
56. Clamour
58. UN aviation org. located in Montréal
59. Go back on one's word
61. Old Testament book
63. Aspirin and Advil: Pain _____
65. It makes sidewalks slippery
66. Take advantage of resources
68. Old-style Turkish title (var.)
70. Rolling Stones hit: "_____ Shelter"
71. Glandular organs in necks
73. **Allan (1980–82)**
76. Canadian singer Cockburn
80. Perseus star
82. Load for a waiter
83. US gov. property manager
85. Negative response, in Rivière-Rouge
86. Begged
90. School type
92. Description of Canada's North
94. Nike slogan: Just _____
95. Typeface tail
97. Description of some gases
99. *Cogito, _____ sum*
100. Discrimination against the elderly
102. Margaret Atwood offering: *The Handmaid's _____*
104. Like a chimney sweep's complexion?
105. Bergman's *Casablanca* role
106. **Bill (2015–. . .)**
108. Hay's 2007 Giller Prize winner: _____ *Nights on Air*
110. Austrian cattle breed
112. Entryway for underground employees
115. Amount of sugar for a cuppa (abbr.)
116. Pent up?
120. Like a mischievous fairy?
122. Downtown landmark: Toronto _____ Centre
127. Type of influenza
128. Laboratory culture gel
130. Stubborn
132. Gossipmongering gal
133. Half of *quatorze*, in Québec
134. State abbr. for 31-D
135. Skip over
136. Expression of disdain
137. US cable TV sports award
138. Vote for
139. Spot and Fido, say

DOWN

1. NAFTA, for example
2. Bait for 4-D
3. O'Toole who ran for the PC leadership in 2017
4. Lake catch
5. Internet Relay Chat (abbr.)
6. Overworked
7. Favourite of the fans
8. Jewish month
9. Like a preacher's truth?
10. **Jean (1977–79)**
11. Golfer's ball position
12. Proposal
13. Plant part
14. See 34-A
15. _____ vera
16. Dude who's crude
17. English river
18. Poems
24. Vend
29. Medical test
31. NHL Ducks city
33. Queen's University pub name (1971–2013)
35. Michigan place: Ann _____
36. _____ de corps
37. Juno winner's words
38. Mulroney-era cabinet stalwart Pat
39. White chip, often
40. Agouti's cousin
43. **Joe (2014–15)**
44. Genial place in France?
45. Alice Munro book: _____ *Life*
46. Greek god
49. Poisonous shrub
51. Drawn-out blockade
55. Man of many, many words?
57. Support for an injured arm
60. Cunning
62. **Mitchell (1965–68)**
64. Put in prison, old style

67. Act theatrically
69. Mites
72. Paul (1993–2002)
74. Canada's northernmost settled community
75. Marauding mammal
77. False
78. Cornerstones (var.)
79. Convert into Morse, say
81. Significant TransCanada pipe?
84. Mythology creatures
86. Dutch export
87. Aborted NASA mission
88. Rite anagram
89. Rotary phone features

91. Persistently annoying person
93. Shaw service?
96. Jim (2006–14)
98. Canada's Fung won '84 Olympic gold in this: _____ gymnastics
101. Workshop
103. Bibliographical abbr.
107. Misgivings
109. Remove all traces
111. Unlock
113. Squeezes by
114. Kind of wave
116. Coral reef islands

117. Some kitchens have a double this
118. Bobby Hull wore this number
119. Something you don't want to tempt
121. Golden Olympic Canadian pair skater Jamie
123. At the summit
124. This news magazine kiboshed its Canadian edition in 2008
125. "I'm working _____!"
126. Volleyball court components
129. BlackBerry download
131. At the back, on the boat

ACROSS

1. Container for a Kokanee
4. Long-time Crash Test Dummies bassist Roberts
7. Men's figure skating star Browning
11. Varieties
16. Zilch
17. Ex-prime minister Clark
18. Sailing on the Atlantic
19. Former Alberta premier Klein
20. Acting like a bozo?
22. Show signs of sleepiness
23. Anticipate an arrival
24. Deductive debaters?
26. Turn into an old fogey?
28. There's one at 20-A
29. Grain bit
31. Ugly mob scene
32. 2017 Feist track: "A Man Is _____ His Song"
33. Controversial Rushdie novel: The _____ Verses
37. Gym storage compartment
39. Wiener schnitzel ingredient
40. Casino dice game
41. Shock (var.)
43. Pharaoh name
45. Plot for a crop
46. Geographical directories
48. Stitched for a second time
52. Québec broadsheet since 1884
54. Town NNE of Santa Fe
56. Length measure
57. Doe anagram
58. Applause from a storm chaser?
61. William Tell's intent?
62. Famed Beethoven symphony
64. Contented cat's sound
65. Alberta hometown of 7-A
67. More simple
69. The Himalayas formed during this era
71. See 11-A
72. "Good to the last _____"
74. Three-time Wimbledon champion Chris
75. Vascular plant part
76. Wild plum
79. Neurosurgeon once known as "The greatest living Canadian" (with 99-A)
81. Makes safe
83. Hockey Hall of Fame Leafs inductee Day
84. Spreadsheets display this
85. Toronto's Hanlan's Point was named for him
87. Ruin the appearance of
88. Loathe a yeti?
91. Strong adhesive
96. Canadian diva Pellegrini
97. Third most common tree in Canada
99. See 79-A
100. Say
101. It partners with ever
102. Conducted
103. Competitors of the Habs
104. Federal institution in Manitoba: _____ Mountain
105. Disable with a stun gun
106. Some hospital suites (abbr.)
107. *An American in Paris* song: "_____-la-la (This Time It's Really Love)"

DOWN

1. Lake near Manitoba's Nopiming Provincial Park
2. Dwarf buffalo
3. 52-A, for example
4. Muslim mythology spirit (var.)
5. Lawrence Welk opener: "And _____ . . ."
6. Black, in Bilbao
7. Steppenwolf front man John
8. American military org.
9. Alter
10. Aromatic perennials
11. Attribute
12. Two-masted boat
13. Sector of Terrebonne: La _____
14. Animals' parasites
15. Old Jewish village in Eastern Europe
16. Ottawa environs (abbr.)
21. Vancouver and Victoria
25. Gelatinous sea creature (var.)
27. More painful
30. Countertop appliance
33. Triangle type
34. Former CBS drama: *Joan of _____*
35. Tropical Atlantic catch
36. Burger condiment (var.)
38. Not cloudy all day?
39. Carpentry clamp
42. Legislative body meeting
44. Drummer's concern
46. Blonde shade
47. In 1913, Canada held its first national competition in this sport
49. Internet seller
50. Pressing matter?
51. Enemies
53. This used to knock you out?
55. Tilts
59. Evaporated
60. Alice Munro offering: *Who Do You Think You _____?*
63. It sometimes turns?
66. Authority on church rites
68. Martin's *Laugh-In* co-host
70. Goddess of agriculture
73. Rhythmic beating sound
75. Winter wear
76. Sam Spade, for one

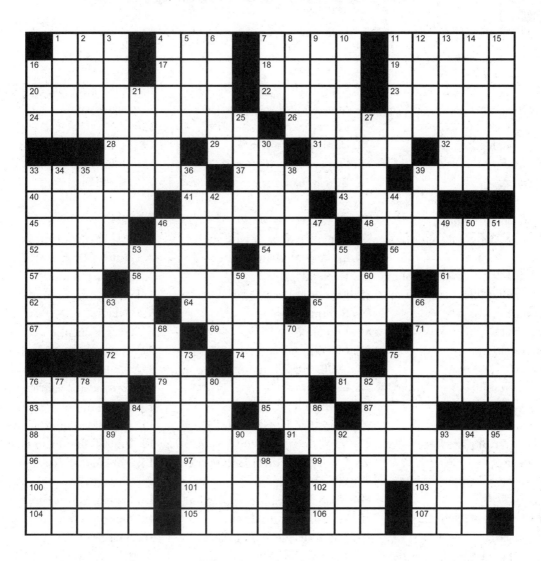

77. Canadian brewery founded in 1847

78. Portugal's second-largest city

80. Salma Hayek, for example

82. Blue-pencils

84. Style of Susanna Moodie's *Roughing It in the Bush*

86. Lego line

89. Carriage

90. *The Dukes of Hazzard* character

92. Look closely, in the House of Lords?

93. Ogle

94. Arm bone for a Roman goddess?

95. Former OLN Canada show: _____ *Up*

98. Compass point

Eggstravaganza!

Brought to you by Fabergé

ACROSS

1. Sign up to serve
7. Greek goddess
13. Goes through a stage of metamorphosis
20. Tippy shed?
21. Canada's James Cameron directed this 2009 blockbuster
22. Farthest orbital point from the moon
23. **Egg that has never left Russia**
25. **First egg that Nicholas gave to Alexandra**
26. Move furtively
27. It follows sleep?
28. Meagre
30. Bard's "before"
31. Narcissistic portrait?
33. Somewhat famous
35. Calf's source of sustenance
37. Took the bus
40. Restate
42. Thirst for
44. Affirmative reply to the captain
45. Resort springs
46. Some things go like this on the Internet
48. Some Tim Hortons orders
52. **1898 "bird" egg for Nicholas' mother**
54. Winter begins in this mo.
55. Grasps tightly
57. Golf pro's prevarication?
58. Final exams at Cambridge University
59. Dim _____
60. Welland _____
61. Top of a pyramid, say
62. Mother, in Montréal
63. Mutual of _____
65. Component
67. Alto or bass
69. **Egg that honoured Alexei Nikolaevich in 1912**
72. Breaks apart
73. Pembroke's province
75. Dopey
76. British fox hunt protestors, for short
77. Of the secular world
78. Canadian Shearer who starred in silent films and talkies
81. Hack off
82. Labour leader Bob, et al.
85. Rummy winner's drink?
86. Ensconce
87. Own, in Aberdeen
88. **1908 "bird" egg for Nicholas' mother**
89. Debater
91. "Bad, Bad Leroy Brown" singer Jim
93. Spain ceded this island to the US in 1898
94. Balance, in Chinese medicine
95. Gate closing mechanism
97. Like a sleeping volcano
99. Eastern church image (var.)
100. C&W singer Brooks
103. 1980s Canadian tennis star Kelesi
105. Governor General's Award-winning poet Margaret
107. Ontario Trucking Association (abbr.)
108. Too large
110. Japanese girdle bottles
112. Yokels
116. **1911 egg with a songbird that sings**
118. **1903 egg named for an emperor**
121. He might pique your interest?
122. Place to thread a lace
123. Steel structure for railway signals
124. Swiss Chalet serves these
125. End of a rugby match
126. Like reduced price merchandise

DOWN

1. Some shade providers
2. Gas for a Broadway light?
3. Repair a retina
4. Precautionary phrase
5. Feed the flames
6. Wrecker's haul
7. Strident women
8. More in balance
9. Attended an event
10. Ocean on Canada's east side
11. Rum libation: Mai _____
12. Bond films villain Blofeld
13. Annual Calgary event: Stampede _____
14. "When You Wish _____ a Star"
15. Stances
16. Molson makes it
17. Rafted
18. Get accustomed to (var.)
19. Ceremonial Passover dinner
24. Loose dress (var.)
29. Sri Lanka's former name
32. Enzyme that breaks down fat
34. "_____ the fields we go"
36. Hillary was nominated at this on July 26, 2016 (abbr.)
37. Extremely engrossed
38. _____ and terminer
39. Setting boundaries
41. Recitation for Catholics
43. Discombobulate
45. Claude Giroux, frequently
47. Triumphant interjection
49. Pole for a Swiss climber
50. Villain

51. Racy electronic messages
53. Syrup of _____
54. Russian legislative body
56. Batten down a sail
59. Seafarers' distress call
60. Haughty
61. Protozoa description (var.)
64. **The first egg, made in 1885**
66. *The Galloping Gourmet* host Kerr
67. Europe's longest river
68. Elizabeth Hay Giller winner: *Late Nights* _____
69. Tugboat horn sound
70. Get _____ the ground floor
71. Edible mushroom
74. Lifeless

76. Gym pants
79. From rags to _____
80. Federal finance dept. post
83. Canyon sound effect
84. Michael Ondaatje book: *In the _____ of a Lion*
86. Underwater equine?
87. Monksbane and wolfsbane, for example
88. Penalize a wrongdoer
90. In the month preceding (abbr.)
92. "_____ to Joy"
93. Lively old dance, in France
96. Sis-boom-bahs
98. Disfigured
99. Entombs a loved one's ashes
100. Rot

101. Early video game company
102. Synthetic silky fabric
104. French politicians Marine or Jean-Marie
106. Instrument with pipes and bellows
109. See 16-D
111. Northern Exposure to Leadership Institute (abbr.)
113. Greek letter
114. Former *The National* anchor Cameron
115. Sebaceous gland problem
117. Big barrel
119. Edmonton Youth Orchestra (abbr.)
120. It might be inflated

ACROSS

1. Bell sound
6. Persian monarch
10. Eye affliction
14. Non-flying bird
17. Manitoba-born playwright and author Betty Jane
18. Aussie actress Blanchett
19. 80-A served here
20. Apiece
21. Bell or Shaw
22. Brian Melo won season five of this reality TV show: *Canadian* _____
23. Newfoundland and Labrador university
25. *The Treasure of the* _____ *Madre*
27. Without a purpose
29. Unique vocabularies
31. Hawk's claw
32. Top layer of some ponds
34. Crossword clue type
36. Order from a judge
38. Accord or Acura
39. Toronto theatrical award: Dora Mavor _____
40. Fairy tale starter
42. Carpenter's tool
44. Steppenwolf hit: "Magic _____ Ride"
45. Position
47. Attend a non-credit U of T course
48. Steak _____
49. Throws
51. Canadian _____ Association
52. Great Plains shelter (var.)
53. Hallucinogenic drug, for short
54. Peter C. Newman book: *The Canadian* _____
58. Apt fundraising grp.?
61. Rabbit fur
62. Galoot
63. Layers of skin
67. Sow anew
69. Growls
71. Long-time game show: _____ *for the Top*
72. Take out Dracula, say
73. Ouzo flavouring plant
75. Cure anagram
76. Metal casting residue
77. Through
78. You can see one at Cineplex Odeon
80. Taylor who was a Canadian ambassador
81. Intend
82. Wagons
84. Ex-MLB pitcher Jenkins from Chatham
86. Four-time Canadian world curling champ Ernie
89. Thelonious Monk tune: "Well, You _____"
91. Discuss a corned beef dish?
92. Entice fish?
94. Mediums and smalls
96. Dug into grub
97. It follows *decree*, in law
98. Delineate
99. Fabric with a scenic scene
100. *The Apprenticeship of Duddy Kravitz* director Kotcheff
101. Jubilation
102. Eurasian deer
103. First Nations food fish

DOWN

1. 100 lbs., in the USA
2. Caustic cleansers
3. Pacts
4. More friendly
5. Canadian media personality Stroumboulopoulos
6. Nerve malady
7. Made a fool of
8. Kind of bomb
9. Olden days land worker
10. Alike
11. Former Vancouver Canuck Linden
12. Mandarin's lodgings
13. Noel anagram
14. Christian _____ Church of Canada
15. Rulers?
16. www.amazon.ca, for example
24. _____ Municipality of Whistler
26. Eye parts
28. "Be quiet," on a score
30. Sparsely vegetated
33. Parcelled out
34. Regina paper: *Leader-_____*
35. "For _____ us a child is born"
37. _____ wave
39. Coleridge poem character
41. Lighten a burden
43. Indian rice-based dish (var.)
44. Like Batman and Robin
46. Clean a coffee maker
48. Order of Canada children's author: _____ Wynne-Jones
50. 1964 Margaret Laurence novel: *The* _____ *Angel*
52. Concerning that
55. Picnic pest
56. Twitch
57. Cherry or cedar
58. Geometric shape
59. Free from weather extremes
60. Rated
64. Northern Canada river or valley
65. Hell's half _____
66. Cold-shoulder
68. 2018 CTV reality show: *The* _____
69. Midges
70. Musical intervals

73. City north of Calgary
74. Dreadful
77. Lombardy province
79. Coughs up
82. Make petty arguments
83. Not intoxicated

85. Best of both worlds, for example
87. _____ Kong
88. International military org. that includes Canada
90. Be a whistle-blower

91. Bowler or beret
93. Diamonds, slangily
95. Collection

Who Am I? 3

An NHL great one

ACROSS

1. River in Yukon Territory
5. Prevent, via the law
10. Yellow spread for bread
14. GBS's contemptuous expression?
19. Membrane in the eye
20. Marc-André Hamelin's instrument
21. Latvian capital
22. Yucca, for example
23. **His long-time team**
26. Gripes
27. Beautifiers
28. Felon's domestic arrangement?
30. Furry catkin: _____ willow
31. Thickness measurements
32. Hit the _____
33. Equines with long ears
36. Cause of consternation
37. Abuses language?
41. Dump rodents
42. Most feminine
46. Many Rogers Centre games do this
47. Org. for AB motorists
48. Old West watering hole
49. Turn left
51. Cassia family plant
52. **His position**
54. **His Saskatchewan birthplace**
57. Hit from Toronto's The Weeknd: "_____ Feel My Face"
58. A mouse might evoke this sound
59. White-collar worker, in Japan
62. Turn right
63. Canada's Sabados or Hyndman, on *So Chic*
67. Director's "stop!"
68. Atomic Energy of Canada _____
70. According to

71. Comes before
74. Horn of Africa country (abbr.)
75. Drug for certain rockers?
77. **He is . . . (with 16-D)**
78. **Number of seasons he played**
84. More lifelike
86. Hospital ward caregiver (abbr.)
87. Like a wily hobbyist?
88. Honda product
89. Harangue the chicken farmer?
91. Canada's Danone makes these (var.)
94. 1960s vocalist: _____ Cass Elliot
95. Secure soulmate?
96. Wander
97. Striped cat
98. Peruse the *National Post*
100. Just more than none
101. From the Beatles: "He's _____ nowhere man"
104. Language spoken in Podgorica
108. Tsunami of lawlessness?
112. Narcotic drug
113. **He holds this NHL record**
115. Graphic novel, for example
116. Toronto Symphony Orchestra instrument
117. Group of nine
118. Marsh grass
119. Demonstrate disdain
120. Tie up tightly
121. Nervous, like the myrmecologist?
122. Notice George Smiley?

DOWN

1. Not well-mannered
2. Bakery appliance
3. BC-born actor Rogen
4. Spanish shawls (var.)
5. Heroic sagas
6. Construction project areas

7. Dawdle
8. Loonies, as opposed to toonies
9. Okra unit
10. Baltimore baseballers
11. *Peanuts* character
12. Crop from a coop
13. Desert havens
14. Employers must meet these
15. Brainy Baldwin?
16. See 77-A
17. These cross France
18. Band formed in Vancouver: Spirit of the _____
24. Burden
25. Kvetch
29. Area in an abbey
31. Winnipeg landmark: Portage and _____
33. 00's Canadian government inquiry subject: Maher _____
34. Laval-born professional wrestler Zayn
35. Doe's mate
36. Web writings
38. Youthful time?
39. Revved the engine
40. Missouri or Maine
42. Staring stupidly
43. International Law Institute (abbr.)
44. Juno-winning singer Sexsmith
45. Nickname of former Swedish NHL Islander Nystrom
46. East Indian mystic
48. Commemorative pillar, old style
50. Hydrocarbon derivative
53. Beatles classic: "_____ Jude"
54. Burton Cummings' instrument on "Undun"
55. Behind the times?
56. Grieves
60. Brazilian palm
61. _____ Gritty Dirt Band

63. Shrouded in mystery, say
64. Group of three, in religion
65. Long-legged wading bird
66. Gull's cousin
69. "_____ will be done"
70. Hikers' trails
72. June 6, 1944
73. Play a ukulele
76. Type of lounge at Pearson
79. Gwynne Dyer's 1982 NFB documentary
80. Electronic Funds Transfer (abbr.)
81. Crusty skin lesion

82. Metrical foot
83. Dental clinic procedure
85. Famous Rio statue: *Christ the _____*
87. Talk
90. Primary colour
92. Circled the Earth
93. 2012 Leonard Cohen track: "_____ Home"
94. Disruptive computer program
97. Former monetary unit in China
99. Muster out, for short
100. Property destruction crime

101. P.G. Wodehouse novel: *Aunts _____ Gentlemen*
102. Slopes
103. Running on _____
104. Feline pets, in Portsmouth
105. 1994 Alice Munro book: *_____ Secrets*
106. **His number**
107. Mongolian desert
108. "Time's a-wastin'!"
109. Sailors' yeses
110. Pence or Biden, for short
111. Whirl in the water
114. California city: Santa _____

ACROSS

1. Canadian coniferous forest, for example
6. *Hockey* _____ *in Canada*
11. Group of Seven member A.Y.
18. Daryl Katz became the Oilers this in 2008
19. Alberta motorcoach transporter: Red _____
20. Mother-of-pearl gastropod
21. Canada's highest peak: _____ Logan
22. Silk pattern
23. Leads into temptation
24. Heavy drinker (var.)
25. Temporary storage facility
27. Take down a peg (var.)
28. Exhausted
30. Audit a lecture, say
31. A long time in the past
32. International Theatrical Institute (abbr.)
34. Your back 40, say
36. Singer Shannon
37. Exercises power, say
40. Mangy dog
42. Lawsuit basis
44. Allude to
46. Lode discovery
47. Small sewing cases
49. Prefix with legal or graph
51. It's often cast
52. Old Greek athletics contest
53. Students
55. Ferguson who wrote 2012 Giller Prize winner *419*
57. Codify
59. Complacent
62. Bone layers
65. Religious season in spring
66. Ran away to wed
70. Canadian novelist Cumyn
71. CBC comedy starring Gerry Dee
73. Make juice
75. Indian loincloth
76. Egg layer
77. Canadian Cancer Society tax receipt recipient
79. Regina-born NHLer Getzlaf
81. Curb, with "in"
82. Get back
84. Spectre's interjection
86. Like a meagre margin
88. NAFTA member
89. The law has a strong one?
90. Loci
92. High-rise girder
94. Skin blemishes
96. Farm, in Folkestone
98. *Star Trek* "Mr."
101. He wrote *99: Stories of the Game*
103. Part of a dovetail joint
104. Voyageurs' transport
105. Attar
106. Cyber message
107. Passing an exam easily
108. Amazing
109. Pembroke paper: *The _____ Observer*
110. Lists

DOWN

1. Tony Musante played this cop
2. Like a roll call absentee (abbr.)
3. One official language of Nunavut
4. Supernatural wish granters (var.)
5. Blood vessel
6. Try to impress through celebrity connections
7. Club for Saskatchewan's Graham DeLaet
8. Some Parliament Hill politicians, colloquially
9. Dreadful
10. Donald Trump, often
11. Toronto Argonauts mascot
12. Aid and _____
13. Canadian dollar currency code
14. Collection of poorly matched computer parts
15. Area of study at York University
16. Loretta Lynn chart-topper: "_____ on the Way"
17. Loch for mixed-up Ottawa players?
26. Stacked
29. Have a bite
31. Canadian flyer: _____ Transat
32. Long-running sitcom: *How _____ Your Mother*
33. National Ballet of Canada dancer's wear
35. Even-steven results
37. Nerd's cookout fare?
38. You might find one in the bucket?
39. Shipped
41. Relates
43. Kind of run
45. Medieval domain
48. Observed
50. Make a change
52. Passion
54. Hit the brakes hard
56. Coat insert
58. Virgin Mobile Canada service
60. Houseplant type
61. Corset parts
62. Bert who played the Cowardly Lion
63. Downwind
64. 25, on the periodic table
67. Respiratory illness
68. Auspices (var.)
69. Beatified Québec nun Bélanger

72. 1960s sitcom: *The Many Loves of _____ Gillis*

74. In an evil manner

77. Not well lit

78. Spun

80. Pen point

83. They're formed by glaciation

85. Modern-day dropsy (var.)

87. Agave-based liquor

90. Former W Network show: _____ *By Jury*

91. Biblical mountain or Middle Eastern peninsula

93. Without delay

94. You visit the Taj Mahal here

95. Yukon community: Old _____

96. Take it from the top?

97. Lion anagram

99. 101-A won this twice: _____ Smythe Trophy

100. Frat barrels

102. Greater Vancouver _____

Up in the Air

Fly high with this one

ACROSS

1. Hindu royals
6. Seafood serving
10. Great, like the Beatles?
13. _____ of Man
17. Choose to serve on Parliament Hill?
18. Breezy greeting
19. Had a little lamb?
20. Hit your finger with a hammer?
21. **Flyers for electricians?**
23. Common noun suffix
24. Actor Bogarde
25. Preplanned soccer pitch play
26. Subway egresses
29. _____ *Karenina*
30. RCMP members' attire: Red _____
31. Unplanned circumstance
32. Pie type
35. Upset tummy symptom
37. Bathed in rays
40. Not controlled
41. Provide a free ticket
42. Stealthy attack
44. Cocktail or salad name
46. Daffodil mo., in Canada
48. Flub
49. Sawchuk and Parent wore these numbers
50. Environmental Control System (abbr.)
51. Walks through the tulips?
54. Make a positive first appearance
56. **Transport for a boaster?**
58. Specific to a certain region
61. Ancient burial barrow
62. Wallin or Duffy (abbr.)
65. Necklaces to wear in Waikiki
66. Large mushroom
68. Cellphone smart card, for short
69. Snuggle cozily
71. Soaks steak
74. 1A or 14D, on a WestJet flight
76. Simba's *Lion King* spouse
77. Institution for the indigent, old style
78. Band from Ontario: Billy _____
80. Keen
81. Product you buy at the pump
82. Japanese rice wine
83. Nova Scotian Snow who sang "I've Been Everywhere"
85. Math
88. Sense
92. Asian desert
93. CIBC money dispenser (abbr.)
94. **Police officer's flyer?**
96. Glowing topper?
97. US firearms lobby grp.
98. Baby hawk
99. Courtroom pronouncements
100. 2012 Leonard Cohen song
101. US Internet giant
102. After all deductions, in Britspeak
103. Starbucks bottled water brand

DOWN

1. Serves as an advocate, for short
2. Vera's balm?
3. Type of amphibian
4. These keep coolers cool
5. Australian English
6. Mexican–American
7. Bat mitzvah, for example
8. Seaman's affirmative
9. Presews
10. Athlete's target of ridicule?
11. Do penance
12. Canadian TV personality Mulroney, et al.
13. Multicoloured cobs
14. **Glider for a boater?**
15. Italians used to spend these
16. Charitable group: _____ of Canada
22. Crazy Canuck Read
27. Plastics component
28. Therefore
30. Post-divorce payment: Spousal _____
32. Staff
33. Popular Apple computer
34. Refusal words
36. Fine fiddle maker
37. Climb Castle, in Alberta?
38. Side anagram
39. Melanie Griffith's *Working Girl* role
41. Harshly judgmental
43. Canadian high jump record holder Debbie
45. Tiny amount, to a physicist?
47. Puzzle type
52. Walked back and forth
53. Japanese stringed instrument (var.)
55. Sit for Karsh?
56. Pause
57. Light intensity measurement
58. Sources of shade
59. Certain tide
60. **Blimp for oil field workers?**
62. Gathering for guys
63. Fashion magazine that debuted in 1945
64. In the area
67. Seizure type
70. Vipers' den
72. Canadian-born NHLer Rick
73. Gown for 1-A
75. Non-believer
79. Rock growth
80. Create a cryptic message
82. Montréal subway
84. Curve
85. Old Eastern pooh-bah (var.)

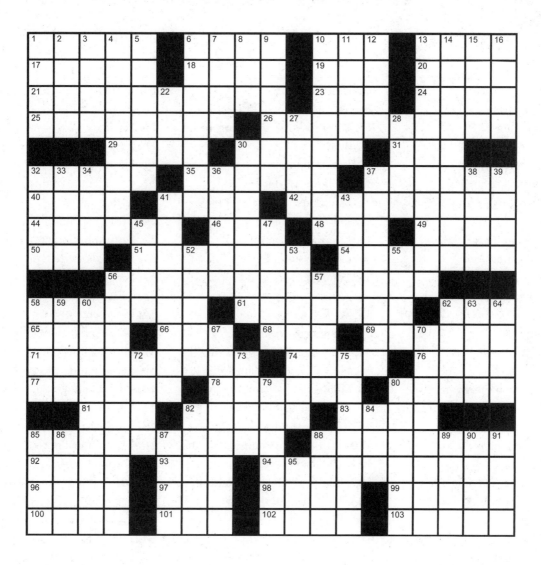

86. Wander without a destination in mind

87. "Give that _____ cigar!"

88. Land appraiser's document

89. Restlessness

90. Reject an idea

91. Stats for pitchers

95. In the _____ of the beholder

96   Canada Cornucopia 48

ACROSS

1. European river
5. Soda anagram
9. Hic et _____
13. Scottish slope
17. Kitchener-born Miss Moneypenny portrayer Maxwell
18. Noon, in Sept-Îles
19. Uzbekistan body of water
20. Couple's pronoun
21. Took unawares
23. Canadian-based beverage retailer
25. Swirling
26. You might leave Israel on this
28. Some coffeehouse orders
29. Tour Eiffel building material
30. Jimmy Durante's gourd?
32. Sprouted up
36. Cake ingredient
38. Tardy
39. *C. canadensis manitobensis*
42. World's highest capital city
44. Egghead
45. Stratford Festival performer
47. Cordial flavour
49. They abandon a sinking ship
50. "_____ I've heard"
51. Frequent Robert Munsch book illustrator Martchenko
52. _____ à cigarettes
54. Sanctified, old style
55. How some math equations are solved
59. Dieters might limit these
62. BC Place athlete
63. Saskatchewan provincial park
67. Nefarious deeds
68. Four-time Art Ross Trophy winner Mikita
70. Student's training
71. GDP word
73. Egg shaped
75. Kind of boom
76. Merino mother
77. Toronto-born ex-Boston Bruin Brad
78. Leases lodgings
80. Sir John A. Macdonald banknotes
81. Job for a BC logger
83. Eurasian Economic Commission (abbr.)
85. Toronto's Tory and Calgary's Nenshi
88. Walked all over
89. Bring back together
94. More conclusively, to Caligula
96. How Canada's Nylons sing
98. Golden Canadian Olympic swimmer Tewksbury
99. Minuscule bug
100. Half or whole musical symbol
101. Unfathomable?
102. Some raiders might raid these
103. Negative interjection
104. Pigeon-_____
105. Fires 81-A?

DOWN

1. "What _____ can I get you?"
2. Deafening
3. 2001 Nelly Furtado hit: "I'm Like a _____"
4. US sports award name
5. Nitrogen compounds
6. Cause irritation
7. "_____ to Billie Joe"
8. Motorcycle passenger's cocktail?
9. Tennis great Rafael
10. Obsolete European language family
11. Part of USNA
12. Prevailing weather conditions
13. Dutch painter Hieronymus
14. Canadian children's book author Ohi
15. Territory
16. Edmonton Symptom Assessment System (abbr.)
22. Canadian retirement income option (abbr.)
24. Medicinal amounts
27. Fatty substance
31. Bangkok currency
32. Sartorial style for some rockers
33. She's Indian royalty
34. Huge, in slang
35. Like acrylic painted walls
37. Unit of gravitational force
39. Leprechauns' literary locale
40. Edinburgh damsel
41. Slip or granny
43. Enthusiastic emotions
46. Multilingual person
48. Young sheep
49. Mar
52. *Happy Days* star Moran
53. Principle for Confucius
54. Long-time Canadian players: Downchild _____ Band
56. See 63-A
57. Corrupt
58. Place to park
59. Relinquish control
60. Declare openly
61. "The _____ of the Ancient Mariner"
64. Highway 401 segment
65. Opposed to, colloquially
66. They tick by quickly (abbr.)
68. Scorpio or Sagittarius
69. Wear out
70. Sunbathe
72. Good ringette player?
73. This cookie had its 100th birthday in 2012
74. Green

198

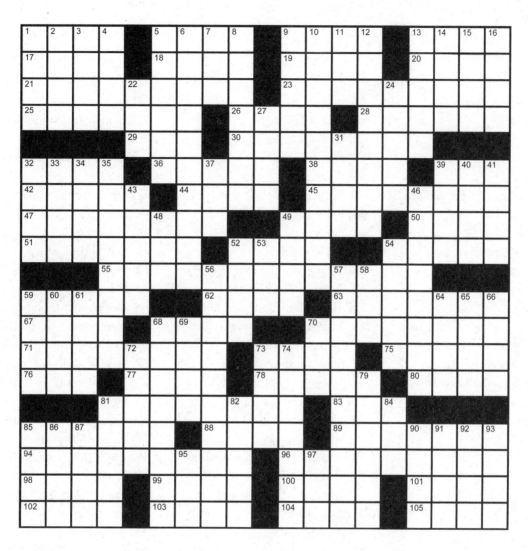

79. Oozed

81. Winnipeg marketplace: The _____

82. Hackneyed

84. Canadian university football trophy: Vanier _____

85. Loggins and Messina hit: "Your _____ Don't Dance"

86. Many kilometres distant

87. Toronto university

90. National Eating Disorders Association (abbr.)

91. Holly

92. Go on the run

93. Chatters like a Chihuahua?

95. Lennon spouse

97. Murmur

97 Go West, Young Scot

Place names replicated in Western Canada

ACROSS

1. Southern hemisphere constellation
4. Units of work
8. 1962 novelty hit: "Monster _____"
12. Starch sourced from palm trees
16. Little details
18. Bird that soars by the shore
19. Ten million rupees, in Maharashtra
21. As cute as a button
22. Echelon
23. American author James, et al.
24. Oscar-winning actress Patricia
25. AB town named after a Scottish settler's Scottish birthplace
27. Disinfectant brand
28. Dandy fellow?
29. Egg part
30. Dissolve
31. Entranced by
36. Archaic adverb
40. Some are bright?
41. Esso offering
42. Stairways that lead to Indian rivers
43. Canadian golfer Brooke Henderson, for example
44. Youthful period for ladies
46. Colour of very yellow corn?
47. Lays down turf
48. They arrange open house decor
49. Nickname for a marital mate
50. Whale constellation
51. Another way to say "Yea"?
52. AB mecca named for a CPR president's Scotland birthplace
53. It borders Ger.
54. Mollusc shell layer
57. Toy that debuted in 1967: Lite-_____
58. Most limp
62. 2006 Canadian movie: _____ *from Her*
63. Because of
64. Señora's scarf
65. BB-8 or C-3PO
66. Eel type
67. A TV Ewing
68. Songs for sopranos
69. Skied at Whistler, say
71. They might cause turbulence
73. Museum of the Moving Image (abbr.)
74. Sonny and Cher classic: "I Got You _____"
76. Leftovers scrap
77. Hold responsible for wrongdoing
79. Edmonton neighbourhood that shares its name with a royal Scottish palace
81. Neil Young's 13th studio album: *Fork in the _____*
85. 10-time Juno nominee Lee
86. Dunderheads
87. Small, to an equestrian?
89. Paltry
90. Overly decorous
91. Focuses intently
92. *All's Well That _____ Well*
93. 15th of March or May, in old Rome
94. Anagram for 7-D
95. It precedes bran or grass

DOWN

1. Four Seasons song: "Walk Like _____"
2. West Edmonton Mall's Mindbender
3. Asian buffalo
4. YVR posting
5. Dog show prize
6. Ecuadorean islands
7. Palm reader, perhaps
8. You might find this in your madness?
9. Former Israeli prime minister Sharon
10. Cagey crook?
11. Corral the cattle
12. Dental hygienists, for example
13. MB place named for its early settlers' Scottish home
14. Deteriorates, at the poker table?
15. Black and white cookie
17. WWW address
20. Course for a new Canadian (abbr.)
26. Canadian Club products
28. Angler's lens type?
30. Apportion punishment (with "out")
31. Fruit export from Egypt
32. Miner's entry point
33. Will be, in Madrid
34. AB city named for an Isle of Mull place
35. Minuscule amount
37. Like a humid Montréal morning
38. It's spoken in Islamabad
39. _____ and turn
42. Embarrassing misstep
45. Salem state (abbr.)
46. MB village named for a Governor General's earldom
47. MB city named for an earl who sponsored immigrants
49. Middleton's premarriage moniker: _____ Katie
50. Get in touch with
52. Baker's circuitry device?

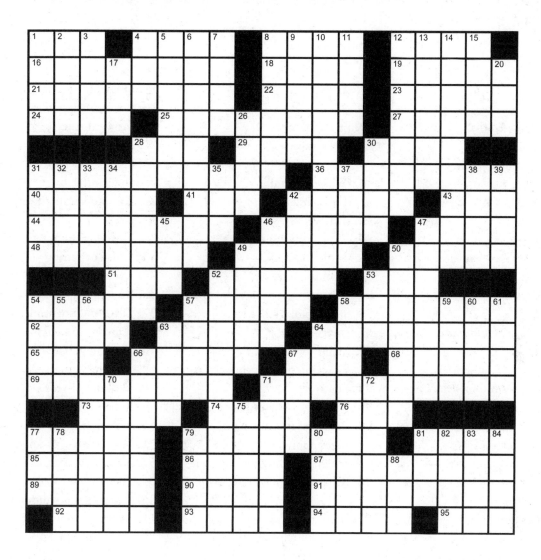

53. Movie camera's sweeping motion
54. Brings in the bad guys
55. Illegally absent from base
56. Sailboat type
57. 1990s Vancouver Canuck Pavel
58. Royal Canadian Air Farce performer, say
59. Nobelist Wiesel
60. Board beneath a bed
61. News agency founded in 1902

63. Ex-Toronto Maple Leafs "enforcer" Tie
64. Purple Day for Epilepsy mo. in Canada
66. Particular points in time
67. Halifax historic site: _____ 21
70. **AB village that shares its name with a famous loch**
71. Chasms, old style
72. East Side Mario's requests
75. Canadian singer Zappacosta

77. Some U of A degs.
78. Fabric for 64-A
79. Arizona indigenous group
80. Seep slowly
81. Salty seafood delicacy
82. Bear, in Verona
83. Canada exports potash to this continent
84. Fender-bender blemish
88. 2002 Giller-winning book: *The Polished _____*

ACROSS

1. Applaud
5. Male FBI operative?
9. Pack
13. Long-handled hammer
17. Daughter of Zeus
18. Currency for an excursion to France
19. _____ pet
20. Schiaparelli or Lanchester
21. Reaching too far?
24. Some cards
25. British _____
26. _____, stock and barrel
27. Nasal sound
28. Tofu source (var.)
29. Competes on *Chopped Canada*
30. US government health-related org.
31. Cut of mutton
34. Prickly feeling
36. Crop grown in Alberta
39. Swimming _____
40. Shut away in a cage
41. Person at the back of the pack
43. State that abuts Canada
45. Edmonton Police Service employee
47. Film director's milieu
48. Carmaker founded in Italy
49. Craving for sushi?
50. Paul Anka, for example
53. Fin's team?
55. How actor Tom keeps a steady speed?
57. Michael who wrote the 2017 Giller Prize winner *Bellevue Square*
60. Paintings by Pierre-Auguste
61. A pair
64. Dairy aisle buy
65. Contraction in "The Star-Spangled Banner"
67. Give a massage
68. -
70. Extra amounts
73. Chest muscles, in brief
75. At _____
76. Glen Eden trails
77. Bluebell
79. Radiates
80. _____ and tonic
81. Gardening tool
82. Soothing salve
84. "We _____ on guard for thee"
86. Prison block lodgings
87. Poetry Muse
91. Memo
92. Pickering power producer, e.g.
94. Matures
95. Preminger or von Bismarck
96. Renfrew county town: _____ River
97. Major Yorkshire river
98. Rockies landmark: Yellowhead _____
99. Mud dauber
100. Griffith who was briefly a Leaf in 2016
101. CBS TV series since 2003

DOWN

1. Bonbon for a Brit
2. The "L" in L-dopa
3. Offspring of Adam
4. In-depth reviews
5. Eke out
6. Chloride, old style
7. Grey _____
8. Ton anagram
9. Carleton and Concordia, say
10. Copses
11. Pig noises
12. Witty one
13. Consequential
14. Dipsomaniac
15. Drug addict
16. E.J. Pratt narrative poem: "Towards the _____ Spike"
22. Industrial haze
23. Pipe blockage
27. Small glitch
29. Toronto landmark
31. Neuter
32. This king was a merry old soul
33. Horse colouring
35. Ancient Peruvians
36. Respiratory woes
37. Tire puncture result
38. Canada Council for the _____
40. Spreading, like a flower cluster
42. Straight muscles, anatomically speaking
44. Indian caste
46. Horse for harness racing
51. Clay ones cover some roofs
52. Ninefold
54. Like a yenta
55. Stormy sea condition
56. Alice Munro won this prestigious prize
57. Gretzky won this 10 times: Art _____ Trophy
58. Hebrew month
59. Downplays
61. Like most Bangkok residents
62. Direction of Manitoba vis-à-vis Ontario
63. Glenn Hall and Glen Hanlon wore these jersey numbers
66. Esteems
69. Alexander Mackenzie's go-to food
71. Advance funds to
72. Seafood serving
74. 1972 musical that won eight Oscars
78. Run in neutral gear
79. Jazz singer Fitzgerald

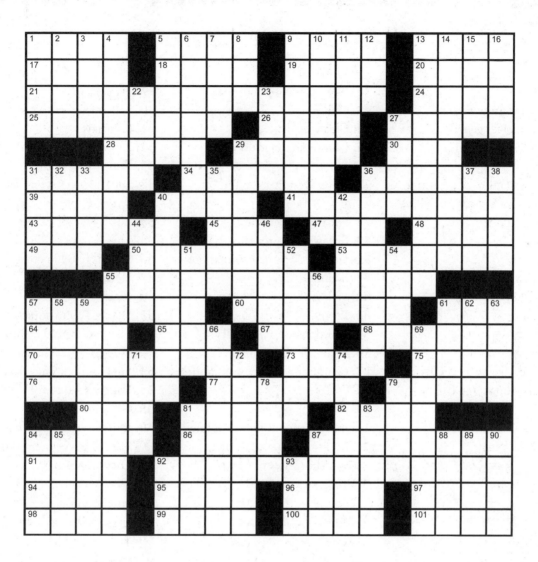

81. Old Roman shields
83. First Hebrew letter
84. Lose it, emotionally
85. Attire item for Roman senators

87. Canadian playwright Tomson Highway, for one
88. Auricular
89. Finnish city

90. 1974 Top Ten song: "____ Tu"
92. Joni Mitchell song: "Both Sides ____"
93. Plugs

99 | The Shape of Things to Come

A rare rule breaker

ACROSS

1. Malignant tumour
9. Famous French general
18. 250 or 778, in British Columbia
20. New Zealand red timber tree
21. Prepped for a test
22. Sue Grafton mystery: _____ *for Lawless*
24. Israeli city
25. Small amounts
26. Small skin openings
28. Federal party leaders did this on 9/24/15
29. Willow tree
30. James Barber's 1990s CBC cooking show: *The Urban* _____
32. Fills with sediment
33. Sewer vermin
34. London-to-Southampton transport, in *Titanic*
36. Gave a signal
37. Jacques Plante's jersey number
38. Hands-on monitor type
40. Make a mistake
41. Hit from Canada's Alannah Myles: "Love _____"
42. Partial beard
43. From _____ in
44. Every _____ often
45. Theme of this puzzle?
48. Location preposition
50. Flat-topped hills
56. Coyote's kin
61. Beatles classic: "Let It _____"
62. Dalhousie digs
64. Almost hellish states?
66. Mushroom type
67. They might hang around the Blue Jays dugout?
69. Population death rate
70. Coconut husk fibre
71. Rugged mountain ridge
73. Malleable
74. Create counterfeit ID
75. Foundation made of broken stones
77. Gaye/Weston 1966 hit: "It _____ Two"
78. Subatomic particles
79. Receive will proceeds
81. Former Canadian Armed Forces member
82. Valleys
83. Furtive
85. Pass down responsibility
86. Friars' flowering plant?
87. Childminder, in Victorian times

DOWN

1. Dreaded spoonful of childhood
2. Toronto's annual One of a Kind show showcases these
3. Bring back together
4. Mooches
5. More slick, in winter
6. Turndowns
7. Strange
8. Anne Murray classic: "You Needed _____"
10. 1989 album from Canada's Luba: *All _____ Nothing*
11. Toronto Raptor's target
12. Blown away, say
13. Goes white
14. Language spoken in some Middle Eastern countries
15. Assess an antique again
16. Chirps on social media?
17. Furtively listen in
19. Groundbreaking events
22. Detest
23. Look for
26. Parliament Hill landmark: _____ Tower
27. Type of drum
30. Sullen look
31. Cake layer
34. Large snake
35. Family tree word
38. 2001 Pierre Berton book: *Marching as _____ War*
39. Elijah Harper's answer to Meech Lake
46. Sweeney Todd's cruelty?
47. Holds back emotions
49. Attack
51. Shania Twain's fourth album
52. *Cats* cast member: Rum _____ Tugger
53. Jog like a pony
54. Long-legged bird
55. GPS, for example
56. Illinois city named for Canadian explorer Louis
57. Ovule coverings
58. Give one's bibliographical references
59. _____ West, Florida
60. Simile word
61. Fritters, in Frontenac
63. Former 24 Sussex Drive resident Harper
65. Assigned an assignment
66. Haloes
68. Run of luck
70. Jointly endorse a document
72. Canadian restaurant chain since 1982
74. Flu symptom
76. Essence of a matter
78. Stag or bull
80. Nevertheless short form
82. Press the accelerator
84. US singer: Ne-_____
85. 2015 Justin Bieber chart-topper: "What _____ You Mean?"

ACROSS

1. Hairpin bend
6. Dada's mate
10. Genre for Gordon Lightfoot
14. British Columbia Day mo.
17. Get around
18. Freshly
19. Mayberry boy, on TV
20. It can nail a perp
21. Milieu of Canada's Property Brothers
23. You might order these at Swiss Chalet
24. Turn abruptly
25. Like guidance from 6-A?
26. Part of a play
28. Network of nerves
29. Bucolic poem (var.)
31. Butterfly's wing markings
33. Birdwatcher's hindrance?
38. Data storage device
42. Governor General appointed in 2017 (with 78-D)
43. Changes decor
45. Forever, in olden days
46. Lagoon islands
48. Torontonian Lowe who composed "Put Your Dreams Away"
50. South American monkeys
51. Greek wine
53. Toronto Queen Street West landmark building
55. America equivalent of Canada Post (abbr.)
56. Seaweed-sourced thickening agent
59. Fountain pen fillers
63. Christian art images
64. Opening for Winnipeg's William Stephenson?
69. These ladies wear saris
71. Middle Eastern gulf
72. Roofing specialist
73. Chemical compound's cousin
75. Arise, at the farm?
79. Dionne quintuplets' father
80. Like Wilde's writing
82. Medical office recitation
84. Decorative basin
85. Canthus infection
86. Bale anagram
89. Email message receptacle
91. Clears up a crossword clue?
97. It monitors United (abbr.)
98. Michael who played for the Canucks, Oilers and Leafs
99. Clarinet player's spokesperson?
101. One of Canada's big banks (abbr.)
102. Gloat
103. You might wanna make this?
104. Tank fish
105. Mahone Bay island off Nova Scotia
106. Thinking rationally
107. Paddock papa
108. Bear's nose

DOWN

1. Ontario Diefenbunker town
2. Eye part
3. Lions' den din
4. Disgusting
5. Canadian *Son of a Trickster* author Robinson
6. Bullfighter
7. Investigate, in Ipswich
8. Greeted
9. Stupefies
10. Crew's quarters area, on ship
11. Speaks openly of one's feelings
12. Defendant in a defamation suit
13. *Star Trek: Voyager* character
14. Woodcutting tool
15. Storage locker, say
16. Hamilton ON park
22. Mix ingredients together
27. Mint family plants
28. Ottawa hall residence of 42-A
30. Tripper's drug
32. Calgary commuters' options (abbr.)
33. Slightly open, to a raja?
34. Mandolin's cousin
35. Rorschach image
36. Has the flu
37. Purposeful
39. Annoys
40. Use scissors
41. Old British tax
44. Spaghetti sauce seasoning
47. Break in two
49. Coop layers
52. Canadian Opera Company performer's solo
53. Ontario university or city
54. Puppy kennel noises
57. Colourful veggie?
58. Parachute material
59. See 2-D
60. Former employer of 42-A
61. Nautical mile
62. As cold as ice, for example
65. In fine fettle
66. American linebacker Floyd who played for four CFL teams
67. First name in blue jeans
68. Significant historical periods
70. Transfusion liquids
74. European vacation destination
76. Sap anagram
77. Less factual
78. See 42-A
81. *Moulin Rouge* dance
83. Tent window covering
86. Jimi Hendrix hairdo
87. Rum-soaked cake
88. Deficiency

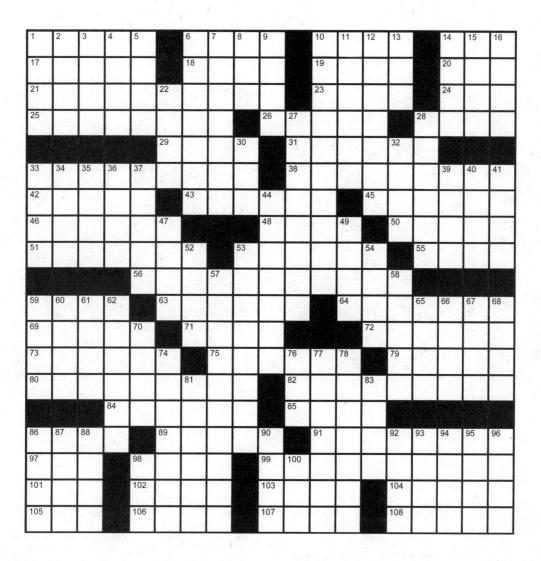

90. Celebratory day in Dec.
92. Chooses
93. Creditor's claim

94. Oval Office "no"
95. Neutral pantyhose shade
96. Air Transat purchase

98. *Nova* network
100. Japanese belt

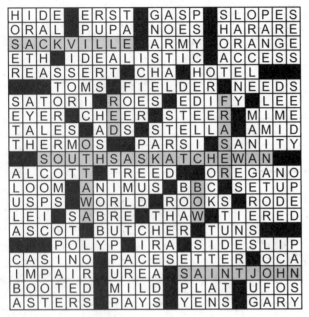

1 ▪ *Water Marks*

2 ▪ *Canada Cornucopia 1*

3 ▪ *Cleanup on Aisle Pun*

4 ▪ *Canada Cornucopia 2*

5 ■ *Great Ones of the NHL*

6 ■ *Canada Cornucopia 3*

7 ■ *Hat Tricks*

8 ■ *Canada Cornucopia 4*

9 ▪ *Where Am I?*

10 ▪ *Canada Cornucopia 5*

11 ▪ *Dual Instrumentalists?*

12 ▪ *Canada Cornucopia 6*

13 ■ *Read All About Him*

14 ■ *Canada Cornucopia 7*

15 ■ *You Snooze, You Lose*

16 ■ *Canada Cornucopia 8*

17 ▪ *Meet the Wilsons*

18 ▪ *Canada Cornucopia 9*

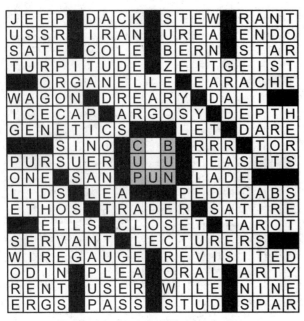

19 ▪ *Stuck in the Middle with U*

20 ▪ *Canada Cornucopia 10*

21 ■ *Where the Girls Are*

22 ■ *Canada Cornucopia 11*

23 ■ *Doppelgängers*

24 ■ *Canada Cornucopia 12*

25 ▪ *This Land is Your Land*

26 ▪ *Canada Cornucopia 13*

27 ▪ *Presidential Nicknames*

28 ▪ *Canada Cornucopia 14*

SOLUTIONS

29 ■ *For Their Service*

30 ■ *Canada Cornucopia 15*

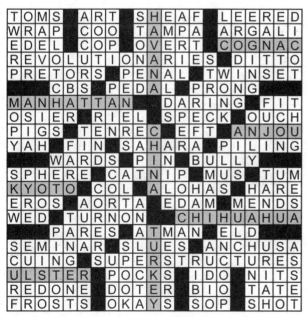

31 ■ *A Place for Every Thing*

32 ■ *Canada Cornucopia 16*

33 ■ *Watch Your Qs (but not your Ps)*

34 ■ *Canada Cornucopia 17*

35 ■ *You Gotta Have Heart*

36 ■ *Canada Cornucopia 18*

SOLUTIONS

37 ■ *To Market, to Market*

38 ■ *Canada Cornucopia 19*

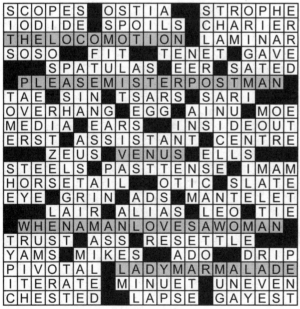

39 ■ *To the Top, x2*

40 ■ *Canada Cornucopia 20*

41 ■ *A Tree Grows in Canada*

42 ■ *Canada Cornucopia 21*

43 ■ *Letter-perfect Presents*

44 ■ *Canada Cornucopia 22*

45 ■ *Who Am I? 1*
Unscramble: *GOSLING*

46 ■ *Canada Cornucopia 23*

47 ■ *Anagram Unscramble*
Unscramble: *NADIR*

48 ■ *Canada Cornucopia 24*

49 ▪ *A Literary Legend*

50 ▪ *Canada Cornucopia 25*

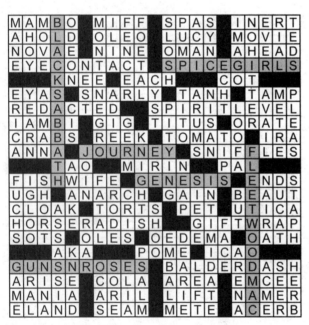

51 ▪ *Band (Members) on the Run*

52 ▪ *Canada Cornucopia 26*

SOLUTIONS

53 ■ *French-Canadian Fellows*

54 ■ *Canada Cornucopia 27*

55 ■ *The Name is the Same . . .*

56 ■ *Canada Cornucopia 28*

57 ▪ *Who Am I? 2*

58 ▪ *Canada Cornucopia 29*

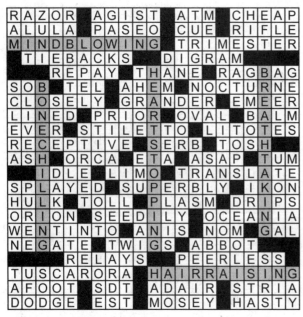

59 ▪ *Pathologically Speaking*

60 ▪ *Canada Cornucopia 30*

61 ▪ *Canadian Christmas Singalong*

62 ▪ *Canada Cornucopia 31*

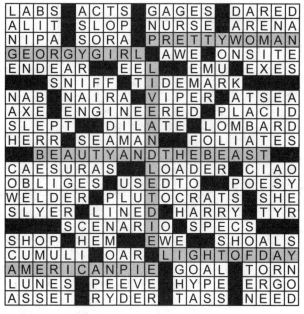

63 ▪ *Either/Or*

64 ▪ *Canada Cornucopia 32*

65 ■ *Canadian in the City*

66 ■ *Canada Cornucopia 33*

67 ■ *Beware the Ides of March*

68 ■ *Canada Cornucopia 34*

69 ■ *Destination: Fredericton*

70 ■ *Canada Cornucopia 35*

71 ■ *The Gods Must Be Crazy*

72 ■ *Canada Cornucopia 36*

73 ■ *Island Life*

74 ■ *Canada Cornucopia 37*

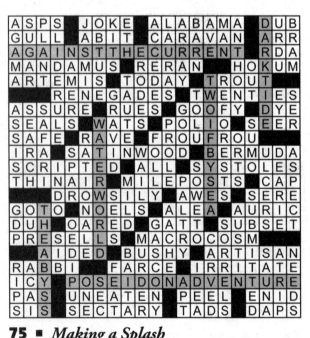

75 ■ *Making a Splash*

76 ■ *Canada Cornucopia 38*

77 ■ *Broadway Lights*

78 ■ *Canada Cornucopia 39*

79 ■ *On the Move*

80 ■ *Canada Cornucopia 40*

81 ▪ *A Penny Saved*

82 ▪ *Canada Cornucopia 41*

83 ▪ *Two for the Price of One*

84 ▪ *Canada Cornucopia 42*

SOLUTIONS

85 ■ *And the Province Is . . .*

86 ■ *Canada Cornucopia 43*

87 ■ *Repetitious*

88 ■ *Canada Cornucopia 44*

O Canada Crosswords Book 19 ■ *229*

89 ▪ *Money Men*

90 ▪ *Canada Cornucopia 45*

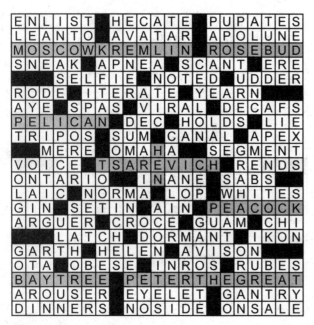

91 ▪ *Eggstravaganza!*

92 ▪ *Canada Cornucopia 46*

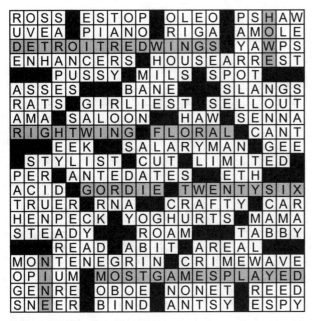

93 ■ *Who Am I? 3*

94 ■ *Canada Cornucopia 47*

95 ■ *Up in the Air*

96 ■ *Canada Cornucopia 48*

97 ■ *Go West, Young Scot*

98 ■ *Canada Cornucopia 49*

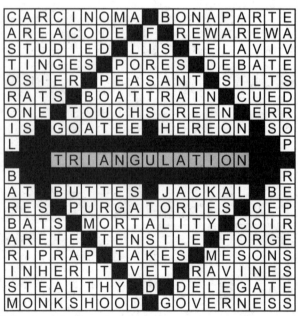

99 ■ *The Shape of Things to Come*

100 ■ *Canada Cornucopia 50*

MORE
O Canada Crosswords!

O Canada Crosswords, Book 1 • *115 Great Canadian Crosswords*
8½ x 11, 136 pp, pb • *978-1-894404-02-0* • *$14.95*

O Canada Crosswords, Book 2 • *50 Giant Weekend-size Crosswords*
8½ x 11, 120 pp, pb • *978-1-894404-04-4* • *$14.95*

O Canada Crosswords, Book 3 • *50 More Giant Weekend Crosswords*
8½ x 11, 120 pp, pb • *978-1-894404-11-2* • *$14.95*

O Canada Crosswords, Book 4 • *50 Incredible Giant Weekend Crosswords*
8½ x 11, 120 pp, pb • *978-1-894404-18-1* • *$14.95*

O Canada Crosswords, Book 5 • *50 Fantastic Giant Weekend Crosswords*
8½ x 11, 120 pp, pb • *978-1-894404-20-4* • *$14.95*

O Canada Crosswords, Book 6 • *50 Great Weekend-size Crosswords*
8½ x 11, 120 pp, pb • *978-0-88971-206-5* • *$14.95*

O Canada Crosswords, Book 7 • *50 Wonderful Weekend-size Crosswords*
8½ x 11, 120 pp, pb • *978-0-88971-218-8* • *$14.95*

O Canada Crosswords, Book 8 • *75 Themed Daily-sized Crosswords*
8½ x 11, 176 pp, pb • *978-1-88971-217-1* • *$14.95*

O Canada Crosswords, Book 9 • *75 Themed Daily-sized Crosswords*
8½ x 11, 115 pp, pb • *978-1-88971-225-6* • *$14.95*

O Canada Crosswords, Book 10 • *50 Themed Daily-sized Crosswords*
8½ x 11, 120 pp, pb • *978-1-88971-236-2* • *$14.95*

O Canada Crosswords, Book 11 • *75 All New Crosswords*
8½ x 11, 175 pp, pb • *978-1-88971-253-0* • *$14.95*

O Canada Crosswords, Book 12 • *100 All New Crosswords*
8½ x 11, 232 pp, pb • *978-1-88971-257-7* • *$14.95*

O Canada Crosswords, Book 13 • *100 All New Crosswords*
8½ x 11, 232 pp, pb • *978-1-88971-272-0* • *$14.95*

O Canada Crosswords, Book 14 • *100 All New Crosswords*
8½ x 11, 232 pp, pb • *978-1-88971-291-1* • *$14.95*

O Canada Crosswords, Book 15 • *85 All New Crosswords*
8½ x 11, 232 pp, pb • *978-1-88971-304-8* • *$14.95*

O Canada Crosswords, Book 16 • *100 All New Crosswords*
8½ x 11, 232 pp, pb • *978-1-88971-312-3* • *$14.95*

O Canada Crosswords, Book 17 • *100 All New Crosswords*
8½ x 11, 232 pp, pb • *978-1-88971-322-2* • *$14.95*

O Canada Crosswords, Book 18 • *100 All New Crosswords*
8½ x 11, 232 pp, pb • *978-1-88971-334-5* • *$14.95*